SYLVIA FRASER was born in Hamilton, Ontario in 1935. She spent her childhood and teenage years there. She graduated from the University of Western Ontario with a B.A. in English and Philosophy and worked as a journalist until the publication of her first novel, *Pandora*, in 1972. Her other works of fiction include *The Candy Factory*, *A Casual Affair*, *The Emperor's Virgin*, and *Berlin Solstice*. She has been awarded the Canadian Authors Association's prize for non-fiction for *My Father's House*. Sylvia Fraser lives and writes in Toronto.

Margaret Atwood has described *My Father's House* as having 'the tension and pace of a detective novel – except that the detective is a part of the narrator's self, and so is the murder victim. A beautifully written, heart-wrenching and untimately healing story by an amazing and courageous woman'. As an adult, Sylvia Fraser had no recollection of a sexual relationship with her father; for forty years the existence of her other self and the secret life she led had been unknown to her. Yet some connection always remained – pain, terror, and guilt were never far beneath the surface.

   With tremendous candour, power, and eloquence, she breaks through her amnesia to discover and embrace the tortured self she left behind. *My Father's House* is at once a terrible coming-of-age story told with lyric beauty and intensity and a story of love and forgiveness.

D0715931

My
Father's House

A Memoir of Incest
and of Healing

Sylvia Fraser

Published by VIRAGO PRESS Limited 1989
20–23 Mandela Street, Camden Town, London NW1 0HQ

First published by Doubleday Canada Limited, Toronto
1987

Copyright © Sylvia Fraser 1987

All rights reserved

A CIP catalogue record for this title is
available from the British Library

Printed in Great Britain by
Cox & Wyman Ltd. of Reading, Berkshire

To Margaret Laurence,
the wise and loving leader of our tribe

Acknowledgments

I wish to express my appreciation to the Canada Council. My thanks also to Sterling Lord, Lily Poritz Miller, Jennifer Glossop and Philippa Campsie for editorial advice. A special thanks to novelist Adele Wiseman, whose incisive knowledge of English prose is unsurpassed. I am, of course, deeply indebted to all my friends, as well as to my sister and my mother, who have become better friends.

CONTENTS

Author's Note

The story I have told in this book is autobiographical. As a result of amnesia, much of it was unknown to me until three years ago. For clarity, I have used italics to indicate thoughts, feelings and experiences pieced together from recently recovered memories, and to indicate dreams. It is important to keep this device in mind while reading this book.

To provide focus and structure, I have used many of the techniques of the novelist. I have also adopted fictional names and otherwise disguised persons who appear in the narrative. No attempt has been made to create full or balanced characterizations, only to portray such persons and myself as our lives relate to this difficult story. However, to my knowledge, I have not exaggerated or distorted or misrepresented the truth as I now understand it.

That my father did sexually abuse me has been corroborated by outside sources. Our family secret, it appears, was not such a secret after all.

REMEMBERING

SECRETS

My father's house was a three-story, frame building on a shady street in Hamilton, Ontario. Though our family found it hard to grow grass because of maple roots, our lawn was always neatly trimmed, our leaves raked and our snow shoveled. No one drank in my father's house, no one smoked and no one took the Lord's name in vain. My mother planted a victory garden and canned the tomatoes. My sister and I made seasonal dandelion chains, leaf piles and snow angels. Though my father worked on shifts at the Steel Company of Canada, he always wore a white shirt, navy suit and tie to his job as a steel inspector—trace-memory of a family that had once been prosperous.

Geographically, Hamilton is defined by a three-hundred-foot escarpment, which everyone calls the Mountain, and Lake Ontario, which is its northern boundary. My father's house was located directly under the Mountain brow. I was born into my father's house before noon on March 8, 1935. . . .

I sit on my daddy's lap playing ticktacktoe under the glare of a fringed and faded lamp. I have the Xs, he has the Os. I get three across: "I'm the winner!"

There's not much room on my daddy's lap because of his big tummy, held up by a black belt. His tummy feels warm against my cheek. The buttons of his shirt are pearly in the light. I run my fingers down them singing: "Tinker, tailor, soldier, sailor."

My sister Helen, who is four years older, says: "When you run out of buttons that's the man you have to marry!"

Helen takes me to kindergarten at Laura Secord Public School the very first day, holding me firmly by the hand for the two blocks, as she has been instructed. To bolster my courage I run a Popsicle stick along the spike fence around St. Cecilia's Home for Cripples and Incurables, which all us kids call the Cripples' Home.

We line up outside the big double doors marked GIRLS till a teacher lets us in. Then we march left right left right down the long hall as she bangs her pointer. I am in Room 1. Miss Potter has rings on every finger and hair like butterscotch-ripple ice cream.

I sit in a circle with fifty other kids and we model with Plasticene. Miss Potter lets me play the tambourine in the rhythm band and we learn about the Big Dipper by pasting stars on the floor. Some kids cry.

Granny Cragg lives on our second floor. She has a Singer sewing machine with a treadle and a jar of buttons for stringing into beads and a rag box where old clothes die and patchwork quilts are born. When Granny Cragg tells fortunes from teacups I point to pictures in the leaves. She does jigsaw puzzles from which Helen and I always hide the last piece.

Twice every Sunday my family drives to St. James' United Church in my daddy's secondhand Ford-with-a-running-board. I wear white stockings and carry my Dionne Quintuplet handkerchief with a nickel tied in one corner. That is for the collection. My father and three other gentlemen carry the silver plates tramp tramp tramp up to the altar where Reverend Thwaite blesses them, "Thank you, Fatherrr, forrr yourrr bountiful blessings." He means God.

When my mother sings hymns, she throws back her head so far the notes fly up to the ceiling where Jesus dies on the Cross for our sins. "I love you, Lord Jeee-sus . . . ."

While Reverend Thwaite preaches the sermon, all of us children go down to the Sunday school room, where the organist's wife teaches Bible stories by sticking flannel figures on a board. We learn how Satan tricked Eve into eating his apple and God took off her clothes: "You've been bad, go naked!" Then we have chocolate milk and wafers. Magda

Lunt, who is poor, steals some for her brothers. Sometimes I give her mine, but not often.

We drive home past the statue of Queen Victoria with a bird's nest on her head, and the sixteen-story Pigott building, which I know to be the tallest in the world, and the Palace and Century theaters, where it costs twice as much for half as much as at the Delta, with my daddy honking every time we get stuck behind a belt-line streetcar. At the foot of Wentworth Street, he points to a pile of weathered boards on the side of the Mountain. "That's where the old incline used to run."

Since he says this often, as if showing off something important to tourists, I know by now he means a cable car that once ran on a track to the top. Pressing my face against the glass, I stare at this heap of boards, buried in undergrowth. Try as I do, I can make no connection between what I see and the wonder in my daddy's voice. Yet his reverence for things that once were and can never be again inspires my favorite name, the one I use to baptize my oldest and dearest friend: Teddybear Umcline.

Down down down the stairs I go, dragging Teddy Umcline by one ear. It is midday. My daddy, who works the night shift, is in his blue-striped pajamas. I hitch at the pink sunsuit that Granny Cragg made for me, waiting to be invited into his bedroom. My daddy gives me candies. My daddy gives me chocolate-chip cookies. Of all the people in the world, I'm my daddy's favorite. *My daddy and I . . . .*

Helen and I go with my mother to Loblaw's groceteria. I like running my hands along the colored boxes and choosing my cereal according to the prizes imagined inside. I start to sing: "No, no, a thousand times no. I'd rather die than say yes." It's the only line of that song I know, so I shout it louder. A lady with red fingernails plays with my hair. "What lovely golden curls, just like a fairytale princess." She searches her purse for a toffee.

When my mother returns with her stewing beef, a ring of smiling ladies applaud as I swivel in my Sisman scampers, singing "Run, Rabbit, Run" and the rest of my brief repertoire. I know from my mother's corkscrew mouth that she is not pleased. My sister frowns behind her gold-rimmed glasses. I turn to the lady with the toffees but she is already at the cash register. The spotlight goes out. I feel bedraggled. As the toffee bursts sweetly in my cheek, I comfort myself: Who's little girl are you? My daddy loves me!

Down down down the stairs I go, dragging Teddy Umcline by one ear. My daddy sits framed in his doorway in trousers and undershirt. As I scuff my running shoe over the brass strip marking the threshold, he puts out his black shoe, which he has trouble reaching because of his tummy. I get down on my hands and knees to tie his lace. My daddy smells of Lifebuoy soap. He rubs his face against mine. That's a whisker rub. "You're tickling me!"

My daddy plays with my blond hair. "I had curls like that when I was your age." He plays with my belly button and jiggles pennies in his pocket. My daddy squeezes my legs between his knees. I count my pennies, already imagining them to be blackballs and red licorice from the Candy Factory. The breeze through the window smells of lilacs. It blows the curtains inward like Rapunzel's golden hair, giving me goose bumps.

My daddy and I share secrets.

My mother tries to pull my flannel nightgown over my head, pretending it is a white angel. I push her hand away. "Why doesn't Helen have to go to bed yet?"

"Helen is four years older."

I clean lint from between my toes. I push my mother's hand away. I fish blue corduroy from my belly button. I push my mother's hand away. I open my legs and—crack! My mother's hand strikes my cheek. "Filthy filthy!" Helen looks up from her Golden Window reader. Blushing, she ducks her head.

Panicking, my mother strikes my other cheek. "Don't ever let me catch you doing such a dirty thing again!"

Now I lie in the dark, between cool sheets, with my dirty dirty hands between my filthy filthy legs. Defiantly, I sing: "Don't ever let me catch you! No, no, a thousand times no!" twisting my lips like my mother twisting clothes. The space between my legs feels soft and warm, not hard and cold like the steel hole of my wet-ums doll.

My mother and Granny Cragg take Helen and me to see "Snow White." I like it when Snow White sings the wishing-well song, but if Snow White is a real princess, why does she have black hair? All fairytale princesses have blond hair. All are the youngest in the family. That I know for sure.

When the queen turns into the witch while dunking Satan's apples like my mother scalding tomatoes, I scream and scream and have to be taken from the theater.

The Goodfellows live across the street in a small stucco house with a big backyard where I am sometimes allowed to go. Arlene, who has spatter-paint freckles and frizzy copper hair like a Kurly Kate fresh from the package, is one year older. When we climb her apple tree, her brother Sidney tries to see up our skirts so he can make the shame shame sign.

Our hide-and-seek world goes from the Goodfellows' back porch through a hole Sidney has cut in their board fence. First comes a muddy ditch, then four sets of railway tracks, then the Mountain. Some day I will climb to the top just like Teddy Umcline!

My mother sprinkles my father's starched white shirts with water from a vinegar bottle. She is reciting a story I know ends with a mouse piping: "Gee whillikers, an owl's egg!" I rock on a hamper of freshly washed clothes, pretending to listen but really worrying if I'll be smart in school.

My Grade One teacher is Miss Warner, who is like a barrel with no neck and no waist. Arlene Goodfellow says once when Miss Warner was giving the strap her pants fell down to her ankles! Now I go to school all day instead of just in the mornings, like the kindy-garden babies. I have my own desk and flip-up seat and blue-lined notebook and pink eraser and black pencil as thick as licorice.

Twice a day I skip to school past the Cripples' Home, reciting the names and numbers of all the teachers in Laura Secord Public School, from one to twenty-four: "Miss LaStrobe wears glasses on a chain. Miss Willis spits when she speaks. Miss Macintosh has a red slip that shows."

I am the first to learn all the voices of the vowels and to read the adventures of Dick and Jane and Spot and Puff through to the end. In the cloakroom I teach the other kids to tie their shoelaces in a double bow just like my daddy taught me.

My daddy plays with my belly button, my daddy plays with my toes as he did when I was little: "This little piggy, that little piggy . . . ." Now I lie on my daddy's bed, face buried in his feather pillow. I shiver, because the window is open, the lace curtains are blowing and I haven't any clothes on. My daddy lies beside me in his shorts and undershirt, smelling of talcum. He rubs against me, still hot and wet from his bath. My daddy breathes very loudly, the way he does when he snores, and his belly heaves like the sunfish I saw on the beach at Van Wagners. Something hard pushes up against me, then between my legs and under my belly. It bursts all over me in a sticky stream. I hold my breath, feeling sick like when you spin on a piano stool till the seat falls off. I hear God say: "You've been dirty, go naked!" When I pull my daddy's pillow over my head I get feathers up my nose.

I cry when my mother puts me to bed. I didn't used to be afraid of the dark but now I know that demons and monsters hide in the cubbyholes by my bed. I'm afraid one will jump out at me, and rub dirty dirty up against me with its wet-ums sticking out. I beg my mother to stay with me but she says, "Such a fuss!"

I have a scary night. My pillow tries to smother me with its dead feathers. When I wake up I am facedown in vomit. It smells like chicken guts.

My father tramps the aisles of the market, pricing turnips, while I drag my Sisman scampers around the slimy puddles. I hate the market with the toothless people huddled against the sleet, their noses like potatoes, their cheeks splotched with beet juice, their rooty fingers wrapped in rags. Stoically, I await my reward, that moment when I can stick my fingers through the slats of the kitty cages with their homemade FOR SALE signs, calling down blessings on their sweet heads while trying not to see the squawking chickens smothering in their cages.

I dust the legs of our dining-room furniture—twenty-four of them, all with knobs and dents and cracks. I do the top of the tea wagon and the buffet, even lifting the doilies. I polish the see-no-evil, hear-no-evil, speak-no-evil monkeys on the radio console, along with the souvenir ashtrays no one ever uses. I even attempt the tri-lamp with the cellophane shade, the bookcase of Encyclopedia Britannicas and the piano with pedals and keys, which only Helen uses.

As always, the object of such determined goodwill is my mother, now bent over her darning egg, making tiny stitches across the worn black heel of my father's sock. Our conversation is already well launched, which is why I am running out of dusty surfaces to clean.

"But who would look after it?"

"I would."

"You know that wouldn't last. Its food would have to be added to the grocery bill."

"It wouldn't eat much." I bubble with generosity. "It could eat my liver."

"Where would it sleep?"

I want to say: on my bed. More wisely I plead: "In the cellar. I'd make a bed for it with rags from Granny Cragg's rag box."

My mother's voice sags in the middle as it always does when we can't afford something. "I don't know. There's more to having a little pet than you imagine."

"Please . . . ."

Here, puss puss puss puss. A fluffy gray kitten follows me home from school one frosty day. He sleeps in a carton by the furnace for several nights before making the permanent trek up to my attic bedroom. I brush him with my own hairbrush and festoon him with ribbons from Granny Cragg's rag box, where Helen says I was born. This I know for sure: Smoky loves ME.

I lie naked on my daddy's bed, clinging to the covers. His sweat drips on me. I don't like his wet-ums. His wet-ums splashes me. The scroll on my daddy's headboard looks like my mother's lips, scolding: "Don't ever let me dirty dirty catch you!" I try to count my pennies but my mind gets frightened and goes away like when the big boys at Beechnut playground push you too high on a swing and you scream to get down. I'm afraid to complain because daddy won't love me won't love me love me.

Sometimes on Fridays my mother and Granny Cragg take Helen and me to see double features at the Delta Theater. We see the first picture and then the second one and then the first one again. Then I crawl under the seats looking for Granny Cragg's shoes with the bunion holes in them. Sometimes we go to Melrose drugstore for butterscotch sundaes. Granny Cragg likes westerns. My mother likes love stories, as long as they aren't "smutty." Helen likes Abbott and Costello and I like cartoons.

*

*Now when daddy plays with me I keep my eyes tightly
scrunched so I can't see. I don't want his pennies or his candies
or his cookies. Mostly I leave them by the pillow while he
swallows me. I hold my breath to keep from crying because
daddy won't love me love me love me.*

I am running running running. My rubber boot catches an
invisible wire, pitching me forward on my belly. When I come
to I am lying in the snow screaming while my hands tear at
bare branches. My sister fetches our mother. "She's having
another fit. She's turning blue!"

My mother holds down my tongue with a wood stick.
Granny Cragg thumps my back. This is what the doctor has
ordered, yet now it's impossible to catch my breath. My fear
turns into rage—at my mother, at Granny Cragg, at Helen.
I fight back. My arms are held. I kick my heels.

*Desperation makes me bold. At last I say the won't-love-me
words: "I'm going to tell my mommy on you!"*

*My father replaces bribes with threats. "If you do, you'll
have to give me back all your toys."*

*I tot up my losses: my Blondie and Dagwood cutouts, my
fairytale coloring book, my crayons. "My mommy gave those
things to me. They're mine."*

*"I paid for them. Everything in this house belongs to me.
If you don't behave, I've a good mind to throw them into
the furnace."*

*I think of my beloved Teddy Umcline, his one good eye
melting in the flames. "I don't care! I don't care! I don't
care!"*

*"Shut up! What will the neighbors think? If you don't shut
up I'll . . . I'll . . . send you to the place where all bad children
go. An orphanage where they lock up bad children whose
parents don't want them any more."*

"My mother won't let you!"

*"Your mother will do what I say. Then you'll be spanked
every night and get only bread and water."*

That shuts me up for quite a while, but eventually I dare to see this, too, as a game for which there is an answer: "I don't care. I'll run away!"

My father needs a permanent seal for my lips, one that will murder all defiance. "If you say once more that you're going to tell, I'm sending that cat of yours to the pound for gassing!"

"I'll . . . I'll . . . I'll . . . ."

The air swooshes out of me as if I have been punched. My heart is broken. My resistance is broken. Smoky's life is in my hands. This is no longer a game, however desperate. Our bargain is sealed in blood.

I kick my heels and scream—I no longer quite remember why. Now when the resuscitation squad gathers around, worried frowns are replaced by scowls and pursed lips. My fits have been reclassified as temper tantrums. This is easier on everybody. Now my behavior can be dismissed as bad. Now I can scream as I sometimes must without having my tongue pulled out and a Popsicle stick thrust down my throat. Besides, anger feels better than anguish. To be angry is to be powerful like daddy, not helpless *like . . . like . . . .*

Smoky has been missing for three days. I've looked under the back stoop by the pail where I'm hatching pollywogs for a frog circus. I've knocked on every door on the block and ransacked every garbage pail clear through to the setting sun, sometimes crawling on all fours. "Here, puss puss puss puss."

I know if Smoky's dead it must be my fault, but I can't remember telling anything unless I've accidentally whispered it at night to the monster in the dark. I can hear the monster in the cubbyhole by my bed, even with my fingers in my ears. I can see his big hairy belly, even with my eyes scrunched. I can smell his stink like chicken guts. He's killed Smoky and now he's coming for me. I know if I fall asleep with my mouth open he'll crawl inside me forever, and then I'll grow crinkly hair and a slimy wet-ums.

Something wet and hairy and stinky brushes past me. It's

the monster! His red eyes glow in the moonlight. No, it's not a monster! It's Smoky! Smoky has come home. I hug his warm, furry body to me. Till death do us part.

I lie on my stomach on the living-room rug, coloring in my fairytale book. I color the hair of all the princesses with my yellow crayon—Cinderella and Sleeping Beauty and Rapunzel.

My father sits in his fetch-me chair working a crossword puzzle. His pencil snaps. He grunts: "Fetch me a paring knife."

I color Cinderella's eyes blue, then turn the page to Sleeping Beauty.

"I'm talking to you!"

I color Sleeping Beauty's eyes blue.

The floor trembles under my tummy. "Fetch me a paring knife."

I shuffle to the kitchen, s-t-r-e-t-ching the seconds like a rubber band, enjoying the terrible tension while wondering when it will snap. I hand my father the knife with the blade toward him, then return to my spot on the floor. With a black crayon, I outline the naked bodies of Cinderella and Sleeping Beauty and Rapunzel, right through their clothes, repeating ME ME ME. Then MINE MINE MINE.

My father sharpens his lead pencil. "Take this back."

Grumbling, I trudge to the kitchen, clutching the knife in my fist. As I return it to the drawer, I see red on the blade. I run to my mother, who is sewing a triangle insert under the sleeve of my daddy's white shirt.

"What's the matter?"

I show her my bleeding palm, my voice edging toward hysteria. "My daddy has stabbed me!" On my insistence, she applies a Band-Aid. I return to my coloring book, nursing my injured hand. Sleeping Beauty has also pricked her finger and must sleep a hundred years. Staring at my father's black boot, I boldly form the thought: I hate you! . . . God does not strike me dead. I do not turn to stone. I repeat: hate hate hate hate hate, enjoying the sharp taste of the word like a lozenge in my mouth.

*

My arms stick to my sides, my legs dangle like worms as my daddy forces me back against his bed. I love my daddy. I hate my daddy. Love hate love hate. Daddy won't love me love me hate hate hate. I'm afraid to strike him with my fists. I'm afraid to tell my mommy. I know she loves Helen because she is good, but she doesn't like me because I am dirty dirty. Guilt fear guilt fear fear dirty dirty fear fear fear fear fear fear.

One day I can stand it no longer . . . .

THE OTHER

When the conflict caused by my sexual relationship with my father became too acute to bear, I created a secret accomplice for my daddy by splitting my personality in two. Thus, somewhere around the age of seven, I acquired another self with memories and experiences separate from mine, whose existence was unknown to me. My loss of memory was retroactive. I did not remember my daddy ever having touched me sexually. I did not remember ever seeing my daddy naked. I did not remember my daddy ever seeing me naked. In future, whenever my daddy approached me sexually I turned into my other self, and afterwards I did not remember anything that had happened.

Even now, I don't know the full truth of that other little girl I created to do the things I was too frightened, too ashamed, too repelled to do, the things my father made me do, the things I did to please him but which paid off with a precocious and dangerous power. She loved my father, freeing me to hate him. She became his guilty sex partner and my mother's jealous rival, allowing me to lead a more normal life. She knew everything about me. I knew nothing about her, yet some connection always remained. Like estranged but fatal lovers, we were psychically attuned. She telegraphed messages to me through the dreams we shared. She leaked emotions to me through the body we shared. Because of her, I was drawn to other children whom I sensed knew more than they should about adult ways. Hers was the guilty face I sometimes glimpsed in my mirror, mocking all my daytime accomplishments, forcing me to reach for a counterillusion: I was special in a good way. I was a fairytale princess.

Since I didn't know what or whom I truly feared, I feared the house we shared, which by guilty association became the house that knew. In my imagination, monsters prowled its cubbyholes—my monstrous secret, my monstrous other self, turned into something outside me that I could fear. Even to bring someone into my father's house threatened exposure. Thus for me the usual childhood reality was reversed. Inside my own house, among people I knew, was where danger lay. The familiar had proven to be treacherous, whereas the unfamiliar, the public, the unknown, the foreign, still contained the seeds of hope. My world was a photographic negative of my playmates' worlds: for white, read black.

I skip to school singing, "Step on a crack, break your mother's back." I am in Miss Macintosh's room, which is Grade Two. Miss Macintosh has a face like a jolly red apple and a pancake hat and a raspberry slip that shows when she bends over. Miss Macintosh never gives homework or the strap. She uses yellow chalk and sometimes calls us kids.

Most weekends after Sunday school my family visits Grandmother Pearl, my father's mother and hence my other grandmother. She has been bedridden so long I attach that description to her name: Other Grandmother Who-Is-Bedridden. Prying our way into the skinny Victorian house, lavishly trimmed with black iron, often takes as long as the Sunday visit. Around and around we go, rattling windows and banging on doors, trying to rouse Aunt Estelle.

"Are you sure she knew we were coming today?" ventures my mother.

"Of course I'm sure!" snaps my father, adding in a grumble: "Estelle does it to spite me."

After the usual poundings and pryings, a loose window is found into the cellar. Being smallest, I am hoisted inside.

"Hurry, hurry!" commands my father, his face hanging upside down like a bat in the window.

Other Grandmother's cellar smells of worms and toads. A skimpy light illumines dead peaches, dead pears, dead plums in glass jars. Laying my palms against the trapdoor, I shove. The door creaks open, sending a slit of moldy light skittering across the brown linoleum. I dash for the front latch, with the cold biting through my soles: why is it always winter in Other Grandmother's house?

Other Grandmother lies propped in bed, petting a white dog so old I've never seen its eyes open. Her arms are long and lean and white, like marble. Her teeth are large, like tombstones. Frosty hair frames a thin white face.

My father approaches the bed, carrying his gray fedora. "Good day, mother."

Other Grandmother strokes her little white dog.

"She doesn't hear," whispers my mother.

"Do you always have to state the obvious?"

Father kisses Other Grandmother on her chalk cheek. Startled, she turns. "Upon my word! When did you get in?" She embraces him with marble arms, suddenly supple. "You'll be the death of me yet, David. Couldn't you even spare your mother a postcard?"

Father reddens. He hates it when Other Grandmother mistakes him for Uncle David, who ran away. "No, mother, it is I, Lyle. It is not David. Mother, I am Lyle."

Other Grandmother's milky eyes begin to clear. "Who?" Her voice croaks: "Oh, Lyle."

We hear a noise. Aunt Estelle—as skinny as my father is fat—stands in the doorway, her black-wire hair parted down the middle and coiled into earmuffs. "Sorry. I didn't hear you. I was scrubbing mother's bedpan." She sets her lips like the wringer on my mother's washing machine. "Somebody has to do it."

We settle in a crescent around Other Grandmother's bed. Aunt Estelle plumps her cushions. "Comfy, mother? I'll do your hair."

Like a salesman with his foot in the door, my father persists: "I've brought the wife and family to see you."

Other Grandmother stares past father at the rest of us. "Ah, yes. How very nice."

Too eager to please, he yanks Helen from her chair. "Go see your grandmother." Helen approaches Other

Grandmother's bed and is stiffly embraced. He tips my chair. "Hurry, can't you see? Your grandmother knows you!"

I make myself rigid with courage.

"Well, well, well," says Other Grandmother, her crystal voice jagged with pain. "Well, well, well, how you've grown." Cocking her head on the same angle as mine, she transfers a pearly comb from her hair to mine as if looking into a mirror. She confirms: "You get your blond hair from your father and from me." She runs her icicle fingers through my hair, spinning it into snowflakes. "Just like a fairytale princess."

I scamper back to my chair, pearl comb perched on my head like a crown, repeating my talisman: just like a fairytale princess.

My father supplicates: "You're looking better today, mother." He turns to the rest of us. "Isn't she looking better?"

I don't think she looks better. Other Grandmother's bones are creeping out of her flesh like the skull and crossbones on the iodine bottle, which I know to be poison.

While the adult talk halts and starts, I look through a photograph album which I know by heart. Other Grandmother smiling from under a parasol, her blond hair twisted like Aunt Estelle's. My father in a Buster Brown suit, with a primly starched Aunt Estelle. Uncle David, six years older, with his foot on his Model T. Grandfather Jonah, in top hat and spats, pointing to the gold-lettered sign of a business he once owned: BAVARIAN IMPORTS, LTD.

I close the photo album, forcing myself back to the here and now. My father is exclaiming: "Nobody cooks dumplings like mother!"

"Look this way, mother," says Aunt Estelle. "You know you love to have your hair combed."

Every time my father says one thing, Aunt Estelle says another, pulling on Other Grandmother's uncertain attention like scrappy dogs on two ends of a tatty towel. I try to catch Helen's eye to grin, but she is thumbing National Geographics. My mother is embroidering a luncheon cloth for a shower gift. No matter how I concentrate on such details, I can't divert my mind from what I know will happen next. Aunt Estelle signals it: "We musn't tire her . . . ."

Soon, soon will come that unspeakable moment when we line up, in order of size, to kiss Other Grandmother's cheek. I struggle against the heaving of my stomach, the yammering of my heart, trying not to experience, before I have to, that instant when the sweet smell of Other Grandmother's gardenia powder overwhelms me and my lips are swallowed in the decaying pulpiness of her cheek. Why this revulsion for an old woman's kiss? I do not know. I cannot say.

This truth belongs to my other self, and it is a harsh one: Other Grandmother's caved-in cheek is the same squishy texture as daddy's scrotum.

At recess the girls of Room 7 cluster around Ruth-Anne Baltimore and me, shouting: "Can I play? Can I play?"

Ruth-Anne folds her skipping rope into a rosette. Since I am her best friend, I get first choice. Seven others grab a loop to see who are the enders.

Ruth-Anne skips. We sing:
>"A house to rent,
>Apply within.
>If you don't pay the rent,
>WHO will come in?"

"YOU will come in," shouts Ruth-Anne, pointing to me.

I jump into the rope as she jumps out. Encircling me are the other players and, beyond that, those no one ever invites: Flora who is fat and Lily who is silly and bucktoothed Magda Lunt from the church. My friends chant: "WHO will come in?"

I catch Magda's pleading eyes—one of which has been blackened. I point to Magda: "YOU will come in."

Everyone is scandalized. Who? Who? "She's not even playing," protests Sharon Battersea, who's so stuck on herself she thinks everyone else is.

Magda glows. Ten minutes later, when Miss Sissons blows her end-of-recess whistle, Magda rushes toward me with outstretched hand. "Be my partner? Be my partner?"

Of course, I can't. "I'm sorry but—" Ruth-Anne and I join hands, like all the other best friends. Magda tries to sneak in behind us. With a blast of her whistle, Miss Sissons jerks her thumb to the end of the double line. "Partners, please!"

As Magda slinks back to Fat Flora and Silly Lily and the other rejects, one slightly behind the other in a straggly line, Sharon Battersea sneers: "Magda's father beats her up. Phew! Magda stinks of fish."

Several girls giggle. I scuff my shoes on the sidewalk, avoiding Magda's craven eyes as she treads her shadow at the raggle-taggle end. Magda doesn't stink of fish. I know that smell. I've smelled it on myself. It's the stink of . . . *fear*. It's the stink of . . . *daddy won't love me love me* . . . .

I stand in front of my vanity mirror, examining myself with Sharon Battersea's merciless eye. My hair has been twisted into bona fide curls, even tied with a yellow ribbon. My bright-penny public self, newly buffed and polished, stares back at me, and yet, and yet . . . . A spot clouds the mirror. I rub. It grows larger. I scrub harder. Now I see a smudge where my face used to be. For an instant, it turns into a girl who looks like Magda, with thumbprint bruises and fangs for teeth. When I try to rub her out, she lays her warty palm against mine: "I'm your partner! I'm your partner!"

Squinting so I can't see her face, I brush my hair till it shines, then I crown myself with Other Grandmother's pearl comb, trying not to think of the bird's nest sitting on Queen Victoria's head in Gore Park, making everyone laugh.

I hear my daddy calling. I go downstairs . . . .

After school and on weekends I play with Arlene and her brother Sidney in their backyard. Whenever we can, we sneak out the hole in their fence to the railway tracks. Sometimes we skip along the rails, trying to push each other off. Sometimes we play on the dead cars parked on the siding. Sometimes I lie on my back between the tracks and let the trains shunt over me, feeling the earth growl and the silver rails hum, *making contact through the thrill of danger with my other self.* Arlene cries when I do this. Sidney dares me but he won't do it himself. Sidney is a sis.

My mother is making shortbread on the kitchen table. I hear the top dint down as she leans into it with her rolling pin, then spring back with a tinny plock. Though the table sounds angry, her tone is smiling. "We can seat eight with the extra leaves. I'll borrow Mrs. Newton's folding chairs and—"

Sweat trickles from my armpits. "I don't think I want a birthday party."

"All your friends have parties. Why don't you ever bring anyone home to play?" My mother's voice hardens like the protesting table. "You're not ashamed of our house, are you? I hope you're not turning into a snob!"

"It's not that. It's, it's . . . ." What? I don't know. I can't say. I stare at our patch-on-patch chintz chesterfield; the threadbare rug whose pattern was always beyond imagining. Am I a snob, as my mother says? Is that why my stomach goes woozy every time someone from "out there" threatens to come "in here"? I look at the see-no-evil hear-no-evil monkeys on the radio console and then at my father's fetch-me chair, sagging under his weight even when he isn't in it, then back at the monkeys. My stomach flips then flops. *Just as everyone is deaf at Other Grandmother's house, everyone is blind in my father's house.*

Next day I cross the threshold of Room 7 with seven birthday invitations in a brown lunch bag. Grimacing, I trudge the aisles delivering homemade invitations in grubby sealed and resealed envelopes. "It's not really a party. Mother just said I could have a few friends in." And then, so as not to make too dismal a job of it: "We're having both cake and banana cream pie." My last invitation goes to Magda Lunt, arms covered in thumbprint bruises, instead of to Sharon Battersea.

Once again the social structure of Room 7 is rocked to its foundation. All week, Sharon whispers in everyone's ear: "Don't go . . . ." And then: "Bzzz," which I can't hear but which turns everyone's face red.

All week, Magda Lunt tries to grab my hand at recess: "Be my partner! Be my partner!"

All week I take off my coat in subzero weather in fading hopes I'll be struck dead with pneumonia. Yet, no matter how slowly I drag my galoshes through the gutters, one day leads inevitably to the next and soon it's Friday.

The attic is cold when I awake—the folly of central heating that ends on the second floor. Measuring the distance to my wooly bathrobe, I put out one foot then dash. With a dirty sock, I clean an eyehole in the frosty window: more snow than I've seen in my life—a blizzard!

My mother breaks it to me gently. "The radio says it's the worst storm in twenty-one years." Schools are closed, roads are blocked, buses aren't running, telephone wires are down. "I guess you'll have to cancel your party."

That morning I'm about the only thing moving on the streets of Hamilton as I plow through snowdrifts, face buried, red parka thrust into the howling wind, joyfully retrieving invitations from those who can't be reached by phone.

After church on Sunday Magda helps polish off the birthday cake and banana pie, stuffing her mouth and pockets at the same time. "I'm sorry, Magda—about the party."

She shows me a plastic ring I know came from a box of CrackerJacks: "This way I get to keep your gift!"

The party is never rescheduled. I am ecstatic: for white, read black.

Other Grandmother's corpse is laid for viewing in the parlor of her *hear-no-evil* house, now opened, aired and dusted.

After the visitors shuffle off, the relatives collect in the kitchen for tea and my mother's shortbread.

I creep from the curtain behind which I have been hiding. Other Grandmother's coffin gleams like an altar in the candlelight. I can see the lid, lined in puckered satin. I can't see Other Grandmother. As I tiptoe forward, Aunt Estelle enters the parlor.

"Ah, I've been locking for you." Grabbing me by the seat of the pants and scruff of the neck, she hoists me like a kitten up the side of the shiny coffin. "This is your last chance to kiss Grandmother Pearl good-bye." As I suck in air the texture of hot syrup, I see the gaunt death's-head floating inches beneath me—a yellow death's-head, since Other Grandmother died of jaundice. I know, as sure as I know anything in my life, that if I am forced to kiss Other Grandmother's corpse, I will go somewhere far away inside myself and never come back. I scream—a silent exhalation struggling to become sound. I scream just as my father enters the parlor. I scream in that deaf house and I am heard!

My father speaks eight words: "I don't think that will be necessary, Estelle." Then he yanks me from her hands. Crumpling to the floor, I seize my daddy's leg and will not let go until my fingers are pried loose. *In those few seconds, my other self reconfirms—if ever she doubted it—the wisdom of serving power in a precarious world.*

MR. BROWN

Who was my other self?

Though we had split one personality between us, I was the majority shareholder. I went to school, made friends, gained experience, developing my part of the personality, while she remained morally and emotionally a child, functioning on instinct rather than on intelligence. She began as my creature, forced to do what I refused to do, yet because I blotted out her existence, she passed out of my control as completely as a figure in a dream.

She was a servant of the house we shared, both useful and dangerous to me. There she remained a prisoner—or did she? Like a dog that sometimes slips its tether, did she ever run free? I can never be sure. I do know this. The first night I slept in my father's house after my memories had begun to return, I did not dream of my father. I dreamed of Mr. Brown.

Halfway through the summer of '44, my mother rents the two rooms on our second floor where Granny Cragg lived before she died. I hear my mother tell Mrs. Newton, our neighbor lady to the right: "What with the wartime housing shortage, I feel it's my patriotic duty." As she also explains: "I advertised no children, but I felt so badly turning down this nice young woman with a little tyke and her husband in the service that I rented to the very next couple that came— a Mr. and Mrs. Brown from the west. He's a plumber. They have a boy who's three."

I sit on our veranda watching the Browns move in while pretending not to. Mrs. Brown has false teeth and dyed-red sausage curls. Mr. Brown has nicotine teeth and five strands of black hair like a music staff across his bald head. I don't like the Browns much, and neither, as it turns out, does my mother. As she later informs Mrs. Newton, while hanging out her wash: "It's not the same having strangers in your house."

What she means is that Mrs. Brown is nosy, snippy and gossipy, while Mr. Brown is mean-tempered, unshaven and can't keep a job. "He says he's 4-F because of his nervous stomach." That means he drinks, which we all know because of the smell and the bottles. Privately, my mother calls him shiftless, meaning—I suppose—he doesn't have my father's shifts at the Steel Company.

The Browns fight a lot and their son, Barry, cries all the time. One day at the very end of August, while I am polishing my shoes for the start of school, I hear my mother confide to Mrs. Newton: "Mrs. Brown is in the family way. She's expecting in January."

Her sidelong look, accompanied by her voice vibrating with suppressed sin, warns me to keep on polishing. I try the word out on Helen, who has been picking tomatoes as a farmerette for the war. "What is Mrs. Brown expecting in January?"

Helen's answer is remarkably straightforward: "Mrs. Brown is expecting a baby." Her expression also warns me: go no further.

I am in Miss LaStrobe's room, which is Grade Three. At recess Ruth-Anne Baltimore and I set up our joint kingdom, just like last year. All the girls of Room 9 gather around: "Can I play? Can I play?"

As we return to our seats, Miss LaStrobe, who wears glasses on a chain, whispers to me: "You're to transfer to Room 11. Don't take anything but your jacket. You've been chosen to skip a grade."

I clutch my desk, feeling my universe tremble. Skip? Skip? Suddenly, all is explained—mysterious conversations between my mother and Principal Burns, and tests only I had to take. I walk down the long hall, with all the doors closed, dragging my jacket by the collar as if it were Teddy Umcline. Miss Buchanan, noted for her stiff spine and strange love of English grammar, introduces me to my new class. Thirty-six pairs of eyes stare at me over their Grade Four readers: freak!

Miss Buchanan announces: "We're going to have a spelling test." A couple of kids shoot dirty looks my way as if I am to blame. Miss Buchanan smiles at me: "Just do your best, dear."

Though I am nervous, I discover that "elephant" is still "elephant" with a ph and not an f, even in Grade Four. When I get my paper back from Lulu Lawson, who has marked it, I am the only one with no mistakes. Miss Buchanan rubs out Tonya Philpott's name from under STAR SPELLER on the blackboard, and inscribes mine in red chalk. Several kids look at me as if I must have cheated, including Tonya Philpott. Plastering over the cracks in my face with a bold smile, I write under my name in my scribbler:

Grade 3–4
Room 9–11
Laura Secord Public School
Hamilton
Ontario
Canada
North America
Western Hemisphere
Planet Earth
Solar System
Milky Way Galaxy
Universe.

After class Miss Buchanan writes "1/4" and "1/2" on the board.

"Which is larger?" she asks.

As four is larger than two, I point to "1/4."

Miss Buchanan asks: "Which would you sooner have, half a pie or a quarter of a pie?" A light flashes, and that's it for fractions.

The rest is not so easy. I always used to be tallest in my

room. Now I'm almost the shortest. I can't play with my old friends in Miss LaStrobe's room now that I know fractions. Since no one will pair with me at recess, I'm stuck with Magda Lunt at the end of the line. When I get ten out of ten in arithmetic, "Joker" Nash makes a sucking sound with his hands. He says what the other kids are thinking: "Tit sucker!"

I try singing the teachers' names with their room numbers, the way I used to, but now there's a gap between grades Two and Four, like when you lose a tooth. To be smart used to mean being popular, but now. . . . My school world, which I count on for stability, has turned unpredictable.

I groom Smoky with my own hairbrush, even tying a pink ribbon around his neck. Smoky stretches, purrs, rolls over, offering up his fat, warm belly. Smoky loves me!

With a leap, surprisingly swift for one of his corpulence, he streaks downstairs. I give chase—through my mother's room, then into the hall. As I dive for Smoky, he shoots into my father's room. He settles on his haunches under my father's bed, still wearing his pink ribbon.

"Here puss puss puss."

Through the bathroom door I hear my father splashing in the tub. Holding my breath, I slide under his bed, grabbing for Smoky. Now the bath plug is being pulled. With a gurgle, the scummy water sucks down the drain.

By the time daddy stomps out of the bathroom, saronged in a towel, my other self is curled on his feather pillow, sucking her thumb and wearing Smoky's dirty pink ribbon. A breeze blows the curtains inward, just like the hair of a fairytale princess, giving her goose bumps. Whose little girl are you?

Now that I am too old to leave with the babies during Reverend Thwaite's sermon, I sit with Magda Lunt in the balcony where we can count the people who fall asleep. This morning, Reverend Thwaite is preaching on "Sins of the Flesh—Lust and Adulterrry." Though I make no sense of it beyond the

story of Samson and Delilah, something about the way everyone is squiggling in their pews makes me think to whisper to
Magda: "Mrs. Brown is expecting."

Magda's swift reply—"I'm sure glad ma isn't!"—suggests
greater knowledge, tempting me to go further.

"How does someone 'expect'?"

With an indelible pencil, which she licks first, Magda draws
a woman with a potbelly on her church program. My eyes
bug—Mrs. Brown, exactly!

"How does . . . ?"

Magda makes another drawing. This time—

I start to giggle, and can't stop. I try to hold my breath,
then start sneezing. After that, it's the hiccups, with Magda,
her mouth an indelible purple, banging me on the back. I end
up down in the basement being sick in the toilet. *My other
self shakes and shakes*. I cannot stop.

On Monday, I make an excuse to go over to Magda's. She
gives me the whole story, and it's a pretty sordid one. Now
I'm beginning to understand the insults hurled by boys; the
actions of the dirty men who haunt the bushes in Gage Park;
the filthy words scrawled on walls; the squishy white balloons
tossed into alleys; the hushed adult conversations that end
when I enter a room.

Over the next month, I chart the expansion of Mrs. Brown's
stomach to the last centimeter. It seems to grow right before
my eyes, like a beach balloon with a tire pump attached. First
she can't do up her skirt buttons, then the zipper won't close.
In the mornings I stand in line with my toothbrush while she
is sick in the toilet. How could I have been so stupid not to
guess?

I draw pictures of Teddy Umcline with a big fat belly. One
day the belly explodes. Out pops—Mr. Brown with horns
and a forked tail!

*

Miss Buchanan slides into my seat beside me. Though the bell has not yet rung, most of the kids are already in the room, whispering. "I know what a curious mind you have," she says, as she unscrolls a map. "Do you know where China is?"

I nod, aware of a growing puddle of silence around me. Everyone knows where China is. If you dig through the earth you get to it.

Her sturdy finger traces a crooked red line running like blood across the map. "This is how Marco Polo traveled to China. If you were still in Grade Three, you'd be taking this now. It's a fascinating story. I thought maybe you might like to follow the journey anyway, in your spare time. There's a text that goes with it."

I look with longing at the wonderful map, covered with strange names and exotic pictures. As I reach out to touch it, I hear a gentle suck suck suck from two seats over where Joker Nash is sitting. Fighting to exist on the only terms possible for me, I demand in a loud voice: "Am I going to have to write an exam on this?"

"Well, no, dear, I just thought—"

I fold over the map. "Then I don't want it. I'm in Grade Four."

Now when Miss Buchanan speaks to me outside of class, I duck my head. I never put up my hand to answer questions. I talk when she's writing exercises on the board. Eventually, I am moved to the back of the room where the "good heads" like Tonya Philpott and Babs Bertoli hold court.

Lulu Lawson is my new best friend. She has a heart-shaped face and taffy hair, which she wears in a ponytail. Her father is a lieutenant in the navy. She carries his picture in her locket, and one day all the kids in Room 11 write a letter to him for Composition. Both Lulu's parents look like movie stars. Lulu calls them Millicent and Paul, which my mother says is forward. Mrs. Lawson does volunteer work, like my mother, but she gets her picture in the paper wearing a hat with a veil.

I play at Lulu's several times a week after school, and sometimes I sleep over. Though their house is a big white one on Delaware Avenue, most of the rooms are closed up because her mother can't get enough help during the war. The Lawson house reminds me of Other Grandmother's, where Aunt Estelle lives boarded up, except everything is dusted at the Lawsons' because they do have a maid, whom Lulu calls a family retainer. When I stay for supper (which Lulu calls dinner) we sit at a shiny mahogany table with silver cutlery rippling in both directions. Two other places are always set, though Mrs. Lawson usually eats out. As Lulu explains: "We leave everything as it was when Paul went to war. That's for luck."

I'm not used to what Lulu calls fashionable dining. Often it's seven before she presses the lump in the carpet, summoning Miss Mildon (whom Lulu calls Miss Mildew). Eventually, she shuffles into view, bearing two bowls of soup on a silver tray. I know, before I dip my spoon, it will be a) one of Heinz's twenty-seven varieties; and b) barely heated. Tonight it's mushroom. Before we begin, Lulu presses for the next course. Eventually, Miss Mildon reappears pushing a creaky tea wagon with a silver salver, which I know holds two dry sandwiches—tuna or chicken or Spam. Of all the kids I know, Lulu is the only one with a maid and the one who eats the worst.

"The soup was delicious," announces Lulu, "but my companion complains it scalded her tongue."

I sputter into my napkin, frantic to hide the blue teeth that reveal we've also been tippling Miss Mildon's grape cordial in the solarium.

An exasperated Miss Mildon hisses: "Stop your tongue, missy! There's other places crying for help that's been trained in the old country."

Afterward we retire to Lulu's room, housing the world's greatest collection of movie magazines. Sprawled across her four-poster, we look at pictures of Maria Montez and Guy

Madison and Robert Taylor. Holding up a silver-framed photo of her father in his white uniform, Lulu asks: "Don't you think Paul is the deadspit of Clark Gable?"

I point to a Photoplay picture of Vivien Leigh. "Your mother looks like that, too."

"No, she doesn't. Her nose is too large. Grandmother Lawson was the beauty in the family. Everyone says I have the Lawson nose. Here, I'll show you."

We go through a double door into Lulu's grandmother's bedroom which, according to Lulu, has also been kept exactly as it was when she died. "The royal family would have attended her funeral, but they couldn't because of the Scandal."

I've heard this story several times, though the details keep changing. Somebody shot somebody over love, which was why Grandmother Lawson had to leave England.

"The Prince of Wales was involved."

I never know how many of Lulu's stories to believe. Tonya Philpott says she's crazy, but I know her grandmother was an actress—or, as Lulu puts it, a great thespian—because her grandmother's bedroom walls are covered with posters. Lulu likes to dress as Cleopatra, which is the role her grandmother made famous on the "legitimate stage," but I prefer to be glamorous like Lana Turner.

Lulu does the makeup. She's very good at it, especially the black Cleopatra eyes. When her mother drops in to say good night, we are listening to "Double Indemnity" on Lux Radio Theater. Millicent Lawson is always putting on her gloves or taking them off. She does this finger by finger because they are leather, not cloth like my mother's. Every black hair is always in place under her hat with a veil, and when she speaks only her red lips move. "Better turn off your radio, Snooks."

Lulu won't turn out the light till she has found a tattered gray handkerchief which she claims has her father's smell on it. Then she kisses his picture. I lie awake feeling jealous. When she starts to snore, I take her hanky with her father's smell on it, pretending it is mine.

*

The phone rings and rings. When I answer it, I hear a child sobbing: "I want my daddy." A silver-framed picture of Clark Gable falls from the wall, knocking me unconscious.

I awake from a sound sleep—the sun is shining through my own frosted window. Why didn't someone call me? I remember with relief—it's Saturday.

The limbs of the maple outside my window have a new coating of snow. Everybody on the street is bundled against the wind. Since I'm going to a matinee with Arlene, I put on my blue flannel skirt, pink sweater and brown cotton stockings with garters. Then I go down to the bathroom.

My sister's bed is like a cocoon from which the butterfly has flown. Same with my mother's and my father's. The house is quiet except for the Browns' radio. The Browns' two doors, on either side of our shared bathroom, are tightly closed, as usual. Now that Mrs. Brown is in the hospital having her baby, my parents do the Browns' grocery shopping on Saturday mornings as well as ours. Barry is crying in his bed. I suppose Mr. Brown is baby-sitting.

I take a long time in the bathroom, though I'm not usually so enthusiastic about cold water on a cold morning. When I do open the door, the Browns' kitchen door is also ajar. I realize, with a flip-flop of my stomach, that I knew it would be.

Mr. Brown appears in the doorway, chest bare, black trousers held up by a too-long belt that sticks out like a tongue. Everything about him is unkempt, from his caved-in chest to his nicotine fingers and unshaven jaw. He smiles. "C'm in here."

I hesitate, my hand on the knob of the only room in the house with a lock, but I've been trained to be polite to adults, even if they look like Mr. Brown.

I step across the threshold, growing light-headed. Granny Cragg's sink is piled high with dirty dishes, her blue corduroy couch has a hole burned in it, her card table is heaped with dirty laundry—not anyone's fault, I suppose, just too small a place for too many people. My head swivels, looking for her butterfly lamp and her Christmas cactus and—

Mr. Brown grabs me by the wrist. *"Don't try to fool me, kid. I know what goes on in this house."* He kicks the wallpaper wall between his kitchen and my father's bedroom. *"Don't you think anybody's got any ears?"*

My other self whimpers rather than cries as Mr. Brown, trousers undone, rubs up against her, so roughly she can count his ribs, back and forth, back and forth, stinking of smoke and whiskey, while he gets hard, then soft and —ugh!—sticky. Now she knows that she, like Magda, must have fingerprints all over her like the marks tramps put on doors to show where they can expect a free meal. She hears Barry crying in the other room. So does Mr. Brown. It makes him mad. He pulls her hair so tight her eyes slit. His own hair is sticking out in wiggly strands all over his head like snakes. "What are you going to tell your old man?"

"Nothing!"

"You'd better not!"

Yanking his belt from his trousers, he lashes her across the legs. Barry is screaming. Mr. Brown curses. Her legs sting through her brown stockings, then go numb as pee seeps down them. Looping his belt around her neck, Mr. Brown snarls: "You tell anyone, kid, and I'll kill you!"

Mr. Brown keeps looking toward the door, anxious that the grocery shoppers will return. My other self is just as anxious. By now she is more enslaved by her daddy than frightened. She no longer believes he will kill Smoky, who is more likely to die of overeating. She IS afraid of Mr. Brown, who she knows is a nasty, evil man. Hysterical, she runs down the stairs, out the back door into the snow, not even noticing she has wet her pants. By the time she dares return home, her sodden brown stockings have frozen to her dirty dirty legs. She burns them in the furnace.

*

I call on Arlene, panting a little because I'm late. "Sorry, I slept in." Usually we go to a double feature at the Delta, which, at twelve cents, is half the price of the first-run uptown theaters. Her current favorites are Red Skelton, Margaret O'Brien and Van Johnson. Mine are Cornel Wilde, Peter Lawford and Rita Hayworth. My mother likes Greer Garson and Gary Cooper. So does Helen.

After much debate we agree on Abbott and Costello Meet Frankenstein, at the Delta, even though that means also seeing Gestapo, a stupid war movie.

"I'm sick of war movies," protests Arlene.

"Everyone is." Defiantly, I admit: "I'm even sick of the war."

"Everyone is."

"Except," I remind her, "Sidney, who still collects shredded-wheat cards with planes and boats on them."

She taunts me: "Sidney says your father is a Nazi!"

"That's a lie. Only Other Grandmother was German, and she's dead." Putting my hands over my ears, I force the conversation into safer channels. "I'm sick of cutting out pictures of bombed places for Current Events."

"I'm sick of cleaning up my plate because of the starving war orphans in Europe."

"I'm sick of war comics with Nazis that say: 'Vell, Fraulein, ve haf vays und means uf making you convess.' "

"I'm sick of chocolate bars that taste like popcorn dipped in brown wax."

"I'm sick of having people like the Browns living in the same house because we can't get them out!"

The comedy is as funny as we hoped. The war movie is as boring as we expected.

I have bad dreams.

Tramp tramp tramp. Leather footsteps thud up my attic stairs. A Nazi with black snake hair and nicotine teeth yanks me out of my bed. "Ve haf vays und means uf making you convess." He slashes me across my brown-stockinged legs with his belt. Pee seeps down them in a smelly yellow puddle.

"*No, no, no! It wasn't me. It was another little girl. It was . . . It was . . .*" I try to hide in Granny Cragg's rag box, but it is full of dirty diapers. Looping his belt around my neck, the Nazi holds me in front of my dresser mirror. "*No! That isn't me. It was another little girl. It was . . . It was . . . Magda Lunt!*"

I awake in a sticky yellow puddle with the sound of the Nazi strap still ringing in my ears. The same thing happens the next night and the next—the same dream and the same yellow puddle. Mortified, I watch my mother strip my soiled bed, a vivid look of embarrassment on her face. I shout: "I hate brown stockings! Why can't I wear ankle socks?"

My mother tries to remain calm in the face of this new challenge. "Your legs will freeze. They'll grow hairy like an ape's."

"I don't care. I won't wear brown stockings!"

"What's wrong with them? You wore them last week without complaint."

Once again I am left to rationalize the truths of my other self. I search my jumbled mind for some plausible answer, for myself as well as for my mother. "Brown stockings make my legs look like poop!"

By now I'm lying on the floor, kicking my heels. My mother is astounded. She hasn't seen anything like this since my fits.

When I finally run out the door, I am wearing the brown stockings, which I take off as soon as I round the first corner. I am late for school.

My mother is talking to Mrs. Lawrence on the back porch. "The noise from those two rooms is hard to believe. With the new baby some fuss is to be expected, but the blare of that radio is another matter. Last night it was after midnight when they turned it off."

She leans confidentially over her frozen sheets. "The one I feel sorry for is little Barry. The way that man goes after that tyke when he's angry makes me cringe. You can hear that strap all over the house. What could that child possibly do to need that kind of punishment?"

My mother's remark puzzles me. I live in the same house. I hear the radio. I hear the quarrels. How come I never hear the strap?

My other self stuffs her fingers in her ears, the possessor of one more guilty secret she must keep from me.

It is the last day of Grade Four after a very long winter. I sit in the auditorium beside Miss Buchanan, pretending I am listening to Grade Three sing "D'ye Ken John Peel" in three parts, but I am really staring at the minute hand of Bill Bowen's Westclox watch: eleven more minutes till summer!

I might have been enjoying the countdown. I might have been exchanging notes with Lulu about the movie we intend to see or asking Tonya Philpott about summer camp. Instead, I am shifting resentfully on my folding chair, my legs corkscrewed, my hands neatly folded, trying not to look at Miss Buchanan. How this arrangement with the seats came about I am at a loss to say. I was supposed to sit beside Bob Hanna as dictated by the alphabet, but at the last moment Miss Buchanan took his place.

Only seven more minutes. The Grade Three choral singers launch into "Flow Gently Sweet Afton," despite limp applause. If this were morning assembly, the student body would have rung the rafters begging for an encore in hopes of shaving a few minutes off the next class. Now everyone's eye, like mine, is on the clock.

At last, at last. A proctor unfurls the Union Jack. We sing "God Save the King."

The bell rings. Four o'clock on the button. Principal Burns announces: "School dismissed."

With a whoop, everyone races for the exits. I try to join Lulu, waiting at the end of my row, but Miss Buchanan bars my way. "I want to speak with you."

Unfair, unfair! School is over. The principal said so.

Miss Buchanan's voice starts out as if she were dictating history notes. "I suppose you have an interesting summer planned?" Halfway through the second sentence, her voice cracks. Without my understanding how it happened, she is pleading: "Why? Why did you turn on me?"

I stare at her, shocked at this breakdown of teacher-student protocol, all the more painful in someone usually so unbending.

"Why have you been so mean all year? You seem to have developed such a chip on your shoulder. It's as if you've decided not to trust anyone any more."

I shift my gaze to the exit through which the last students are shoving, wretched to have caused this suffering, appalled to have possessed such power, resentful to be called to account.

"If you'll give me some explanation, I'll try to understand. Why do you hate me so?"

Hate? Now I am flabbergasted. I don't hate you, Miss Buchanan. I love you. As soon as these words pop into my head, I know that in spite of everything, they are true. I've always liked my teachers, even crabby Miss Warner, but Miss Buchanan is my favorite. As her voice continues, controlled but still perplexed, the room seems to wiggle like Jell-O. Now Miss Buchanan is staring at me, waiting for some response. My tongue lies frozen in my mouth. *Love hate love hate fear fear fear, it's all mixed up, impossible to sort.*

Miss Buchanan sighs. "I feel sorry for you. If you lock yourself away from everyone who cares about you, you're going to have a hard life."

By now the auditorium is empty. The janitor bangs his broom as if he must begin his summer's sweeping precisely where we are standing, nowhere else will do. Miss Buchanan reddens, then snatches up her papers and strides off. I try to call: "Have a nice summer!" but even these pale words stick in my throat. Scraping my shoes as if to rid them of stickiness, I run out the exit under the glassy-eyed buffalo head.

Lulu is still waiting: "Well, it's about time."

Arlene and I are roller-skating down Lorne Avenue one August day when all the factory whistles in Hamilton start to blow. The neighbor ladies run onto their porches, calling to the mailman and even to strangers: "Have you heard? The war is over! It's official, it just came over the BBC." Cars honk and girls in coveralls pour out of Mercury Knitting Mills and Wagstaff's Cannery.

Helen takes Arlene and me uptown to see the lights come on for the first time I can remember. Suddenly, Eaton's and Robinson's and Cut-Rate Shoes and the Palace Theater flash neon pink and red and gold and blue and green. People with party hats and horns make a conga line through Gore Park. They climb up the statue of Queen Victoria with the bird's nest on her head and drink liquor right from the bottle. Everyone is happy and everyone cries.

Lulu's father comes home from war. The Hamilton Spectator runs a photo of him in his navy uniform with all his medals: WAR HERO PAUL LAWSON BUYS RADIO STATION CHKL. Lulu takes it everywhere with her, the way she used to carry his handkerchief with his smell on it. I am jealous. *My other self thinks about stealing it.*

Two weeks after the end of the war, the Browns move out. My father discovers Mr. Brown has run electrical wires, without insulation, all through the plaster in Granny Cragg's kitchen. As my mother tells Mrs. Lawrence, donning her not-our-sort expression like her Sunday hat: "Our house could have gone up in smoke at any time. It was like a time bomb. That Mr. Brown is a dangerous man."

THE GOLDEN AMAZONS

My sexual relationship with my father had many time gaps, and the older I grew, the more irregular it became. In particular, a break occurred around the time I was ten that lasted about two years. Perhaps guilt caught up with him. Perhaps he feared my maturing body, as I did. Perhaps he feared me. Perhaps he didn't understand that I couldn't confess because I had no idea there was anything to confess. Perhaps he feared my mother, as I did. Certainly, the story of Mr. Brown suggests that evidence lay about the house like an open diary waiting to be read.

Whatever the reason, this hiatus gave me a chance to stabilize, to imitate normalcy, to begin to close the gap in sexual awareness between me and my other self, to escape with relief into my peer group and to absorb its moral values. It did not stifle my anger. If anything, tenuous safety made me more openly rebellious, more disdainful of all authority, more outwardly raging, the way a small dog yaps loudest when a glass door seems to protect it.

When my father attempted to revive our affair, I was no longer the seven-year-old baby who had struck the dirty deal with him in the first place. Just as the emotions of my other self often leaked up into my life, now my moral values began seeping down into hers. Her Garden of Eden now had a very menacing two-headed snake: guilt and fear.

I am in Grade Eight. Every Saturday, weather permitting, Tonya Philpott and I go for a bike hike. This Saturday Tonya and I pump up the Jolley Cut on our way to Albion Falls, our legs straining as our wheels get slower and wobblier. On the Mountain brow, Tonya returns to a conversation begun at the last stop. "We could meet at my place. We should maybe have six—no more than eight or it's too many to stay overnight. We need good heads like Babs Bertoli, not the silly boy chasers. Did you see the ball Babs hit at recess yesterday?"

"Yeah, she's lots of fun. Babs and Arlene Goodfellow."

"The redhead with the frizzy hair and the teeth braces? Isn't she kinda quiet?"

"Not when you get to know her. We practically grew up together."

"Okay. How about Cooky Castle?"

I grimace. "She's a chaser."

"Nah, she's just used to guys because she's got a couple of brothers."

"I really like Lulu Lawson."

Tonya is unenthusiastic but this is a horse trade. "I suppose. Hey, that's six. What we need now is a name." She slides her nut brown fingers through her ducktail. "How about the Purple Raiders?"

"Nahh, that sounds like a boys' basketball team."

"Okay, but let's not choose anything too girlie."

Unhooking our thumbs from the belts of our matching gray gabardine strides, Tonya and I coast down a tunnel of birches, enjoying the slither of cool air against our sweaty cheeks. As I look up into the vibrant golden canopy, I remember the science fiction novel I've been reading in the Toronto Star Weekly:

> Imagine that the future gave to the world a woman
> with the strength of ten men, the science of Einstein
> and the will of an Oliver Cromwell. Such a woman
> lives. Her name is—

Jamming on my brakes, I exclaim: "Let's call ourselves the Golden Amazons."

Tonya turns the name over like a ripe pear, looking for a soft spot. She can't find one. "Yeah, the Golden Amazons."

We have our first meeting at Tonya's place. Main item on the agenda: shall we invite more kids to join?

"What about Barbara O'Neil?"

"That hard rock? Last Friday Miss Sprockett made her scrub off her pancake makeup."

"What about June James?"

"She's okay, but sort of young-acting, you know, silly."

"What about Magda Lunt?" As soon as the words are out of my mouth, I can't believe I've said them. The group turns on me in indignation.

"You must be kidding!"

"Have you seen the way she hangs around with those zoot-suity guys? I'd hate to have her conscience!"

"Her father hasn't worked a day in ten years—he's too drunk."

More tactfully, Arlene points out: "She's not in our grade. She's someone from your past."

No more names are put forward. It seems that membership in our shiny little group has already conferred so much glory that no one, judged from the inside, has sufficient luster to qualify.

Tonya, Lulu, Babs, Arlene, Cooky . . . . As I brush my blond hair into two parentheses, I recite the names of the Golden Amazons into the empty space between them. For the first time since I skipped a grade, I feel safe, legitimate, full of power. Now when I look in my mirror I see Tonya-Lulu-Babs-Arlene-Cooky.

Together, or in shifting pairs, we Golden Amazons hike, bike, bowl, sip vanilla Cokes at the Kozy Korner, swap movie mags and the latest on Ingrid or Rita, swoon over Frankie Lane and Billy Eckstine, discuss the virtues of Frank Sinatra versus Bing Crosby, try to predict the Hit Parade's Top Ten, see the latest movies at uptown prices, wear men's shirts and ties, giggle over dirty jokes Tonya claims are invented by men in prison, tell Little Moron stories and smoke DuMaurier cigarettes (three cents more but worth the price in sophistication).

Increasingly, we moon over who has a case on whom, and

pool our knowledge of sex. As Tonya sums up our growing suspicion: "It boils down to just one thing. No boy is safe. Once a guy gets hot and bothered, he can't control himself."

"Last Saturday night my mom and dad sat in the back row of the Delta, and they were shocked," says Cooky, smoothing her brunette underroll for emphasis.

"When a girl goes to the movies by herself, she's just asking for it," agrees Tonya.

"If a guy goes after you, you should bite him," offers Babs. "Or pull back his thumb."

"I think boys can be as shy as girls," protests Arlene, covering her teethbraces with her hand.

Tonya squelches her. "You've had your head twisted by your brother."

Amazon Cooky reads aloud from a copy of "Love Without Fear," smuggled from under her parents' mattress. "Though it may be difficult for modest and inexperienced young girls to understand, married women who are deeply in love with their husbands may enjoy having their breasts caressed or their nipples kissed as a prelude to lovemaking."

She is hooted down in disbelief.

A similar fate overtakes Amazon Arlene when she produces an even more lyrical manual, acquired on a similar fact-finding mission. Entitled "For Young Brides" and written by "a man of the cloth with impeccable credentials," it declares on page ten: "While toying with lust is a sin worthy of eternal damnation, God Himself hath blessed the overwhelming fire between man and wedded wife."

Cutting through our laughter, Tonya reminds us: "Sex for girls is always serious business. I read about a woman in one of those hot Latin countries who got preggers from a toilet seat. Don't think it can't happen to you." More confidentially she adds: "There's a delivery guy at Macnamara Drugs so perverted he pricks holes in French safes."

On the way home, I brood about my parents: the overwhelming fire between man and wedded wife? I conjure up the lemony mouth my mother makes when she judges a remark "off color" or "smutty." I think of her tone as she dismisses all threat of sexual taint with: "MY girls would never . . . ."

As I turn the corner, I start to giggle, picturing my mother and the other neighbor ladies hanging out their silk drawers each Monday morning, their pink corsets, their brassieres with watermelon cups, their lips set as stiffly as their clotheslines, pretending they can't see or be seen: you don't show me yours, and I won't show you mine! I picture Mrs. Lawrence's oversize snuggle-down nightgown cavorting with Mr. Lawrence's BVDs, all flaps flying, with the wooly arms of the BVDs goosing the bum of the nightgown whenever God happens to break wind in that direction. I am still laughing as I mount the front steps.

Our house is dark—not even a night lamp. I assume my mother is at a church meeting, that Helen, now in high school, has a date, that my father is on the night shift. Retrieving the key from the windowsill, I insert it in the lock, listen to the bolt click right, then slide back. I bound up the stairs two at a time, fifteen of them, curving around. As my right foot touches the top one, I hear the clearing of a throat. The door to my father's bedroom is open. He calls. I freeze.

My other self lies on her daddy's bed, her arms glued to her sides, her legs numb. For the first time, penetration is attempted, though it is by no means completed. She feels as if she were being repeatedly punched in the belly, forcing all air from her lungs. She feels used, not as one person exploited by another, but as a condom is used then discarded in the gutter. Tears run backward down her face into her hair. The emotion she holds so tightly in her chest that it blocks everything else is grief. She is old enough, now, to know about blood and babies. She is old enough, now, to understand how completely she has been betrayed.

The ice at Gage Park is best in the morning when it's flint-hard and glass-smooth. All is possible. You carve out circles and eights, and nothing exists until you put it there. Sometimes you just race around the rink, your legs sliding like they're on elastic bands, with your breath whistling through your teeth like steam from a locomotive, faster and faster.

Soon it's noon. The rink fills with kids in red and blue parkas playing tag or crack the whip.

"Hi!" It's Joe Baker from school. "Wanna skate?"

I prefer to play tag, but I don't want to hurt Joe's feelings and, besides, if I say no to him, maybe Perry Lord won't ask me. Such delicate weights and balances are the stuff of pre-dating, as I am coming to know it. Giving my hand to Joe with a bright paste-on smile, I slow my racing pace to his stodgy rhythm. The sound system squawks out "Oh, How We Danced on the Night We Were Wed" as we skate around and around, like the needle on the record. Joe's silence rattles me. I make chattery conversation. "Did you see The Thing from the Deep?"

By bad luck, the record never ends. The needle hits a crack, repeats "we vowed our true love we vowed our true love we vowed our true love," then jerks into "Don't Fence Me In." Now Joe links arms, forcing me to even greater intimacy and an even slower beat, *and making my other self very, very nervous. She cannot bear to be held or confined.* The game of tag is breaking up. Joe speaks his only sentence, and it is a lethal one. "Can I ah take you home if ah you're not doing anything?"

At the word "home" a cold shiver passes through me. I ransack my head for an explanation for the unpleasant way I am feeling and, failing that, an excuse. "I'll check with Arlene. We came together."

The clubhouse is crowded and noisy and steamy, as always. We jostle for a place on the splintery benches closest to the wood stove. The air stinks of charred wool—someone's icy mittens left too long on top. Joe helps me off with my skates, then unlaces his own while I inform Arlene. "Joe wants to take me home."

"He's cute. You have all the luck."

I study Joe through the lens of Arlene's enthusiasm: brown cowlick in wet spikes from his cap, earnest face bent over the task of knotting skate laces. Cute? Now that I know how I'm supposed to feel, I am reassured. Well, maybe.

We leave the rink just as the gang takes off in a gossipy pinwheel for the Kozy Korner. I think about suggesting we go too, but I'm afraid Joe doesn't have any money and I don't want to seem like a gold digger. Perry Lord tosses a snowball at Cooky Castle but hits Arlene instead. Tonya Philpott zings one back overhand, the way a boy would. I yearn to take up the challenge, but being with a boy obliges me to conform to more ladylike standards. Trapped, I stick my fists in my pockets.

Crunch crunch crunch. Skates knotted over Joe's shoulder, we trudge through the chalky snow. I've already told Joe the plot of The Thing from the Deep, and since I saw it uptown it wasn't a double feature. The silence lengthens with the shadows. Joe doesn't seem to mind. I do.

"Arlene says you got a hundred in arithmetic."

"Yeah. So did you."

"Yeah. But our test was easier."

I make the mistake of taking my hand out of my pocket to brush a snowflake. Joe commandeers it. *My other self panics*. How long before I can brush another snowflake and get it back without seeming rude? As I am working out the etiquette of this, two dogs rush the season by attempting to "do it" on the path in front of us. *My other self slips toward hysteria*. I burst into giggles. The blood rises up Joe's protruding ears. He fumbles with his backside: "Are you laughing at the rip in my ski pants?"

"No, it isn't that." But I can't stop giggling.

"Joker Nash cut it with his skate."

"Honest, I didn't even notice." I stifle more giggles in a sneeze. "Ah-choo!"

We are approaching my house. The giggles stop. Now my anxiety grows so intense I'm afraid I'll faint. Snatching my hand from Joe's, I pick up a stick and drag it ping ping ping along the fence around St. Cecilia's Cripples' Home the way I used to as a kid, pretending this is the most important thing in the world. How can I let you hold my hand when I am busy doing this?

We turn the corner. Now I see it—a sour-cream frame listing with snow like a milk bottle with the cap frozen off. *Home.* I stop, rooted to the spot. For reasons I can't explain, it's essential that Joe go no farther. I reach for my skates. "I live only a couple of doors away."

"I don't mind. I'll carry them to the—"

"No!" I yank the skates from Joe's neck, almost beheading him. "I've got to go—by myself."

Again Joe blushes from his neck through his ears. "Is it because of the rip in my ski pants? You don't want your parents to see—"

"No!" Then more humanely: "Honest. It has nothing to do with you." Pushing past him, I sprint for my father's house, clearing the steps in a single bound. As I open the storm door, the wind catches it.

"Don't slam the door!" roars my father from his armchair.

My other self bursts into hysterical weeping.

"What's wrong?" asks my mother.

Again, I find myself overcome by an emotion for which I must find a reason. Hurling my skates at her feet, I shout: "Why do I have to wear these old things? They hurt my feet."

Wiping her hands on her apron, my mother rallies. "Those skates were new last winter."

"Secondhand from Amity. You said I could have new skates for Christmas."

"You needed other things." By now I'm racked with weeping I can't control. Not about the skates, though I hear a voice I hardly recognize go on and on about them. "I hate these skates." Rage pours out of me like lava, devastating everything in its path. It flows around my father, implacable in his asbestos armchair.

It's a relief to be sent upstairs without supper. Flinging myself onto my bed, I pound the pillow till my body is seized with convulsions, *releasing the rage my other self can no longer control.*

*

I stand in line outside the Delta Theater, shoulders hunched, hands in pockets. I'm not used to attending a Saturday matinee by myself, but Arlene canceled at the last moment with flu, Lulu has gone Easter shopping with her mother in New York, Tonya has a Saturday job at Eaton's and Babs went bowling with her brother.

I examine the NOW PLAYING ads:

> Gary Cooper and Paulette Goddard in
>   UNCONQUERED!
> See the Lovers Plunge Down 106 Feet of Roaring
>   Water!
> See the Slave Auction Where a Man of Destiny
>   Buys a Girl with Crimson Tresses!
> See the Whipping at the Stake—Soft, White Flesh
>   Before the Stinging Lash!
> See—

"Hi, kiddo."

Glancing behind, I see a girl with henna hair, bare feet thrust into huaraches, men's raincoat thrown over an outlaw blouse and cotton skirt.

"Hi, Magda. Gee, you look . . . different."

Magda grins, displaying buckteeth smeared with Revlon's Orchids-to-You lipstick. "Well, yeah, I'm working nights at the Fish 'n' Fries Drive-In now. Long time no see."

I start to let her in, then remember the judgment of my peers: Have you seen the way she hangs around with those zoot-suity guys? I'd hate to have her conscience!

Halfheartedly, I ask: "Want in?"

Magda shakes her frizzy hair, a casualty of the new home permanents. "Ix-nay. I wanna know if you want in." Pointing to a side alley, she announces: "Me and my friends get in for free. The Mole sneaks us in during the news."

"Gee, I don't—"

"Come on." Magda hooks her arm through mine. I allow myself to be propelled on the strength of a quarter saved.

From the side, the Delta is a brick fortress pierced by one rusty door. Here the Technicolor promise of Paulette Goddard's soft, white flesh, parted lips and tousled crimson tresses has been translated, by chalked graffiti, into a more direct offer: I'M HOT, LOVER-BOY! WANNA SCREW? The gun-swaggering challenge of Gary Cooper, Man of Destiny, has been rendered: MY PRICK IS BIGGER THAN YOURS.

Eight potato-faced boys with tiny eyes and Brilliantine ducktails slouch against the wall like suspects in a police lineup, their electric-blue strides, with triple French seams, hung holster-low. As they flick their eyes insolently over me, I conjure up recent headlines:

BARTON BOYS ARRESTED AFTER VICIOUS ASSAULT
SHIV-CARRYING HOODLUMS SHUN REFORM

Is this the notorious Barton Street Gang that Reverend Thwaite has been preaching against as "the true legacy of the war, when mothers forsook the hearth for the greed of the marketplace"?

Magda seems to know them all. "Hi, Ziggie. Long time no see. Hey, Swinger, missed you Friday at the Bright Spot. How's tricks?"

The boys stare, sullen, impassive. One makes a move toward his pocket. I tense, expecting a shiv. Instead he withdraws a rat-tail comb, which he flicks though his pompadour, as slick as licorice. Trying to disappear against the wall, I jiggle my quarter to reassure myself the bargain is worth it. "At least I got my mad money."

"Huh?" Magda is alerted. "Mad money? What's that?"

"Oh." I pull a face. "It means you have car fare if anything goes wrong on a date . . . . I'm only kidding."

Magda whoops: "Hey, that's cool."

I cast my eyes enviously at the line of free souls shuffling past to the box office, reminding myself of the first rule of dating: loss of economic freedom equals loss of personal freedom. Another guy—a head taller and a squint meaner, also wearing blue strides but with his hair cut in a buzz saw—lumbers toward us.

"That's Bullmoose," exclaims Magda. "He's my boyfriend. Hey, Bull, you were a no-show on Wednesday." She nudges me: "Lucky I had my sad money ha ha ha!"

Bullmoose smirks, the rest snicker. Pulling out a star-spattered pouch everyone in the world knows is for carrying Modess pads, Magda passes around a package of purple Thrills gum. "Here, have a Thrill." She winks at Bullmoose. "Don't say I never gave you a Thrill!"

Edging from the group, I wonder how I can escape back to the legitimate line without being rude. In relief, I spy two more girls moseying up the alley. They move in closer. Oh-oh: black strides, black windbreakers, Dragon Lady lips, Boris Karloff eyebrows.

"That's Jackie and Jill," exclaims Magda, adding with awe: "They just got out of reform school."

I roll my eyes, unable to resist: Jackie and Jill went up the hill—ha ha ha! Then I make an overdue decision. "Magda, thanks very much but I think I better—"

A rusty clang like the lowering of a drawbridge. Temptation yawns in the form of an open door. A sharp nose protrudes from the darkness, followed by gleaming eyes and a fuzzy brown head: the Mole. I'm sure of it. I've seen something like this in a Dick Tracy comic strip.

He snarls: "Quick, get the lead out."

The short illicit line shuffles inward, with me sandwiched between Jackie and Jill. I feel a cobwebby curtain slap my cheek.

"Psst, grab a seat. There's Baldy."

Propelled on a tide of arms and legs, I am dumped into a seat. I stand up, looking for Magda. A light beam strikes me in the face. I fall back. It slides into the eyes of the boy on my right then onto Magda.

"Lessee your tickets," rasps an old man's voice.

Bullmoose hands over the stubs passed to him by Mole. As the elderly usher scrutinizes them, his light skitters back over his own wizened features and bald head, reminding me of the newborn mouse I once found in the home-economics flour bin. I hold my breath.

"All right, you punks, but if there's any fuss I'm calling the cops."

The flashlight is extinguished. I exhale, feeling grudging camaraderie for my fellow conspirators, prepared now to enjoy illicit gains.

The newsreel unfolds, way off to the right. Queen Elizabeth, in silver fox furs, and Princess Margaret Rose, in Girl Guide uniform, are opening some exhibition or other, surrounded by members of the British upper crust. Their faces, elongated by my awkward perspective, confirm all those cruel caricatures of the British horsey look.

Soviet warplanes continue maneuvers over the
    Anglo-U.S. airlift corridor to Berlin . . .
Fierce ground and aerial fighting between Israel and
    Egypt thwart cease-fire attempt . . .
Gandhi fasting again . . .
How to stock your A-bomb shelter . . .

The screen explodes in color. "Hi, f-f-folks!" It's Porky Pig, pursued by a wolf with a long black tongue. I feel a pressure on my left knee and draw it away, still watching the screen. The pressure remains. I look down. A hand. A hand on my knee! It squeezes. I push it away. It sticks like a suction cup. Another hand clasps my other knee. The first hand clamps my left wrist to the arm of my seat while the other grabs my right wrist. That leaves two hands unattended. One claws at my sweater while the other dives under my skirt.

My other self is confused. This seems like a call for her services but . . . .

"Th-th-that's all, folks!" Porky Pig waves. I crush my breasts against my knees. "Let me go!" I feel myself passing in and out of consciousness. *My other self struggles to take over.* I struggle to stay conscious, remembering Tonya's scornful judgment: when a girl goes to the movies by herself she's just asking for it!

For every hand I detach, another takes its place. I hear people clapping and want to call out to them, but I am too ashamed. I twist my legs, feeling dizzy once again. The clapping now seems very far away. "Please, I'm only thirteen . . . ." Fingers pull at my pants, touch flesh. Shocked, I bend double. Now I bite a hand, tasting blood.

An outraged cry.

The row is suddenly illuminated. "What's going on?" demands the raspy old man's voice. "We'll have none of that in here."

Yanking free, I slide to the floor, then wriggle under the seats.

"You punks! You think you can come in here and do any dirty thing you want."

Propelling myself with my elbows, I navigate through popcorn and puddles of Coke, my hair brushing a fortune in secondhand gum, remembering how I used to slide under these seats as a child, looking for Granny Cragg's shoes with the bunion holes cut out. The scrape of my bosom against the sticky floor reminds me how times have changed.

I bolt for the exit then pitch against the metal door. Daylight! Hard to imagine there's still such a thing. I streak for Main Street, feeling my cheeks burn with humiliation *while the shoulders of my other self shake with hysteria.*

I dream: *Magda Lunt runs down the aisle of the Delta pursued by Bullmoose in Nazi uniform. He yanks off her outlaw dress. "Please, I'm only thirteen!" Tonya Philpott shines a flashlight in her face: "Do you think you can do any dirty thing you want?"*

My mother walks by, wearing white stockings and her Sunday hat. "MY girls would never do such a thing."

*

I refuse to go to church on the grounds of having exposed myself to Arlene's flu, but really I'm afraid of seeing Magda. Curled on the chesterfield, I read the final chapter of The Golden Amazon:

> "Why can't you be content with an ordinary life? What more do you want?"
> The Golden Amazon tosses her blond curls.
> "Power—more power than has ever been achieved by our sex. The power to rule and to destroy, if necessary."

The phone rings. My mother calls: "It's for you."

Eyes still glued to the page, I pick up the dangling receiver, dusted with flour from the piecrust my mother is making.

"How ya been, sewing machine?" A hoarse chuckle. "What happened to you yest'dy, kiddo?"

I glance nervously toward my mother. "Nothing happened. I just left, that's all."

"Lucky you had your bad money, eh? Ha ha ha!"

I switch the receiver from my right ear to my left—six inches farther from my mother.

"Say, listen, kiddo. You missed a real neat time. Afterward we all went to the Chicken Roost. Jujube was asking about you. He thought you were a real slick chick."

"Who?"

"Jujube. He was sitting right beside you. You couldn't miss him. The redhead."

"Oh." The hand with the warts. The one I bit.

"He was real disappointed."

"Yeah, I'll bet."

My mother is peeling Spy apples into perfect Shirley Temple curls with the exaggerated concentration of someone who is listening—a technique I recognize.

"Say, the-reason-I-was-calling—I gotta watch the little buggers this eve. I thought maybe you and me could spin a couple of platters and—"

Clamping the receiver to my ear so as to contain the tinny voice, I croak: "I'm busy."

"What about tomorrow night?"

"No, I'm busy tomorrow, too."

"What about next Sat'day aft—"

"I've seen it. Thanks for phoning, but I've got to go."

As I hang up, my mother calls: "Come here, will you please, dear?"

That word "dear" alerts me. My mother never calls me dear. I shuffle into the kitchen.

"Who was that on the phone?" she asks.

"What?" I correct myself: "Pardon?"

"That person on the phone. Who was it?"

"Oh." I help myself to a peeled apple, hoping to draw my mother's fire. She smiles as if she'd prepared the apple for just that purpose. "Mmm," I mumble.

My mother's ears are remarkable organs. "Did you say Magda Lunt? Mrs. Lunt's Magda from the church?"

"I guess it could be the same."

"You know very well there couldn't be two Magda Lunts!" Her knife flashes. "Why were you so rude to that poor girl?"

"I wasn't rude. I just don't feel like spending a Sunday evening on—"

"What have you got to do that's so important?"

"You know I always listen to Charlie McCarthy and Our Miss Brooks on Sundays."

Scoring a perfect circle in her pastry, she explodes: "I swear I don't know how you and Helen ever got to be sisters."

I steel myself against the familiar refrain, despising myself for letting it hurt so much after all these years.

My mother continues as reasonably as if she were proving the existence of Satan to her Sunday school class: "Helen goes out of her way to be nice to people like Magda but you think only of yourself." She spoons brown sugar over her pie. "Mrs. Lunt came over in church this morning to say how thrilled she was that you and Magda had had such a lovely time."

"I don't want to chum with Magda. You don't understand."

"I might if you told me. If you gave me a chance to understand."

For a dangerous moment I consider unburdening my conscience, but what could I say about yesterday afternoon that wouldn't horrify my mother into forbidding me from attending the Delta ever again? Finding anything to confide would be like trying to pick candies out of cow dung. Besides, why should I tell her anything when she's always throwing Helen up at me?

Placing one crust over the other, she continues: "You're the most stubborn child I've ever known. You think the world was made to accommodate you."

I put my hands over my ears. "Okay!"

"Okay, what?"

"I'll call Magda and make a date for some time next week."

"What's wrong with this evening? That's when she invited you." Pricking her crust to release the steam, my mother reminds me: "You used to be very good friends not so long ago."

I slouch down the street in my raincoat, past unpainted houses jammed against the sidewalk with their garbage cans on their stoops, each smelling of its last meal. Magda opens the door before I can turn the bell. "Hi, kiddo!" She's so thrilled to see me that I drop my resentment, which is just a pose anyway. What I really feel is confused.

Eyes in pairs stare at me through the broken banister. "G'wan, you brats. Remember what I told you about having my friend over."

The Lunts' living room, lined in greasy floral wallpaper, is almost bare except for a startling red velour sofa with fluted back won in a raffle. As silence lengthens between Magda and me, at either end, I remember the radio programs I am missing. "Would you mind if we turned on 'Charlie McCarthy'? That is, if you haven't anything else planned."

"We don't have a radio. The store took it back." Magda

grins: "I thought maybe we could phone." She tosses me a list of names and phone numbers, wrapped around a toilet roll—Bozo, King, Mouser, Dogo, the Blimp. "These are my boyfriends."

"There must be hundreds!"

"Two hundred and twelve. Jackie and Jill traded me a bunch for some lipstick."

"You mean you don't know these guys?"

"Not all of them. Not till I call them."

"You mean you call boys you don't know?"

Again, Magda is perfectly plausible. "How can they call me if they don't know me?"

Bouncing up from the red velour, Magda wraps her skinny legs around a stool that was once a high chair, then runs her chipped Paint the Town Red fingernail down the scroll. It stops, reverses, settles. "Flattop. I haven't called him in weeks. He must be wondering what's happened to me." Adjusting the mouthpiece of the wall phone, she dials. "Hiya, Flattop. Long time no see. It's me—Magda. I saw you at the Bright Spot with Oiler . . . . Yeah, you got a purple jacket, don'tcha?" She cracks her gum. "Yeah, that's me. Magda." Her face falls. "Am-scray, huh?" Good-naturedly, she signs off: "See you soon, Honeymoon, ha ha ha."

Pulling down the bracket of the receiver to get a dial tone, Magda dials her next number. "Hiya, Digger. Long time no see. Watcha doing?" Holding the receiver back from her ear, she exclaims: "Hey, we was cut off." She redials. "That's funny. Line's busy."

Magda dials another number, then shoves the receiver at me. "Here, kiddo. I run out of things to say but I bet you're a swell talker."

I drop the receiver. It dangles between us as a deep voice shouts: "Hullo, hullo."

"Pick it up! He's calling you."

The gruff voice, so like my irritated father's, continues to demand: "Hullo, hullo. Hey, who is this?"

Giggling, Magda croaks into the receiver: "Here's my friend.

She's a real cutie! She's fifteen."

I accept the phone, feeling a surge of anonymous power. "Hi—"

"Rosco," mouths Magda. "His name's Rosco."

I wet my lips the way I imagine Ava Gardner might do it. "Hi there, Rosco. Is that really you?"

The gruff male voice assesses. "Say, who is this?"

I answer musically: "You should know, Rosco. You asked me to call."

Now hopeful: "Loreen?"

Tossing the mouthpiece a smoldering pout, I confirm: "I knew you wouldn't forget me, Rosco. I couldn't forget you!" I lower my lids, playing up to Rosco's gullibility and Magda's glee. "Well, uh, sug-ah, I'm not sure about this evening. Call me back in an hour, will you? Here's where I'll be." I rattle off a number posted by Magda's phone—Reverend Thwaite's number, also prominently displayed by my own home phone. "Now don't forget, Rosco, baby. I'll be waiting." Convulsed, I hang up.

Magda is ecstatic. "I knew you'd be a good talker. Here, try this one." She dials another number, then shoves the receiver into my hand.

I am already planning my next gambit—"Hello, this is your Avon Lady calling"—when a tired woman's voice answers. "Hullo?"

Pointing to the receiver, I mouth to Magda: who?

"Bullmoose! The dreamboat."

I blanch, the all-too-real image of Bullmoose—gross, mean and hairy—flashing into my mind. I am about to claim a wrong number but the woman has heard Magda. In a reedy voice she calls: "Bill-eee!"

I toss the sweaty receiver from palm to palm, wanting to hang up but afraid of losing face with Magda.

A phlegmy bass: "Bullmoose here."

"Ah . . ." I continue to sweat it out. "This is, ah, your Avon Lady calling!"

"Look, broad. Watchaname?"

I close my eyes, seeking new inspiration. It comes in the form of the title of the latest hot movie. "Amber. You don't know me but I feel I've known you—forever." I flounder: "That is, I saw you once at the Delta." Uh-oh. The Delta, like Bullmoose, is too real. Closing my eyes, I imagine the receiver in his hairy hand, his thick lips pressed to the mouthpiece. "Hey, uh, I think maybe I got the wrong number. Is this Bullmoose, uh, Jenkins? Because it's Bullmoose Jenkins I want, not any other Bullmoose."

A long hot pause in which the receiver sticks to my ear. Bullmoose clears his throat. "Look, broad. I know who this is. It's the smart-mouthed little bitch who ran out on Jujube yesterday. Next time you better be wearing tin pants because we're gonna work you over so good you'll—"

I slam down the receiver.

"Hey, what happened? Did you really kid him along?"

"We were cut off," I insist, still hearing Bullmoose's voice throbbing in my head.

Magda is crestfallen but understanding. "Yeah, it happens a lot, don't it?" She picks another number. "Here, try—"

"No!" I brush aside the toilet roll. "I think I better go home." I am adamant. "I know I better go home."

As I run through the slippery night, I picture my mother's unlined face, haloed by braids. How come you stay so untouched by everything since the Garden of Eden? How come you never protect me? *How come I have to protect you? How come it's me who—*

Though I have run out of reasons, my rage builds, *fueled by its secret underground source.*

Helen has not yet returned from Hamilton High, where she is in her third year. My mother is visiting a friend in the hospital.

My other self lies numbed on her daddy's bed, but with ears pricked like a dozing cat. Listening has become an obsession with her. Listening for footsteps, for creaks in the floor, listening, listening for—

A loud metallic click. She stiffens—the downstairs latch. She hears the door open. Simultaneously her father leaps up, snatching for his trousers. "Get out!"

The downstairs door closes. Footsteps up the stairs, fast and light—one, two, three, four . . . . They stop directly outside the bedroom door. They pause—a long and awesome silence. A rattle. The doorknob begins to turn. Her father shouts: "Don't come in, I'm dressing!"

The knob stops, then rattles again, as if a hand were still holding on. My other self stands perfectly still, like an animal caught in headlights, her pleated skirt in one hand, her sweater in the other.

My mother has promised to buy me a pair of oxblood loafers with slots for nickels, but first we have to stop at Dr. Miller's so Helen can have her tonsils checked. As I read True Romance, which Dr. Miller, being modern, has in his waiting room, I'm surprised to hear my mother discussing me instead of Helen. "She used to have convulsions right up to the time she went to school."

Convulsions—what are they? As my mother explains them, they sound important and vaguely glamorous. "She would fall on the ground, screaming and choking, unable to catch her breath." This is the first I have heard of them. I listen, fascinated.

Next thing I know, Dr. Miller instructs me to undress, while my mother continues to discuss me as if I can't hear. "It started out with a bout of whooping cough when she was a baby. We were afraid she would swallow her tongue. Our family doctor told us to hold it down with a depressor."

I am indignant and humiliated as I slough off skirt and sweater and slip. I never get undressed in front of my mother any more, or even Helen, and certainly not in front of a man, a doctor or not! *My other self is on red alert.*

Feeling very peculiar, as if I were about to faint, I climb

onto Dr. Miller's steel examining table, trying to keep my legs from shaking, seeing the doctor approach me matter-of-factly with a tongue depressor. It is then I notice, from the direction he is moving and the struggle my mother is having to disguise her familiar look of sexual distaste, that it is not my throat he is going to examine. As he spreads my legs, *I disappear. My other self takes over, quivering in dread. She knows why she had convulsions. She fears . . . .*

Face blank, Dr. Miller removes his rubber gloves. Mortified, I climb down from the table, feeling light-headed and confused, as if I were returning from a long distance, aware—not for the first time—of having lost a couple of minutes of my life. As usual these days, my rage focuses on the safest detail: this isn't even my appointment. Do you hear me—it isn't my appointment! How could you?

A month before graduation, we Golden Amazons hold our last pajama party, at Cooky Castle's. We've spent the evening fox-trotting to our favorite records—forehead to forehead, breast to breast—with all the formality of asking and cutting in. Now, at ten, just as the yawns outweigh the giggles, a war whoop blasts the air. Someone is banging on the back door at the same time as the front bell peals—not once but over and over.

"There's Iky Mason," exclaims Arlene, hanging out a window.

"Perry Lord's at the back," squeals Cooky, hanging out another.

"And Joker Nash and Joe Baker—it's a raid!" announces Lulu.

We flutter from window to window like hens before the foxes. "Shall we open the door?" Apart from any social niceties, there are the neighbors to consider.

"If we don't they'll break it down," Babs asserts enthusiastically.

"We can't ask them in like this," gasps Arlene. "The whole school will know the color of our pajamas."

Hastily we exchange flannelette tops for blouses, yank out metal wavers sticky with green Hollywood waveset. Babs stuffs Kleenexes under her armpits. Cooky seems to be padding her bra with socks.

More banging.

"Answer it!" squeals Lulu.

"You answer it!"

The door bursts open. Six boys sail through, on a rush of spring wind and adrenaline. "Where are the eats?" asks Joker Nash. This demand proves a clever and distracting male ploy. Soon Cokes are being guzzled, Honey Dew donuts wolfed. Peanuts, potato chips, Cheesies disappear by the bagful. The invasion is complete. We Amazons, with the honorable exception of Tonya, are thrilled to be of service.

The boys bunch in the dining room, talking loudly about baseball. We girls spread ourselves over the living-room sofa and chairs. We cross and uncross our ankles. I drag on my DuMaurier, remembering it cost three cents more.

"Are you sure my sweater isn't too tight?" whispers Arlene.

"Relax," Babs assures her. "If it were any looser we could hold the party in one of the sleeves." Pitching her voice, she demands: "Who knows any good jokes?"

Joker Nash shouts back: "What did the football player say to the cheerleader?" He answers himself: "If your skirt were any higher, you'd have two more cheeks to powder."

Babs hoots: "Har-de-har-har." The rest of us avert our eyes. Tonya mutters: "That's an old one. Bob Hope got cut off the air for telling it, except he used a playboy and a glamor girl."

The boys grow rowdier and more exclusive. Tonya signals me to a conference in the kitchen. The others crowd around.

"Go back," I insist. "We can't all hang out in here. Let's play records or something."

Tonya and I boldly stack records in tens for the Castles' new combo.

"Some enchanted evening . . ."

At last the boys break their huddle to stretch along the

wall. A certain vulnerability can be read into their Brylcreem brush cuts and wispy mustaches. Still, they possess that magnificent male trump card—the power of choice.

"Circus, life is a circus, a hectic thing . . . "

Humiliated at having to hang around like merchandise when nobody is buying, we commiserate out the sides of our mouths: "What are we going to do?"

"Isn't this ghastly!"

Can it be? Iky Mason separates from the tight formation, butts his Lucky Strike and hitches his droop-loop trousers. He ambles like John Wayne toward Tonya, who blushes for the first time anyone can remember. Arlene humanely douses the lights as Iky and Tonya shuffle onto the floor.

"Tea for two, and two for tea . . . "

Babs remembers the Kleenex stuffed up her armpits and surreptitiously removes them. Cooky tightens her waist cincher a notch. Lulu expels her cigarette from her holder, burning a hole in the Castles' broadloom.

I see Joe Baker yearn toward me and shift ever so subtly away. Catching the glance of Perry Lord, elegant in the manner of Peter Lawford, I hook him with a sideways sweep of my eyes, rather like trolling for fish.

"Blue Moon, I saw you standing alone . . . "

"Would you care to . . . ?" One of Perry's hands clasps mine while his chin settles against my forehead. I register a faint heartbeat under lamb's wool, the hint of Wildroot Cream Oil. All too soon, the record ends. I ask Perry a question about baseball—enough to keep him talking while the arm of the Castles' record player lifts then lowers.

"I've got a crush on you . . . "

Over Perry's shoulder I keep track of the politics of the room. Joe Baker has asked Arlene. Herbert "Muddy" Swamp is pursuing Lulu, who cringes behind the kitchen door. Babs is guffawing too loudly at Joker's jokes. Cooky is also pretending to flirt with Joker while staring after Perry and me.

Perry and I dance the next record, the next and the next. From what I can see, Perry is probably no better a dancer than Joe, but Perry thinks he's superior in all things and I accept his lie.

"I'm in the mood for love . . ."

Unaccountably, I grow restless, become frightened of my own success, break off with Perry to powder my nose, then take a spin with Joker, flirting with all the boys at the same time, feeling arrogant and powerful one minute, mean and self-contemptuous the next.

"You made me love you, I didn't want to do it . . ."

Midnight. Our guests disappear in another swoosh. Did it really happen? At school the next day the boys pretend it didn't. We girls talk about nothing else. Now it can be stated from womanly experience that Perry has bedroom eyes. Joker eats more than anyone else, and with both hands. Joe Baker is the politest. Now having a crush could be dangerous since it might be requited.

Most scandalized talk centers on Herbert alias Muddy Swamp, possessor of a chronic and sweaty case of Wandering Hand Trouble. "Getting him off me was like scraping gum from my sweater," testifies Lulu.

To everyone's surprise, the invasion breeds Grade Eight's first full-fledged romance. Iky, a brawny Li'l Abner type, invites Tonya on a bona fide movie date for the very next Saturday. What's more, we suspect Tonya is wearing Tangee Natural lipstick, though she insists it's only moisturizer for chapped lips. What is certain is that she has converted her ducktail into a poodle cut.

The Golden Amazons share one of the Kozy Korner's famous one-dollar Idiot Delights. As we dig in with six spoons, Tonya delivers our reviews. "The guys said the party was okay, but they don't think that's how they want to spend another Saturday night."

"What? That's all they said after the food they wolfed down? The boors!"

"Well . . . ." Tonya is insufferably coy. "That's all I'm allowed to say."

"Unfair! Give, or we'll slip you a fat lip."

"Are you sure you want to hear this?" Waving her spoon at Arlene, Tonya pronounces: "The boys think you're the nicest."

"Oh!" she blushes in relief.

"They also think you've got the best figure."

"Oh, good grief!" Arlene hugs her chest. "I knew my sweater was too tight."

"Babs, the guys think you're the most fun to kibitz with."

"Oh, har-de-har, thanks a lot! Maybe next time someone will ask me to dance just once." Taking a giant spoonful of chocolate fudge, she manages to look mollified.

"Lulu, they can't figure you out. You're always acting."

"Good. I can't figure me out either."

"Cooky." Eying her with disapproval: "They think you're the feminine one but they don't like you patting them so much and fiddling with their hair."

"Oh, su-gah!" exclaims Cooky, patting her own flawless brunette underroll. "I was only trying to help."

Tonya fixes me with a scowl. "I can't remember what they said about you."

"Oh, yes, you can," insists Babs. "You never forget."

"Maybe she did this time." I squirm. "Maybe they didn't say anything."

"Come on, you told on the rest of us!"

Tonya shrugs like a dentist forced to deliver bad news. "All right. The guys like you the best because they say you're the sexiest."

"What?" I'm genuinely shocked.

"Don't blame me." Tonya shrugs. "That's what they said."

The sexiest. A warning bell goes off in my head, leaving me both pleased and queasy. I imagine Rita Hayworth tossing her hair in Gilda, Jane Russell throwing out her bosom in The Outlaw, Marilyn Monroe jiggling her hips in everything she's been in: what is sexy?

The talk flows on, mostly about next week's graduation. Catching sight of my reflection in the mirror, I note with alarm that the space between the blond brackets, where I used to see the Golden Amazons, is blank once again. I study the faces of my friends, still puzzled or glowing from the male judgments passed upon them. Tonya, Arlene, Babs, Lulu, Cooky. I have a sudden sad insight: we Amazons aren't going to be able to help each other much anymore. Already we are beginning to see ourselves and each other only as the boys see us.

RED SHOES

I have a shirt box full of old photographs. I spread its contents around me—blurred black-and-white pictures taken with an assortment of Brownie box cameras. Myself in sloppy-joe sweater and saddle shoes with hair draped over one eye like Veronica Lake. On the steps of Hamilton High in red-and-yellow cheerleading outfit. In red strapless velvet: Fall Frolic '52. Always I am smiling, my lips a scarlet bow even while my teeth are clenched and my eyes closed against the sun.

I say these pictures are of me but they are not. They are of the "glamor girl" I glued together out of tinselly bits cut from movie magazines—Marilyn Monroe's sultry eyes, Rita Hayworth's mouth, Lana Turner's sweater. Like the fairytale princess I once fancied myself to be, this glamor girl was an alter ego I created to hide my shadow-twin. I invented her to fool myself as well as the world. I invented her to paste over the pictures that do not appear in this box—dark photos, still underexposed, of my other self and daddy daddy won't love me love me love me.

The job of my glamor-puppet, whom even then I called Appearances, was to demonstrate that everything was super keen while I was most despairing. I ran her in school elections, entered her in popularity contests, placed her on athletic teams, bought her a cheerleading outfit. For several years she won the trophies and garnered the votes, but she had an inherent flaw. She did not react to real circumstances out of real emotion. She was programmed like a computer and, like a computer, she played to rule. Since dating was the standard by which Hamilton High judged a girl's popularity, she filled her date book like a junkie.

So now there were three of me, all vitally connected yet somehow separate. Like my other self, Appearances began as my servant and then I became hers. Her strings were live wires that burned my hands. Increasingly, I danced as fast as

I could in her red shoes while she pulled my strings, always upping the stakes whenever she grew bored or became frightened. Though I frequently lost control of her, I never lost conscious contact with her, as I did with my other self. I always knew—painfully—what she was up to because I always had to pick up the pieces from her disasters. If my other self was my shadow, then she was "our" billboard— one that increasingly advertised the wrong things. Red was her color. The color of the lipstick smear on a Coke glass, of blood, of fire, of violence, of craziness, of the letter on my cheerleading sweater, of Other Grandmother's satin pumps, of dancing feet on a hot stove.

Even now my high-school years are the most difficult for me to remember. Though sexual contact between my father and me must have been very infrequent, the threat of it was constant at a time when fear of penetration and pregnancy had escalated the risks. Because I now hated my father without knowing why, I hurled myself into extracurricular activities, spending as little time as possible in his house. However, now that sex had also invaded my peer world, that world had become almost as threatening. Because of overlapping territories, what had begun as a leakage of emotion between my other self and me had become a hemorrhage. Never was it more necessary for me to keep my personalities separate, yet never was it more difficult.

I call for Arlene. Lulu calls for Babs. They call for Cooky. We meet at Tonya's place. We walk to Hamilton High, hugging our loose-leaf notebooks to our chests in the female style, thus squelching any rumor that we might have breasts, bunching at stoplights and spreading out in different sets of twos and threes. We climb the steps of Hamilton High, an imposing red sandstone, with a thousand-student enrollment, for our final year. Senior boys in faded red and gold jackets hang around the Roman portal, taking last drags on their cigarettes. As they look us over, we pretend not to notice—the accepted ritual.

The din in the halls is deafening as we select lockers by the boys' trophy case in the first-floor rotunda, Action Central. I nudge Arlene. "Look, freshettes. You can tell by the way they taste their lipstick that they're not used to wearing it." Some even sport freshly pressed school ribbons. "Were we ever as green as that? Dear dead days!"

The bulletin board is already bristling with notices: "Football tickets now on sale. Don't Forget the Fall Frolic. Cheerleader Tryouts. Nominations for Students' Council."

We see Joker Nash and Joe Baker.

"Oh, there's Iky," exclaims Tonya. She runs to join him.

"If only Perry Lord were here," says Cooky. "Private school—what a waste!"

"Don't look now, but who's that guy beside Iky?" demands Babs. "He's the deadspit of Guy Madison!"

I follow her lascivious gaze. A lanky boy with dark blond hair, and a clean-cut profile ending in a cleft chin is tossing books into a locker.

"That's Daniel Hobson," whispers Lulu. "His family just moved onto my street. His father's a doctor."

"Drool, drool, now that's my idea of a dreamboat," exclaims Cooky.

I study Daniel Hobson with averted eyes. All of us do. Since the basic social unit at Hamilton High is the couple, we girls are, of necessity, passive predators.

Our classrooms are the same as in public school, except the seats are larger and the inkwells have been painted over now that everyone uses a fountain pen. Lulu, Babs and I choose three together, hoisting our ankle-length, pencil skirts. Joe Baker takes a seat beside me. I turn to him with a dazzling smile. In fact, I am really smiling past him at Daniel Hobson—a familiar female ploy, since at Hamilton High even speaking first to a boy you know is deemed to be a sign that a girl is on the make: "Have a good summer, Joe?" Though his reply is drowned by the bell, I do catch Daniel Hobson's eye, and see an answering flicker.

Miss Dowling enters with her Medieval History tucked under her arm. Though nearing retirement age, she cuts a romantic figure with a youthful face framed in shingled gray hair. Her flapper dress, lengthened with a six-inch border for Dior's "New Look," now five years old, is in itself an archeological treasure.

"Her fiancé was killed in the war," whispers Lulu.

"Which one?" demands Joker Nash. "King Arthur's?"

Babs gives Joker the eye: "Har-de-har-har." She is also playing to Daniel Hobson. Like sunflowers, we have turned our faces to the new sun king.

Placing her notes on the podium, Miss Dowling announces: "And now we can begin . . . ."

Cooky Castle, three other cheerleaders and I lounge against the glazed-brick wall of the girls' gym, wearing our gold sweaters, scarlet skirts and dyed-to-match running shoes. Seventy-three contestants squat before us, wearing baggy gym tunics with their names embroidered on the back. Most are as nervous as beauty contestants. Small wonder. Cheerleaders are the starlets of the high-school system. Cheerleaders get dates.

Miss Joper, gawky in a fitted tunic that reveals the beginnings of varicose veins, sends Cooky to see that no lustful males are lurking in the balcony. Then she addresses the hopefuls, drawing out the tension with all the sadistic fervor of the chronically unattractive chosen by fate to cast judgment on the more fortunate. "Remember, girls, though it's our boys who carry the ball, we're the ones who give them the will. Every cheerleader has a responsibility to Hamilton High, to her squad and to herself. You will be marked on poise, on talent, but most of all on enthusiasm! Number in twelves, and we'll assign you to a leader from last year's squad."

I collect my group under the balcony clock. Since the honor of cheerleading is withheld until third year to lessen its moral dangers, I know most of the candidates from having refereed their basketball games. "Okay, we'll do 'Give 'em a kick,' first in slow motion, then up to speed." Some of the girls are actually quaking. "Hey, don't worry. No one gets it right the first few times."

>Give 'em a kick,
>Give 'em a shove . . .

The contestants rubberleg their way through. Cooky stage-whispers to me: "Do you think they're ready yet for Suzie-Q?"

Scowling, Miss Joper publicly reprimands her: "You should be aware, Miss Castle, that Suzie-Q has been banned. The school board objected—quite wisely—to some of the, uh, more provocative buttock motions." Now striding up the ragged rows, she makes initial eliminations: Mavis, Myra, Fanny, Joan. Despite the advertised conditions of poise, talent and, above all, enthusiasm, it's clear what the real standard is: too homely, too short, too tall, too busty, too pimply.

After three hours, nine girls remain—seven as regulars, two as subs. Once again checking the balcony to foil prying males, Miss Joper slips on harlequin glasses, hung by a shoelace around her neck. "Congratulations, you are the chosen ones! As cheerleaders you are part of a well-disciplined athletic team. You are not—I repeat—not burlesque queens. The stadium is a public place. Sometimes emotions, uh, run high. At HHS, we expect our girls to be ladies. When not actually cheering, you must keep your legs concealed under a coat or blanket."

Miss Joper hitches up the gym bloomers, in which she has been known to ply the corridors of HHS, her long legs pumping like the oars of a rowboat. "And another thing: it's important that we always wear a firm uplift." Floating her fingers down her concave chest, she testifies: "I have found French brassieres the most reliable, especially when tied so three fingers can be comfortably inserted between the laces and the skin—not so tight the flesh bulges, the breasts have to breathe too, you know, but not so loose that we, uh, flop around out there." She delivers her bombshell. "Some of you may not think so, but boys notice things like that and may even remark on it!"

Several of the new girls, unprepared for Miss Joper's "frank" style, gag as if they've swallowed frogs. Though I've heard all this before, I can't stifle my fit of giggles. I touch off Cooky, sitting beside me, and soon the whole row goes down like dominoes.

Miss Joper reprimands: "Girls, girls! I thought I was addressing adults." She returns to her prepared text. "As for those to whom God has been less generous, to you I say be proud. Throw back your shoulders, throw out your chests, but please understand that I absolutely forbid the insertion of foreign matter in the brassiere. When God decides, God will provide." Lowering her voice, she continues: "Now, as to the use of a good depilatory . . . ." All but whispering: "As for cheering on 'difficult' days . . . ."

Without warning, Miss Joper blasts her whistle. Fourteen girls jump higher than they've jumped in their lives. "Now then, all together, the new and the old, let's give a cheer, and let's put some oomph into it."

The 1952–53 Hamilton High cheering squad spreads out across the gym floor.

> One ahacka, two ahacka sis boom bah.
> Stallions, Stallions, rah rah rah!

I do the regulation cartwheel, then another and another, right out the gym door into the locker room, partly fueled by exuberance, partly by release of tension, partly by a self-mocking awareness of the colossal hypocrisy of which we are the eager butts. Body arched, I finish with a high jump. CRASH! My hands strike a light globe. Glass cascades. Blood splashes my sweater with its scarlet letter.

"Get a towel!" shrieks Cooky. "There's been an accident. Oh God, look at all the blood!"

I see worried faces staring down at me, a smear of red on white tiles.

I am in my family's bathroom—a white porcelain corridor with a dome. When I straddle the hole serving as a toilet, blood pours down on my head. I look up. The naked bodies of Alfred Hitchcock and a blond girl are stuffed in the dome. Shocked, I ask my mother: "How come no one notices them?"

She replies: "Oh, everyone knows they're there, but they've gotten used to them." It's then I see a trail of bloody footprints leading from the bathroom up my attic stairs.

Babs, Arlene and I squeeze into a soundproof booth at Moody's Record Bar, listening to "Slaughter on Tenth Avenue." At least, the booth is supposed to be soundproof, but from the musical catacombs we can hear the Weavers bawling "Goodnight, Irene," Rosemary Clooney shouting "Come On-a My House," Percy Faith fiddling "Song From Moulin Rouge" and Johnny Ray sobbing "The Little White Cloud That Cried."

Yanking a Coffee Crisp from her saddlebag, Babs offers it around.

Arlene shakes her head: "Not me, I'm on a diet. I want to get into my formal—if someone asks me."

"Don't say that word," Babs shudders.

"Which? Diet or formal?"

"Both!" She takes a large bite of chocolate. "I need some advice. Joker says he isn't going to the Fall Frolic because he can't afford it. What if I took the money I made this summer and—"

"You can't ask a boy to a formal," protests Arlene.

"Well, I can't put in another year like the last one, either! Hell's bells, I had exactly two dates, and neither guy asked me back."

"It's better to stay home than to go with someone you don't like," I assure her, knowing that I'm lying. All social life at Hamilton High is strictly two-by-two, as in Noah's Ark. Not to date is to be an object of scorn or pity.

"Oh, sure! Thanks a bunch." Babs leans moodily against

the perforated wall of the booth, eyes closed. "Know who I'd really like to ask me to the Fall Frolic? Daniel Hobson. He's spoken to me three times—one hello, and two hi theres. I thought the last hi there sounded kind of interested."

Arlene's strange expression reveals that we are all angling for the same fish. Laughing, I come clean: "Counting me, that makes three."

Babs opens one eye. "Three? Have you noticed Cooky breathing heavily whenever he comes near? Make that twenty-three. All the girls are smitten—he's so damned nice." She sighs. "What I wouldn't give to be going steady with anyone just to get out of the rat race."

Arlene turns to me. "How come you've never gone steady?"

"Yeah, how come?" echoes Babs. "You get such a b-i-g crush on a guy, then when he likes you, you don't want him anymore."

Arlene's overcasual inquiry followed by Babs's too-quick follow-up warns me that they've already discussed this between themselves. My reply is cautious: "Maybe I've just never met anyone I've liked well enough. Say, what is this— the Spanish Inquisition?"

"Don't get huffy, old girl," exclaims Babs. "We're just asking. Everybody does. The guys say you go out with them a couple of times then you ditch them. They say you use them."

"That's exactly what I don't do! Why not check out the going-steady girls? Half of them admit it's just for the social security."

"Going steady doesn't have to mean you're madly in love," protests Arlene. "It just means you like one boy better than the rest."

"Well, I don't. They all bore me. They're so possessive. They make me"—*panic as if I were smothering*—"bored!" I stand up, feeling my head spin with the record. Perforated walls, *the color of flesh*, press in upon me. "Phew, it's hot in here—" Knocking the phonograph needle across the record with a loud screech, I claw my way out of the booth.

*

I run up the attic stairs with my books under my arm, then stop so abruptly I almost tumble down. My father, wearing once-good trousers held together with patches and pins, is lying on his side replacing floorboards. *"No! no! no!" shrieks* my other self. "This is MY *room. It belongs to* ME!" Now, no place is safe. My other self has caught the virus of terror, and she is infecting me.

The football team exercises in a lopsided circle under the library window with Coach Jacobson barking orders. I divide my attention between Shakespeare's *Julius Caesar*, being tempted by Antony to accept the Roman crown, and Daniel Hobson, doing push-ups on the playing field. It is not a fair division. Though the object of my obsession can't see me for the perspiration dripping into his hazel eyes, I have managed to convince myself that staring at him, whenever and wherever possible, will extract from him the desired invitation to next week's Fall Frolic. I am not alone in such practices or beliefs. Many's the sweated hour I have spent with my hands on Arlene's Ouija board as she pleaded: "Will I be invited to the . . . ? Who will invite me to the . . . ?" Magic—last refuge of the powerless.

Tonya sits down opposite me. "Psst!" she taps her hard-boiled egg on the library table. "Babs and I nominated you for Students' Council."

"Thanks, but no thanks. I don't want to run this year."

"Why not?"

"Nothing mysterious. I've been secretary twice and vice president once. I'm bored, that's all."

Tonya grins. "We've nominated you for president."

"You know that has to be a boy."

"Not according to the constitution. Here, listen to this. 'The President shall be that student of good academic standing who receives the most votes as outlined in Section III.' That's student, not boy."

"You know what the tradition is. Hey, don't look at me. I've had enough."

"Can you guess who'll get in if you don't run?"

"Joe Baker, I suppose."

"No, Joker Nash. All the heartsick Grade Niners will be thrilled to vote for a football hero."

"If that's what the majority wants."

"How can you say that? You know he won't do any work. What we need is a female reform candidate. Every year anyone who wants to play sports has to buy a five-dollar membership in the GAA or the BAA, but instead of each group getting its own fees, we girls get one dollar per card and the boys get the rest. They say we don't need more dough because we don't go out of town, but we don't go out of town because we don't have the dough. Heck, we can't even afford Airwick for the locker room. As for gym time—"

"Look, Tonya, if you're so keen on making a point, then you run."

"I couldn't win, but you could."

"I'm flattered, but please leave me out." I return to Julius Caesar, thrice offered the crown by Antony just as the bell rings.

Tonya picks up her books. "Ready for the caf?"

"I think I'll snooze in the lounge. I'm not feeling so great." I give a sigh of female complaint. "You know."

Loosening my girdle, I stretch out on a horsehair sofa, my stomach crampy and bloated. Everything about my body seems strange, as if it were not really part of me. Through the window I can still hear the guttural grunts of Iky and Joker and Daniel and the other football players as they pummel each other just for the hell of it. Something about those animal sounds, so spontaneous and primitive and free, pulls on a sadness buried deep inside me. I muffle sobs in the smelly old horsehair sofa. I cannot stop.

Two other women and I have been purchased as concubines by King Farouk. Farouk chooses me as his favorite. Each night his advances become more demanding—he fondles my breasts, rubs his penis against my vagina. I tell myself I'll run away before I'm forced to have intercourse with him, but

*I can't escape because I'm stuck to the bed. I sob and sob,
and the sound is terrible to hear. When tears drip onto my
white nightgown, I see they are blood. I try to staunch the
flow, but blood spurts through the pores of my skin as if it
were a sieve.*

When I awake, I am lying in a puddle of blood. With
distaste, I clean myself up.

I look at a picture of Marilyn Monroe on the cover of Photoplay. Her flashy silver-blond hair has my undivided attention.
My own has started to darken as if a lightbulb were switched
off in my head, and I hate it. It was blond hair that caused
strangers to ask: "Who's little girl are you?" It was blond
hair that transformed me into a princess. It is blond hair
that—Hollywood still agrees—all gentlemen prefer, even those
with soft beards and barely cracked voices. For Appearances,
it is standard equipment.

Despite the example of Marilyn Monroe and Lana Turner
and Veronica Lake, "nice" girls in Hamilton circa 1950 don't
bleach or dye their hair. That's judged cheap and/or hard—
a blatant advertisement for moral turpitude. Nonetheless, I've
secretly experimented with old wives' recipes of lemon juice
and camomile tea. Perhaps in sunlight at high noon they do
make some marginal difference; however, like most dabblers
in the forbidden, I am growing bolder. Flipping to the back
of Lulu's Photoplay, I sort through mail-order ads for trusses
and bodybuilders to: "Miracle Golden Hairwash—not a dye,
not a bleach, not a tint. Restores radiant, natural color. Preferred by the Hollywood stars. We will send in plain brown
wrapper. $2.95, plus mailing charges. Satisfaction guaranteed
or money refunded."

"Beaky" Beckles patrols the aisles on her stumpy legs. Her
Latin textbook, long since memorized, lies closed on her desk.
What she wishes is one perfect sentence of homework to be
regurgitated word for word, like the segments of a worm,
from each constricted throat.

She chooses her row at random, then moves from front to back or back to front, pausing to mesmerize the occupant of each desk with her yellow eyes. Naturally, as soon as the first choice is made, everyone in the row figures out which sentence will be his or hers and strives to perfect it.

I count out my sentence: bad luck! The faithful Helen, who filled in most of the answers three years ago, has missed this one. I stare at the blank space the way the driver of a speeding car stares at a gap in a suspension bridge.

Beaky is now torturing Lulu, in front of me. To work out my sentence from scratch is hopeless, and I'm in no mood for another confrontation over undone homework. I fall back once again on that ever-chancy skill: mind control. Concentrating full strength, I imagine myself to be invisible. Passover passover passover passover.

As Lulu stumbles to the end of her sentence, I feel a surge of serenity like the music that swells in a Cecil B. DeMille epic when a miracle is about to be performed. I'm not even surprised when I hear Beaky announce: "Next sentence, Mr. Nash, please."

An exhalation from behind, followed by an oath. Heads swivel.

"Hey, what gives?" mouths Lulu, expressing the general consternation. "It's supposed to be your turn." This isn't the first time I've managed this stunt, though it doesn't always work—just often enough. I relax as Joker flounders in his tiny piece of hell and those in the rest of the row hustle to piece together their new sentences before Beaky strikes.

The bell rings. A grateful rush to the door. Daniel Hobson shortens his stride to accommodate mine. "Boy, do you ever lead a charmed life!"

Having just produced one miracle, I am not surprised to find I am to have a doubleheader.

"By the way, the Fall Frolic is next Friday. I was wondering if you would—"

Indeed.

*

My father sits in his armchair as if it were his throne, ordering my mother and Helen and me to fetch for him, as he always has. First it's a drink of King Cola well iced, then the paper from the porch, then his glasses. Old King Cola and his Fiddlers Three!

I draw the assignment of the glasses. My child's ploy of in-a-minute has now escalated into bolder experiments of taunt and torment. "Exactly where on the dresser did you put them? Well, I don't see them now. You must have left them somewhere else. Oh, yes, under yesterday's newspaper. Why didn't you say so? I'll be down in-a-minute."

As I return with the glasses, I match each step to its own bitter complaint, like prayers to beads, *with the voice of my other self chiming in with her even nastier contrapuntal:*

I hate you father. *I hate you father.* Let me count the ways. *Let me count the ways.* I hate the way your gold tooth squeaks as you wolf down bread slabbed with butter *because it reminds me of the way you spread and stab and wolf me down.*

I hate your listing armchair with the broken springs. *I hate your listing armchair with the broken springs* and the way it groans under your weight even when you aren't sitting on it *the way I groan under your weight when you are sitting on me.*

I hate the way *I hate the way* you lumber from bathroom to bedroom, shouting, "Don't look! don't look!" so no one can help but picture what they aren't supposed to see. Behold, *behold!* The Emperor Has No Clothes, *No Clothes.*

Mostly, what I hate *what I hate* is your flesh *is your flesh.* I hate it because ... *because ...*

My thoughts sail off the edge of my known world, leaving me with a bitter aftertaste of guilt. Guilt for what? For father-hate. It is a serpent that turns back on me, infecting me with the poison of self-loathing.

It's a last-ditch stand. I follow my mother from kitchen to dining room to living room, pleading: "Please let me stay out till one o'clock. All the other kids can. There won't be time to eat afterward. Please, mo-ther."

"There'll be food at the dance, won't there?"

"Hardly any. Not enough for the boys."

"Helen always manages to be in on time, and she's in college."

"Helen doesn't have to be in till one, and that's a big difference!"

"I said no and I meant it."

Helen, studying for a geography exam, pretends not to hear her name shouted back and forth, and perhaps by now she doesn't. As I stumble across her feet in hot pursuit of my mother, my voice grows harsher and louder like the siren of a fire engine. "Pleeease, Mother. It'll be so embarrassing. We're driving Arlene and—"

"No. Be in by twelve. That's final."

I know it's useless but I can't stop. I want to scream. *In fact, the scream, with the temporary release it brings to my other self, has become more important than our quarrels.* "Pleeeeeease, I'm on the decorating committee and—"

"No!" My father rears out of his chair, swatting at me with his folded newspaper the way he once swatted the late, much-lamented Smoky. "I don't care if you've been elected school dogcatcher. Be in that door by twelve!"

I smooth a mask of rose-beige foundation over my face, dab rouge high on my cheekbones, then wave a Maybelline wand over my eyebrows in the light feathery strokes favored by teen magazines for nice girls on a special date, for which the Fall Frolic certainly qualifies. I comb my long hair so that it covers one eye, then add my glamor-girl signature—bold lips courtesy of Revlon's Scarlet Lady.

My scarlet strapless formal, trimmed in bunny fur with seams stiffened by steel staves, is clipped to a hanger. I'm already wearing a black Merry Widow with enough boning to classify as heavy armor. Feeling the velvet slither over my back, I remember my saleslady's disapproval:

"Isn't that a little sophisticated? Perhaps you should look in our Young Misses' department."

I check the price, $29.95, reduced from $69.95, slightly soiled from use as a demonstrator model. Already Appearances is imagining the velvet clinging to her body like a second skin as she casts a come-hither glance over her naked shoulders—what Marilyn Monroe wore in How to Marry a Millionaire, or should have.

"I'll take it."

The saleslady's words drop like acid. "No exchange."

Now, burrowing through the fur trim, I hold my breath, hook and zip, feeling belated panic: will it stay up? And then: was the saleslady right? As I stare at my breasts, oozing over the scarlet bodice like marshmallow from a valentine, I feel myself grow dizzy. My face seems to be melting into the quicksilver, revealing something twisted and mocking behind it. Snatching up my lipstick, I slash at my mouth, impaling the red moth before it can flutter away. With savage strokes I darken my brows, pinning them like bushy caterpillars. Closing my eyes, I steady myself against the sharp corner of my dresser, suddenly weary, as if I were preparing for the hundredth performance of a play that wasn't very good in the first place. I don't want to go. I never have a good time, no matter who I'm with, and it's getting harder to pretend.

My mother calls up the stairs: "Your date is waiting."

Putting on Other Grandmother's red satin slippers, I elevate myself by three inches. Out of bravado, I even try a little dance step or two, vaguely recalling a once-favorite fairytale: Karen and the Red Shoes.

Everyone in church looked at Karen's beautiful red shoes, and when she knelt at the altar and the chalice was put to her lips, she thought of nothing else but the red shoes. Outside the church, she took a few dance steps. She couldn't help it. Once begun, her feet continued to dance as if the shoes had power over them. She danced around the church. She couldn't stop.

I make my entrance through the hall curtains, using a shawl to hide my décolletage from my parents. Daniel Hobson unfurls from the chintz sofa, boyish and appealing in his navy

(Dress Optional) suit with one-button roll. His dark blond hair has been slicked back in a single deep wave. His amiable face, made more interesting by a bent nose, wears no trace of get-me-out-of-here panic.

I reach for the first lie: "Mother, I'd like you to meet . . ."

"Oh, yes," she beams. "We've just been talking about my African violets. Daniel's mother grows them, too."

"Oh?" I smile at Daniel in genuine appreciation as I reach for the whopper: "Father, I'd like you to meet . . ." Still in a rage over our quarrel, he grunts from behind his newspaper, held between white fists.

My mother hands me the florist's box, which arrived earlier that day—a gardenia, just visible through dewy cellophane. "Don't be late—please."

As Daniel pushes against our storm door, a gust of wind tugs at my shawl. He reaches for his coat. "Do you want—?"

"No. I don't feel the cold." Or heat. Or rain. Or anything at all.

Daniel is driving his father's metallic green 1951 Buick with a D-for-doctor licence plate. As I slide—ouch!—across the frigid plastic seat, I thank him for my gardenia. "It's lovely. I can smell the perfume right through the box."

We pick up Arlene and Joe Baker. As they come down the Goodfellows' front steps, they are already sharing a private joke. Arlene's easy grasp of the evening arouses my wistful admiration. She had a crush on Daniel until Joe asked her. Then she prepared to have a good time with Joe, even to the extent of playing "Don't Cry Joe" nonstop on her record player. By contrast, I pined for Daniel until the moment after he invited me. Now, still quaking from family quarrels for which, in retrospect, I blame myself, I want only to get through the evening as painlessly as possible.

As we pause for the Sherman-Main stoplight, Daniel reaches for my hand. I surrender it, *automatically withdrawing all sensation, unaware that I am doing so, leaving only the wax model resting against his palm, almost as convincing as one from Madame Tussaud's.* I smile at him in apology, already knowing: you should have invited someone like Arlene. I can't meet your expectations.

The high-school gymnasium is resplendent. Blue balloons dribble from silver basketball hoops. Stars wink from a blue-tissue ceiling. Wrapped in the cool embrace of a crescent moon, the Stan Carter Serenaders play "Moonlight Serenade." The theme of the evening? "Once in a Blue Moon."

"It's gorgeous," exclaims Arlene.

I glance at the pastel swirl of Debbie Reynolds formals from the Young Misses' department, their taffeta skirts fat with crinolines, their sweetheart necklines set with pearls and lockets, their dyed-to-match fabric gloves leaving just three inches bare between cuff and cap sleeve, and I experience self-doubt. The only one who looks original is Lulu Lawson, dressed in her grandmother's Cleopatra getup, with dark eyes and false gold nails. She is with Herbert (formerly Muddy) Swamp, the drippiest drip of Laura Secord Public School, but quite presentable now that he's grown six inches, filled out and calmed down.

"That Lulu is a nut." Arlene giggles.

And getting nuttier. "Always playing a part." Like me.

Daniel reaches for my shawl. Though I resist clutching at it, I acutely feel its loss as it slides down my bare shoulders. "Wow, that dress is a knockout!" he says, beaming proudly.

Gratitude makes my smile brilliant.

A mob scene in the washroom. I pin Arlene's pink-carnation corsage to her pink peau-de-soie dress—the sort my saleslady described as "a perfect pet." Like all the other girls, I know the code: orchids at $4.00 to $6.50 for show-offs; gardenias, like mine, at $3.50 for sophisticates; roses at $3.00 for going-steady couples; $2.50 for casual dates; no corsage—a confession of poverty and/or no manners, an insult.

When we get back to the gym, Daniel and Joe are leaning against the athletic bars, transformed into a silver trellis twisted with blue roses. Safely at a distance, Daniel seems irresistible. As he lays his palm on my bare back to guide me onto the dance floor, *I experience a tremor of sexual arousal which I*

*repress, unaware that I am doing so. On instructions from
my other self, who considers sex her territory, I replace it
with something less dangerous*—ennui.

"When I hear that serenade in blue . . ."

The basketball floor is tacky with powdered wax. I watch
Daniel's lead shoulder dip and spin, following expertly in
Other Grandmother's red shoes.

Other couples shuffle by in variations of the fox-trot, the
girls with their hair too frizzy from an unaccustomed trip to
the beauty parlor, the boys with freshly cropped hair exposing
ears to wind and ridicule. Even the going-steady couples are
a little stiff as they peer over each other's shoulders, trying
on the evening, finger by finger, like a pair of kid gloves. This
is the stuff of tomorrow's cafeteria conversations—who was
with whom, who broke up, who is now going steady—the
female equivalent of refighting the winning (losing) football
game.

The artificiality of the set plays to my strengths. Confidently, I set about to entertain Daniel: "I'm surprised how
great the gym looks, considering. The League of Decency,
headed by Principal Forbes, swooped down on us at exactly
2:17 p.m. He had some little thingamabob he said measured
'candle watts.' Naturally, we didn't have near enough to suit
him. We had to unstuff all the fiberglass from the overhead
lights—after all the trouble we had getting the fire marshal's
approval. Last year at the Harvest Hoedown, Forbesie objected to us using real straw in the haystack for fear of 'ir-
regularities.' The way he pawed through it, I swear he thought
he'd uncover Jane Russell in her outlaw blouse."

Daniel laughs appreciatively. Gratified, I relax.

"Blue Moon, I saw you standing alone . . ."

Though I expect to have to carry the conversation, Daniel
is not reluctant: "You know, I once saw a blue moon—up
north at our hunting cabin. A full moon, as blue as a balloon.
I thought I must be seeing things, but it was reported in the
North Bay paper. Something to do with forest fires."

"Oh, do you go hunting very much?"

"Only till I accidentally shot something. A duck. Its mate flew over our cabin for the rest of the weekend quacking. No one in the family would speak to me. Since I killed it, I figured I better eat it. It tasted rotten."

"Blue velvet, bluer than velvet were her eyes . . ."

Under gentle prodding, Daniel also admits: "I don't like football much, though I play it. I don't like punching people, and I don't like to be punched. I'd be happy to watch the game from the bench, which burns Coach Jacobson. Because I'm big, he thinks I should be aggressive but it's the little guys who are the scrappy ones."

He even confesses to having spent several nights in jail. "Whenever our church basketball team plays Syracuse, we check into the local jail to save the cost of a hotel. If they're not too busy, the desk sergeant takes our wallets and belts then locks us up for the night."

End of first shift: not so bad. In fact, very very good. What was I afraid of? Daniel is fun as well as nice. Not a show-off like other boys. Maybe . . . a hope too fragile to express.

The modernized cafeteria with its fluorescent lights and plywood furniture is too harsh, too real. The girls, in their pastel gowns, look like melting sherbets with maraschino lips. Once again, I feel exposed in my paint-on face and too-naked dress.

"Over here!" calls Babs. She is sitting with Joker Nash, whom she invited against everyone's advice. Trussed in paddy-green satin, which emphasizes her size, she exclaims too exuberantly: "Look at the corsage Joker brought me. Isn't it a riot?" Pulling a plastic daisy from her clutch purse, she aims at him, squeezing the rubber bulb. It backfires. Water trickles down her face. She looks as if she were crying. She probably is.

A gang assembles, with everyone balancing triangular sandwiches, pink lemonade, ice-cream sundaes on paper plates. As I assist Lulu, physically helpless in her false gold nails, she whispers: "Don't look now, but Perry Lord is here. He's sitting with Tonya and Iky. I heard he got expelled from Hillfield for drinking."

Studying his pretty-boy face, frozen in a sneer, I ask myself: What did we all see in him in public school? Aloud, I comment: "We thought he was so sophisticated because he was arrogant and his voice changed first." Of such flimsy material are romantic legends created.

Perry calls Joker to his table, concealing something under his jacket as if it were a football. After much laughing and fumbling, Joker returns with his lemonade stained brown. "Don't drink that pink stuff straight!" he warns. "Forbesie spiked it with saltpeter."

"Saint Peter?" asks Arlene.

Joker laughs with Babs chiming in. She explains the joke to Arlene. "Saltpeter—to calm the guys down."

"At least that's better than Spanish fly!" calls Perry. "We put that in the punch at Westdale last June and half the girls got knocked up."

Joe looks disapproving. Daniel is annoyed. I whisper to Lulu. "He's lying. I've heard that old chestnut about every school in Hamilton."

"Moonlight becomes you . . ."

Daniel's arms coil possessively around me; his lips press against my forehead as we slide back into the blue mush. My claustrophobia builds in direct proportion to Daniel's attraction for me. I look at the clock: 10:35. Like Cinderella, I must be home by midnight, *in my father's house*.

"We'll build a blue room, a new room, for two room . . ."

Couples are rocking now instead of dancing. Daniel's arms feel like clamps, constricting me. I can barely breathe in the narrow space between my face and his chest, *my father's belly, my father's chest*. I see Perry Lord slither by with a confident pelvic wiggle, his date entwining him like a rosebush. Is everyone enjoying this but me?

I cast about for something to break the mood. Fortunately,

our chaperones, Miss Joper and "Geometric" George, en-
trusted with the six-inches-apart rule, have the same thing in
mind. Approaching the bandleader, they request a fast one:
"Oh, there's nothing to be ashamed of,
When you stub your toe on the moon . . ."
Startled couples pull apart as portly George and bony Miss
Joper hit the beat like the bouncy ball in an old-time movie
sing-along. Daniel sheepishly guides us off the floor. "Let's
sit this one out, do you mind? My feet are too big."

Perry Lord, temporarily abandoned, is leaning against the
athletic bars. His sulky stare draws on something perverse in
me. Tugging Daniel by the hand, I tease, "Don't be such a
coward!" I pitch my voice to Perry, sensing he will intervene.
He does. Bowing in mock formality to Daniel, he asks: "Why
not let me take this one for you?"

It is not usual to cut in at Hamilton High, and certainly
not at a formal where the male financial investment is so high.
Before Daniel can protest, I step forward, smiling. "Sure, why
not?" We swirl away in giddy hedonism.

*The red shoes would not let Karen do what she liked. When
she wanted to go right, they danced left. They spun her around
the room, then down the stairs and out the town gate. Away
she danced, and away she had to dance, right into the dark
forest . . . .*

Again the Serenaders settle into something smooth and
mellow. Closing my eyes, I lean against Perry's shoulder,
ignoring Daniel hunched against the athletic bars. The very
quality that makes Perry seem dangerous to other girls makes
him safe for me. He's running, so I'm not trapped. For black,
read white.

"That ole devil moon, deep in your eyes . . ."

Eventually, Daniel approaches, as I know he must. Jaw
set, he taps Perry. "I think you've got my date, fella."

Perry ignores him. Daniel's fingers tighten on his shoulder.
Throwing up his hands in mock surrender, Perry backs off,
exaggerating his drunkenness. "Much obliged, pal." The ar-
got of false camaraderie.

I return—am returned—to Daniel. His body is stiff, my heart resentful: you don't own me. Nobody does. Chatting too brightly, I mention other dances, other boys—casually, anecdotally, fighting for breath in the pulsating blue room, laying out the premises of my life. Don't get serious. I play the field. *Please* . . . .

Frowning, Daniel lays his finger across my lips: Cut it.

Now I feel guilty, *like daddy's naughty girl who's failed to please*. The evening is falling apart. I glance at the clock. It's after eleven. Time is slipping through glass fingers. I'm overcome with sudden loneliness: Daniel's a terrific person, and I've been a rat.

"Good night, sweetheart . . . ."

Daniel and I park outside my house in his father's Buick. It's 11:55. Now that the moment of leave-taking has come, I want only to escape inside. Instead, I slide across the cold plastic seat to Daniel, squeeze his hand. "I had a really good time, Daniel. Thanks for inviting me."

He kisses me. My lips are cold, like plastic. I can't do anything about that. They aren't under my conscious control. We neck a bit more, with Daniel's hand falling across the bosom of my dress. This shouldn't be first-date stuff, but I have been adding up the gasoline and the corsage, my guilt about my withdrawal against his legitimate expectations, and I find something owing which, being an honest tradeswoman, I feel obliged to deliver. I have no discernible sexual feelings. The battle of the car seat, as I know it, is strictly between my date and my parents, represented by the get-in-here lamp in our front window.

Daniel is beginning to breathe too heavily. Alarmed, I draw back, eager to close the account, drugged by the smell of my gardenia now crushed brown, not daring to stay a second longer. I speak the truth: "I have to get in or I'll be in trouble."

When Daniel tries to kiss me on the porch, I reply with more truth: "My parents wouldn't like it." What will the neighbors think? My hand is already on the knob as I repeat:

"I had a really good time. Thanks, Daniel." Don't call me. I can't explain. Even to myself. The more I like you the faster I have to run.

I bolt up the stairs, tripping over Other Grandmother's red shoes, falling flat on my face outside my father's bedroom. I lie on my stomach, feeling the house spin, hearing my father snore. *So off she danced in the red shoes, and off she had to dance, over fields and meadows, in rain and sunshine, and at night it was fearful.*

I try to kick off the red shoes, but they've stuck fast to my swollen feet. Crawling into the bathroom, I seize my father's razor and slit the satin fabric, *watching it bleed*, before passing out once more.

A masked man hurls me across a bed. Ripping off my red shoe, he slashes it with a razor. The sole spurts blood.

Defiantly, I say: "I know who you are, though I can't see your face."

"Then I must cut out your tongue and your eyes."

Behind my back, I hide a dagger: "Some day, monster, I'll stab you through the heart!"

The Hamilton High band struts around Scott Park, playing our victory song. As the notes rise to a brassy crescendo, Cooky Castle and I climb onto the shoulders of two other cheerleaders then clasp hands to form a triumphal arch.

The announcer shouts: "Iky Mason, No. 99, captain and quarterback." Iky sprints through the arch as the band begins a shivery drumroll punctuated by a clash of cymbals.

"Daniel Hobson, No. 91." Drumroll. Clash of cymbals.

Our Stallions line up opposite the St. Pat's Saints as both bands strike up: "God Save the Queen." Joker Nash kicks off for the Stallions: Sissssss-BOOM. The teams shift back and forth across the centerline, grapple in slippery knots, throw fists into faces, knees into groins, oof! bam! boom! Sweaters are ripped from backs, faces smeared, noses busted. Hankies are dropped and retrieved. We cheerleaders cartwheel, split, choo-choo.

At halftime the game is tied. A healthy glow emanates from the boisterous crowd as action shifts backstage to the hot-dog booths.

The Saints kick off—a short one. Stallion fans cheer, then gasp—a fumble. A Saint zigzags through the Stallion team for a touchdown. Again the Saints kick. Daniel Hobson flips to Iky, who tries a long pass. Interception! The Saints roll down the field for another touchdown.

The Stallions disintegrate. So does the weather. Soaked in drizzle, the Stallion stands turn surly. When the Saints' cheerleaders—male, because the nuns won't let girls show their knees—line up before them for the traditional exchange cheer, the fans heckle: "C'mon, boys, lift those legs. Let's see a little garter!"

Three-quarter time. Disgusted Stallion supporters leave or get drunk as their team slides into the mud. Fistfights break out on and off the field. An inebriated voice shouts: "Let's have a li'l cheer. C'mon, girlies, let's hear Suzie-Q!" That voice becomes more personal: "Hey, Blondie, you with the megaphone. Give us a cheer, Blondie. Cartwheels! We want to see pan-ties."

The Stallions kick a field goal. Dutifully, I take my squad onto the cinderpath for a sedate "Sis-boom-bah."

"That's right, Blondie. Get those tits moving!"

The crowd gives a nervous guffaw. Other voices chime in: "Crotch! Crotch! Give us CROTCH."

As the heckling intensifies, my morale collapses. The whole stand now seems unfriendly territory. Huddled in my blanket, I resist the urge to pull it over my head.

The Stallions score another field goal. I lead the prescribed cheer, followed by a string of cartwheels. My tormentor tosses an apple core, catching me in the crotch. Others loose a barrage of programs, popcorn and cigarette boxes.

I stop in mid-cheer, feeling as if my head were caught in a clash of cymbals. All I can see are mouths, hurling down obscenities that unroll like used toilet paper. A dart, spiked with a pen nib, hits me in the forehead. Blood gushes. As I rush off the field I hear a whoop of joy: Iky Mason has picked up a fumble and is dashing toward the Saints' goalposts. From the washroom window, I see him evade one tackler then another, his cleats spewing up gouts of mud: touchdown!

Cooky Castle leads "Go, Stallions" while I am sick in the toilet.

My legs are shaky. My forehead burns. Blood spatters my yellow sweater with its scarlet letter. *Blood, blood, blood, I am drowning in blood.* As I lean against the pock-marked, piss-colored, lipstick-kissed washroom walls, I hear Stallion fans give a high-spirited roar now that they're getting their own way. I kick the overflowing wastebasket, imagining it's my megaphone. Bastards! Cowards! It explodes in crumpled paper and used sanitary pads. Cartwheels! cartwheels!

Game over. The Stallions have won.

I run from the washroom through the smug and faceless crowd, using my head as a battering ram, sending revelers into startled pileups. "Look where you're going, girlie! What the hell."

I bolt for home, fueled by the faceless accusations both inside and outside my head, it makes no difference which, they're all the same, no specific charge I can answer, just guilt fear guilt fear rage rage rage.

I clear my porch steps in a single bound—"Don't slam the door!"—then race up two flights of stairs. I claw through my dresser drawer—old school diplomas, perfect Sunday school attendance certificates and other gold-embossed papers that once looked too official to throw away. My fingers close over it—a bottle of Miracle Golden Hairwash in a plain brown wrapper, "not a dye, not a bleach, not a tint, restores radiant natural color." In bravado, I dump it undiluted on my hair, which I wrap Lana Turner–style in a terry-cloth turban. Then I sit down to wait.

"Hey, what happened to you? Stay out in the sun too long, cutie?"

"Ja-vex! Goldi-locks! Per-ox-ide!"

Sticks and stones will break my bones but . . . but . . . .

"Why did you do it? It's all over school that you discovered you were part Negro."
Sticks and stones will break . . . break . . . .

"Hey, Blondie, you remind me of a movie star."
Marilyn? Veronica? Lana?
"Harpo Marx!"
Sticks and stones will . . . will . . . .

The envelope is lying on the hall table addressed to me in block letters. I pick it up, turn it over. Local postmark. No return address—a bad sign. I stick it in the garbage under some potato peels, then reconsider. What if my mother overturns the brown bag and finds it unopened?

I fish it out, its envelope now wet and brown-stained. My thumbnail catches the sealed flap. I open it. A diagram, very specific, plus a French safe, with caption. No signature, of course. Crying, I rip it into tiny pieces and flush it down the toilet.

They have smelled my fear. I should never have run. I can feel them around me, closing ranks against me. Now they know I'm afraid. I've lost my invincibility. I'm afraid of my own shadow—*especially my own shadow: The Shadow Knows heh heh heh*.

Filthy, stinking, rotten letters, always anonymous, and even worse phone calls. I have to hold the receiver tight to my ear, absorbing the poison so my mother won't hear. And yet, in the halls I see them from the corner of my eye, circling, falling back, and then in a rush: "If-you're-not-doing-anything-Saturday—" How can they persecute me one minute then give me so much power the next?

I awake in a jangle and turn off my alarm, hearing a muffled plock plock overhead. It is raining. A leaden day to be carried in the pit of the stomach. I creep down, ritual by ritual, through the quiet house—my father is on the night shift, Helen is on a geology field trip, my mother is down in the cellar tending the furnace. Truly a nasty day.

Since I must be at school early, I cut through the alley instead of calling for Arlene, past rotting fences and garbage cans stuffed with yesterday's Halloween pumpkins, wearing my see-through puddlers and plastic coat, carrying Julius Caesar in a satchel for my afternoon English Lit. test. Once on pavement, I paddle through the gutters, freeing a Popsicle stick from its clog of leaves for an unimpeded gush down the sewer, reciting my speech for today's auditorium:

"Teachers, students, fellow candidates . . . . *Lend me your ears.*

"I have served on Students' Council for three years. This year my qualifications are the same as last except that now I have an extra year's experience. Instead of dwelling on that, I would like to set before you an issue of considerable importance. It is traditional for the president of Students' Council to be male. Traditional but not constitutional. A careful search of the rule book has shown no such qualification. Therefore, in running for your president, I—yuk!"

I jump onto the sidewalk. A poor little sparrow, eyes glazed, feet curled, is lying in the gutter, its chest wriggling with maggots, and I have stepped in it. Scraping guck from my plastic puddlers, I hurry on. *Beware, beware the Ides of November.*

I pass through the Roman arch of Hamilton High, still reciting my speech. The hall is empty, as expected. The clock over the boys' trophy case reads 8:05. I mount the stairs, past the large Kotex carton the janitor insists on using for garbage. I stop. Something is not quite right, something on the first floor. Backing down the steps, I stand before the bulletin board, gaudy with election posters. My poster has been defaced. My lips have been reddened, my hair painted gold. The caption, EXPERIENCE COUNTS, has been altered to read EXPERIENCED CUNT.

I stare at the poster for a long time, with the water dripping down my plastic see-through hat, my plastic see-through coat, my plastic see-through boots, feeling the floor ooze like mud between my toes. When Tonya Philpott finds me two hours later, I am standing in a shower stall in the girls' locker room, with hot water pouring over my plastic see-through self, clutching my red poster, trailing dye like blood, *drowning in blood*. By then, of course, it is too late for election speeches.

"There is in our midst, gentlemen, a strange and deadly character, a woman of towering arrogance and ambition which she hides behind a cloak of desirability and seduction."

"You mean?"

"Yes. I am referring to none other than ... THE BRASS AMAZON!"

A shudder sweeps the group. "From whence doth this brazen creature come?"

"She cometh from the stars, gentlemen! Specifically, from Regulus, the blue-white heart of Leo the Lion, traveling through purple nebulae, glittering with the iridescence of a million separate suns, traversing eighty-six light years so swiftly in her diamond spaceship that it hath become the day before yesterday."

"But why doth she visit Earth, third planet from our mediocre Sun at the edge of a lesser galaxy some men call the Milky Way? Why doth she bother with this miserable place, ruined by Hypocrisy, Stupidity and Lust, where Men ruleth?"

"I believe her ultimate aim, gentlemen, is no less than the TOTAL DOMINATION OF THIS PLANET. Already she and Tonya Philpott, her loathsome henchwoman, have laid plans to gain a stranglehold on this unsuspecting community through a female takeover of Students' Council. I am afraid, gentlemen, we have no choice but to ...."

One of the conspirators brandishes a dagger.

"No! Her armor is too strong for frontal attack. Our only hope, gentlemen, is to destroy this creature by indirect means, to torment her with all the duplicity at our disposal, to disrobe

her images by the cut and thrust of our tongues, to humiliate her in a way that will play on her secret sense of shame and self-loathing. Do this, gentlemen, and you will see her writhe and wither before your eyes, for I tell you, gentlemen, I have smelled her fear."

The conspirators brandish their daggers. "Revenge! Revenge!"

Again the chief conspirator raises a restraining hand. "No! We do this deed regretfully to preserve the Status Quo Publico to which she is a menace, and for her own good."

The conspirators raise their fists: "For her own good!"

"And now, gentlemen, to the senate." WE ARE COMING TO GET YOU, SLUT, YOU WILL PAY!

LADY MACBETH

Everything about the pristine and unforgiving fifties, with its glorification of a girl's virginity as her most prized possession, was destined to make my other self's fear of exposure an omnipresent terror. Ironically, though I created her to look after daddy's sexual needs so I could lead a more normal life, she was now so remorseful that she functioned as my guilty conscience, using her special knowledge to torture me. She was like a demented Lady Macbeth on the rampage inside me, spewing up her guilt into my personality. By the last few months of high school, I was locked in a morality play in which everything that happened to me—every sideways look, every whistle, every slight—was interpreted as an accusation of my unworthiness.

The Hamilton High morality system was biblical. Though it was the boys' loose talk that undermined a girl's reputation, it was the other girls who publicly brought her down. Our list of sexual pejoratives was suitably long—boy-crazy, fast, cheap, hard rock, man-hungry, pushover, pickup, round heeler, makeout artist. I kept waiting for the first boulder to strike, but it never did. Whatever was happening, or whatever I thought was happening, was being ignored in the give-and-take of female friendships. I was pathetically grateful, but my shaky sense of reality wobbled even more dangerously. Was I just imagining the sexual slurs, the innuendo? Was it all in my head? To all my other fears was added an overriding one: the fear of going crazy.

Hamilton is entombed in ice. It frosts windows and seals mailboxes. It snaps branches, glazes sidewalks, hangs from roofs in skeletal fingers, dripping with malice. Everything is beautiful, brittle, secret and treacherous, visible but inaccessible like flowers encased in plastic.

Tonya, Arlene, Babs, Cooky, Lulu. We walk to Hamilton High, sliding our boots over the glassy sidewalk and around the hissing mouths of sewers, melting the air with our post-Christmas gossip, punctuated by shards of splintered laughter.

Tonya, Arlene, Babs, Cooky, Lulu. We enter Hamilton High for our final six months, still talking, talking, talking. Now my feet slide over the polished floor, oiled and waxed for the new year. Arlene feels me stumble, reaches out to catch me. Her hand passes right through me and still we are talking, talking, talking, but saying nothing. Mouths float by.

Lulu is in seventh heaven. She has been chosen by Boris Wayne, the school's acting coach, on whom she has had a passionate two-year crush, for the lead in Romeo and Juliet. Her locker is plastered with posters of his theatrical triumphs, and every other sentence she speaks is preceded by "Boris says . . ."

Since Boris says Shakespeare should be rehearsed in a contemporary setting to overcome any feeling that it's frozen in history, we are getting to know Lulu's role as well as she.

> Poison I see hath been his timeless end:
> O churl! drunk all, and left no friendly drop?
> [Snatches dagger from corpse.]
> O happy dagger! [Stabs self.]
> There rust and let me die.
> [Falls on Romeo's corpse and expires, to loud applause.]

And who gets to play Romeo? Herbert Swamp, in cape and codpiece.

My father calls me into his bedroom. *Since my mother is also in the house, my other self understands it is me he is calling and not her.* He sits on his bed, in front of a dresser drawer overflowing with ties, pulling out one and then another in childish delight. "Look at this. Isn't this a honey?"

I stare at a fat, wine-colored tie spattered with gold stars.

"It's certainly unusual." Though my enthusiasm is as fake as the stars on the tie, my father doesn't seem to notice as he knots it around his fist. "This is real silk. It was on sale for a dime." He pats the bed beside him. "Sit here. I'll show you more." *My other self stares at her daddy's stubby, well-manicured hand. She stares at the place that hand has prepared for her on the bed, deeply sagged under his bulk with fleshy thighs splayed to accommodate an overhanging belly—the bed she knows so well, decorated by her mother's pursed lips.*

I back out of my father's bedroom, feeling sweat bleed from the roots of my hair, feeling as if a bomb were tick tick ticking in my chest, feeling revulsion so powerful that my stomach heaves. My father is still exclaiming, "Doesn't this one knock your eye out? Look at this!"

I collide with my mother, standing in the doorway with a newly ironed armload of underwear. She interprets what she sees: "Why are you always so rude to your daddy? If you'd just go along with him, you'd find he can be generous."

"I don't have a toothbrush."

"I'll give you one."

"I don't have pajamas."

"I'll lend you a pair. Please. Paul is in Vancouver on business and Millicent is shopping in New York. It's spooky staying by myself with Miss Mildon."

It's the same conversation we used to have in primary school. "Okay, I'll sleep over but I'm refereeing a basketball game tomorrow morning at seven."

We lie across Lulu's canopied bed, sipping Miss Mildon's grape cordial. Her movie magazines have been supplemented by Billboard and Variety. The naval picture of her father, Paul Lawson, over which we used to swoon, has been joined by one of him outside Hamilton TV station CHCN, which he owns. "Hey, Lulu, remember when Miss Buchanan's class wrote to your dad in the navy? He still looks like Clark Gable. I'm still jealous."

She corrects me. "Paul looks better than Clark Gable. He's only thirty-seven, after all. Clark Gable is an old man."

All evening Lulu seems subdued. Not once does she tell me "Boris says" anything. In fact, she doesn't mention Romeo and Juliet at all, which seems odd, given her obsession. We have no trouble getting to bed by ten, as promised.

Just past midnight, I awaken. Nothing looks familiar: the canopy of the four-poster bed, the moon shining on the antique doll's house. Then I see "Clark Gable," and I remember Paul Lawson. Ah yes, Lulu's place. I feel for her in the bed. She isn't there. Light slides under the door from her grandmother's room. I tap: no answer. I bang: no answer. Alarmed, I try the knob. "Lulu?"

She's sitting in front of her grandmother's vanity, wrapped in her grandmother's Cleopatra robe, her eyes outlined in kohl, sucking on the tattered handkerchief she once claimed had her father's smell on it. "Are you all right?"

"I've been sick."

"I'm feeling squishy myself—Miss Mildew's revenge!"

"No, I don't mean that. I get sick all the time now. I'm pregnant."

I start to laugh, but her bleak tone and face stop me short. "Are you sure?"

"Yes."

"Do your parents know?"

"Not yet."

"What will you do?"

She shrugs. "I've given up throwing myself downstairs. I guess I'll have to have it." She turns on me. "Just keep your trap shut!"

I lie awake, my heart yammering in my chest, hearing a clock strike two then three then four.

Using a pack of police dogs, a sheriff discovers the body of a teenager buried in our backyard. Her eyes are heavily outlined in black, her blond hair is shaped like a pyramid, her hands are crossed over her chest, and her breasts and sex organs are in an advanced state of decomposition like an Egyptian mummy. Apparently, my father murdered her when she became pregnant. As an observer, I find her horrible, yet fascinating, and oddly familiar. She reminds me of . . . of . . .

I awake at six. Lulu is asleep, or pretending to be. I think about canceling my basketball game, but know I can't get a replacement at this hour.

By 8:50 I'm waiting outside Lulu's first class. I take her arm. "Lulu, you have to see a doctor. Do you want me to go with you?"

She turns on me round-eyed. "What are you talking about?"

I stammer: "You know. What you told me—about being pregnant."

She flares: "I think you've got rocks in your head. I've always thought you were crazy, and now I know."

I am left to bluster. Is this another game Lulu is playing?

And then: did I dream it?

And then: of course, it's true! Lulu's been wearing the same box-pleated skirt and blazer for a month with her books held across her stomach.

And then: am I crazy?

And then: I look at myself sideways in my mirror. Have I gained weight? Everywhere or . . . ? But that's impossible. You can't get "it" from toilet seats, no matter what Tonya claims. Yet my anxiety builds, *fed by the more relevant fears of my other self.*

I go on a diet in which I eat only six apples a day. Babs is also on a diet—her seventy-fifth attempt, I reckon. This time, however, she's molded herself into something the boys don't mind being seen with, so she's getting the Big Rush, spearheaded by Joker Nash. Of course, it's gone to her head, she's failing all her grades and all she can talk about are dates and calories. Even her jokes are about food—sort of.

"It's about this psychiatrist, see? A guy comes into his office wearing a fried egg sunnyside up on his head and three strips of bacon dangling from each ear. He says to the psychiatrist: 'I want to talk to you about my brother.' "

We laugh and we can't stop, and for a while she's like the old Babs, but then she starts to gag, and she can't throw up because there's nothing in her stomach, and then she cries, and she can't stop that either because her nerves are so bad, and her makeup is entirely ruined. *I want to talk to you about my twin sister, har-de-har-har.*

It's hot on the streetcar, and crowded, with dampness rising from slush on the wood floor. Smell of wet fur, wet wool, garlic. I hang from a strap in the rear, surrounded by boys in Marlon Brando jackets and caps, probably headed for the hockey game in the arena.

Every few minutes I wipe steam from the window with my mitt to check for my stop. It's so foggy I can't see the sidewalk, only a sizzle of blue flame from the streetcar arm as it slides along its electric track. Rattle rattle lurch lurch. The motion is beginning to nauseate me, the raucous horseplay of the Marlon Brando gang to unnerve me, the press of bodies to activate my claustrophobia. Sweat trickles inside the sleeves of my new winter-white coat. Bracing my saddle shoes against the slimy corduroy floor, I try to take it off just as the streetcar shudders to a halt. I topple backward, my hands caught in my sleeves. Someone clamps my wrists behind my back. The Marlon Brando gang press against me. A knee is thrust into the small of my back, throwing me off balance. Another pushes between my legs. Hands claw at my sweater, tear at my brassiere. I feel myself begin to sink, as if I were losing consciousness. A face presses up to mine, insolent and confident: "Oh, this one's hot for it. She's really loving it, aren't you, baby?"

Beyond the leering faces, I see a ring of bored passengers, shopping bags on their laps, newspapers in their hands. I try to call out, but feel too winded, as if someone had punched me in the stomach. The streetcar stops. "A-reee-na!" With a whoop, the teenage boys push to the exit. The car empties as rapidly as if someone had uncorked a bottle. I fall backward on the slushy floor. My new coat is trampled, one sleeve torn.

"That's a shame," sympathizes a woman with a goiter. "The way they pack us in, it's like we was cattle!"

Badly shaken, I swab my white coat soiled with muddy footprints, reassuring myself: it wasn't my fault. It could have happened to Arlene or Babs or even Tonya. A voice I've heard a lot lately admonishes me: But why didn't you call for help? Tonya would have kicked someone in the groin. Babs would have hollered. Arlene would have told the conductor.

BUT IT WASN'T MY FAULT!

Welcome to the Streetcar Named Desire har-de-har-har.

Is Lulu crazy?

Am I?

Did Lulu lie the night she told me she was pregnant? If so, why?

Why did she tell me?

Did she tell me?

I hide in the theater balcony and watch Lulu rehearse.

O happy dagger! [Stabs self.]
There rust and let me die.
[Falls across Romeo's corpse and expires.]

Sometimes Lulu swoons so deeply Boris Wayne and Herb Swamp practically have to revive her. Then she looks up at me and winks—or does she? She knows I'm there—or does she? And I know she knows—or do I? I know she's pregnant—isn't she? And she knows I know—doesn't she? But why does she keep rehearsing? She's never going to do this play if . . . if . . .

*

English Lit. We've switched from Julius Caesar to Hamlet.

Was Hamlet really mad?

More likely Hamlet and I and/or Lulu are playing at insanity as a dress rehearsal for the real thing. *Let me tell you about my sister, har-de-har-har!*

The rumor is . . . the rumor is . . . that the plays of Francis Bacon-and-Eggs were written by his brother the Danish Ham Omelet.

My diet is working well. I'm down to ninety-eight pounds. I don't even get the curse anymore. I've made up my mind I'll never have it again. It was a bloody nuisance, ha ha! My friends tell me that I'm crazy, but I'd already guessed that.

I can burn my arm with a cigarette and not feel it. I wrap my mind around pain till it smothers in its own scream. One of these days I'll blot out this whole fucking universe!

I go out with Jim. I go out with Claude.

I go out with Wally. I go out with Rod.

I go out with . . .

Stop! Stop this minute!

I can't! Now the split between what I am and what I pretend to be is so wide I can barely straddle the gap. I see myself dancing across a stage like a stringless marionette, nodding, smiling, joking, laughing with red lips. Once this puppet was my slave, made up of shiny bits and pieces of what other people admired. She performed in my name. I held the strings. She protected me. Now she is a caricature of what I want her to be. Appearances is my enemy, mocking me, serving me up. She is destroying me by destroying herself. Yet I must make her carry me through the school year, one dancing red shoe and then the other, along the tightrope—seconds, minutes, hours, days. Then I will jiggle the rope. Then I'll let her fall while I sail out the scream in her throat. In the meantime, I let her know I'm alive by torturing her. I slop scalding water over her when she's draining the turnips.

I trip her when she runs for the bus. She has broken her strings, but she is not free of me. We are held together by an umbilical cord of pain.

Babs—who else?—told me this one, which she got from Joker: "Two prostitutes go to church on Easter Sunday. One tells the other, 'I'm afraid those people will know we're prostitutes.'

"The other persuades her: 'Nah. Just don't open your mouth.'

"When the minister announces the Hallelujah chorus, the first prostitute keeps her mouth closed, afraid to sing while the other one sings her heart out. Afterward, the minister scolds the congregation: 'There's some who're singing and some who aren't.'

"The first prostitute bursts into tears. 'I told you they'd guess about us.' " Pause. "Don't you get it, dim bulb?" Babs repeats: "There's some 'who're' singing and some 'who're' not, har-de-har-har."

Incredibly, the days are passing like lead soldiers, sent one by one into a battle from which they never return. They're all the same and countable, with a foreseeable end—the day I walk out of Hambone High, a free woman. In the meantime ... I go out with Tom. Dick. Harry. Bob. Somebody. Anybody. Everybody. Nobody. Whomever I'm with. Whoever is with me. What does it matter? They say we're all the same below the neck. I pay them the same compliment: to me they're all the same above the neck, a long line of Wildroot Cream Oil Charlies stretching nowhere.

This time when Juliet swoons, she does not get up. This time the nurse is called.

Lulu has dropped out of the play.

Lulu has dropped out of school.

Lulu has dropped out of life.

There rust and let me die.

[Falls across Romeo's corpse and expires.]

Lulu is over.

She is no more.

Who? That's all anyone can talk about. It's driving everybody crazy.

"She isn't even going steady."

"How could she do it? I mean, the Limit!"

"If my mother hears, she'll make me break up with Jim."

"If my father hears, he'll never let me date again."

"She's always liked attention, and now she's flaunting it."

"No matter what she pretends, it must be killing her."

"I think she did it to get her father's attention."

"I wonder what she'll do—with the baby, I mean."

"I'd kill myself."

"I'd kill it."

"I'd kill him."

"Whoever he is."

Who? Who? Who? Nobody knows for sure, but the rumor is that she is marrying Herbert Swamp.

My other self lies naked on her daddy's bed. He is breathing heavily. So is she. What she feels is rage. Not rage projected against her mother or her teachers or the boys at Hamilton High or herself, which is the kind of rage I always feel. No, her rage is directed at the person who caused that rage, who still causes it. As he rubs up against her with his penis like a poisonous toadstool, she silently repeats her litany: I hate, I hate, I hate, I hate, I hate . . . a choo-choo train getting up steam.

As daddy pushes her head down to his crotch, she at last gets out the words: "I hate you!" She smashes her left fist into his belly. "Touch me again, and I'll kill you!" She punches and punches like her mother kneading bread dough. He doesn't resist. He doesn't fight back.

So that is all it took, would have taken.

*

Exams. We sit in the auditorium, row upon row of chairs with swollen arms for writing. Some of the boys rustle when they walk—cheat notes. Others have inked their wrists.

Today's exam is French. Our professor is "Pop" Overton who eats chalk when he gets mad and looks like the MGM lion with a perm. Wiping his bald head with crumpled foolscap, he puts on the French dictation record. "Ecoutez! N'écrivez pas . . ."

Though it goes against the grain of Hamilton High, I've been studying. Hard. Secretly. Like a solitary drinker. I memorize things: stupid dates and capitals and Latin endings. I stuff them into pigeonholes in my head for easy retrieval. My head is my only battering ram out of this hellhole, and I know it. Out of Hamilton High. Out of Hamilton. *Out of my father's house.*

Wearing my school blazer, its lapels seeded with pins denoting clubs belonged to and offices held, I chat to one group of friends and wave to another, exchanging high hopes and fond farewells, contributing my share to the din, yet unwilling to allow myself relief or hope on this my last day of Hamilton High lest an invisible hand reverse the clock, glue pages back on the calendar, snatching this moment away.

It's a long unwinding. By the time I return to my locker most of the others have headed for Miller's Malt Shop. Unfastening my combination lock for the last time, I take out a bottle of Schaeffer's washable green ink, a package of reinforcements, old gym socks and—pushed to the back on the top shelf—my red cheerleader shoes.

I turn. Someone stands at the end of my row. As I attempt to dart past, his arm goes up, barring my way. He says: "You know, you're really hard to get hold of. Every time I see you, you're with a gang or else you're with some other guy. You're always moving. You're there, but you aren't there. You really sweat a guy out."

"Oh?" I make that sound as small and neutral as possible,

requiring as little expenditure of energy as possible. Over Daniel's left ear I see sunlight streaming through the plate-glass door, a patch of blue sky. All I want is to plunge through that door into that fresh air. I count the seconds, drawing every bit of emotion from the space between us, making it into an impassable mote, afraid of being tracked into some secret lair when freedom is so close at hand.

"You're really a terrific person."

I grip the red shoes, feeling them tremble in my left hand.

"If you're in any kind of trouble . . ."

Don't speak, or you will cry.

Don't cry, or you will never stop.

Don't faint, or you will never get up.

A few seconds more and he'll be gone. A few seconds more and I'll be gone—out the Roman arch, down the steps, *wearing the red shoes, over briars and stubble till her feet were torn and bleeding, on and ever on, she danced, for dance she must, even through the dark nights, forsaken by all the world and cursed by the holy angels of God.*

But Daniel is not gone. He's still standing there. Face grave, he says: "Any guy would be pleased to go out with you. You don't have . . . I mean, you've got so much going for you that you don't have to . . . . You shouldn't . . . ."

"Don't have to what?"

" . . . don't have to . . ."

"Say it!"

" . . . put out for the guys."

So here it is at last, the anonymous accusation translated into words.

Filthy, stinking, rotten letters, always anonymous, and even worse phone calls. Oh, this one's hot for it. She's really loving it, aren't you, baby? Repent, repent! The time of Judgment is at hand. There's some whore singing and some whore not. That's right, Blondie. Get those tits moving! Crotch! Crotch! Give us crotch! WE'RE COMING TO GET YOU, SLUT!

I shout: "It's not true! They're liars!"

He looks at me in surprise, studies my face, then reaches out his hand. I see it coming toward me, ever so gently. He touches me.

I shatter.

I shatter like a reflection shot through with a bullet. I shatter, and no piece remains larger than a thumbnail.

RESCUE

LOVE

I have something to tell you.
Are you going to believe this?

I am in love. I love, and I am loved.

What was the golden arrow that struck me with such force? Simply this—kindness. I denied their lies, and I was believed. I am believed!

Danny comforts me, his arms cradling me as if I were something fragile and very precious. He holds me, binding the pieces of myself together, allowing me to heal. He strokes my hair. He kisses me. His lips are warm. He believes me. He believes in me.

We both get summer jobs at the Sparkling Soda Water Company in downtown Hamilton. Danny drives a truck and I work on the bottling line. For $46.75 a week (minus $10.98 for white coveralls) I stand with nine women along a conveyor belt, putting dirty bottles into the washer, taking clean bottles out, inspecting them as they head for the filling and capping and packing machines.

Clinkety clink. The holes fly by like mouths to be fed. Clinkety clink. A bottle slips through my hands. It explodes on the concrete floor. The women smile their reassurances. The foreman scowls. Clinkety clink. In my dreams, I work the night shift.

Danny and I drive to Burlington Beach in Danny's red MG, a graduation gift from his parents. With hamburgers and milk shakes we park near the Brant Inn on Lake Ontario. Live band music wafts across the moonlit water toward the chimneys of the Steel Company, belching their Stygian fire and smoke.

Danny lays his arm across the back of my seat. I am more shy than wary as he leans over to kiss me. As I grow used to his arms, I cling to him, overriding fear: So this is how other girls feel. Against all the possibilities I am real after all. I am human.

He, too, is three-dimensional, no figment, his body becoming as familiar as my own—the twice-broken nose, the scar on his hand where the pet dog he rescued from a car crash bit him, the crinkly hair on his chest, the beating heart. Though it is dark I see his face more clearly than I have seen anything in my life—the cleft chin, now cupped in my hand; the generous mouth; the thick brows and lashes; the hazel eyes—actually blue with flecks of brown. He is the mirror in which I now see myself, *replacing the accusing eyes of my other self.*

Danny and I spend every free second together. We go to drive-in movies after the late shift. We drive to Niagara Falls or park on the Mountain brow watching the lights of Hamilton blink on and off. The scene shifts but the center holds—Danny and I curled together like two shoots.

All of a sudden, life seems generous and full of ease. There is enough of everything to go around—of love, of laughter, of hope. As we fly around the scented summer nights in his red MG, I have a sense of glamor and of carelessness and of privilege, like a character in a Scott Fitzgerald novel.

The fates are kind. I am to have the whole package, beautifully gift-wrapped. I shake it: it doesn't tick. I open it: it doesn't explode.

Danny invites me to meet his parents. As we leave my house, he warns: "Dad may be in bed. He has to rest a lot since his stroke, and he has trouble speaking. He still thinks he's going to return to work, but no one else holds out much hope . . . . Dad's a wonderful person. I remember going on calls with him. If it was a poor family, we always took clothes, and every Christmas he made dollhouses for the babies he brought into the world."

Danny parks in front of a red brick house with green-roofed gables. A woman with flyaway brown hair and a strong, pleasant face greets us from her rose garden. "I must look a mess! I can't pass this corner without seeing a weed, and I can't see a weed without pulling it out."

We enter the house together. Everything here, as outside, is substantial and traditional—Duncan Phyfe chairs with petit point cushions, Dresden figurines, brocade and velvet sofas, seascape oils in gilt frames, oriental rugs. Danny's father lies in the master bedroom, propped up with pillows. Though looking all of his fifty-six years, with a bald head fringed in silver, he has Danny's open, amiable face and broad grin. Warmly gripping my hand in both of his, he struggles to express what he has already conveyed: "Glad—see you."

Danny's fourteen-year-old sister Kate peeks around the corner, and is beckoned in. Coltish and shy, with Danny's blond hair and long-lashed eyes, she perches on a stool, very close to her father, playing with his bed covers, with his glasses.

The family displays its jokes and legends like heirlooms:

"Remember the day Danny 'borrowed' dad's car? He couldn't have been more than nine! The policeman who caught him couldn't believe what he was seeing."

"Remember when our dog Rusty stole old Mr. Pulford's long johns from the clothesline?"

"Remember how Grandma Hale refused to drink ginger beer because it was called 'beer'? When we pointed out that ginger ale was called 'ale' she stopped drinking that, too."

"Remember the time dad teased Grandma Hobson's monkey by giving it a red onion instead of an apple? Boy, was that monkey mad!"

Dr. Hobson chuckles through the whole recitation. When he attempts to join in, the family waits with patience for the words to form, turning the problem into a game:

"Who do you mean, Dad? Is it anything in this room?"

"Is it the photo album, Dad?"

Afterwards we watch home movies: jerky black-and-whites with each member of the family smiling self-consciously as he or she waves into the camera. "Look, there's Danny hanging by his legs from the old apple tree—that was the house we had in Burlington before we moved into the city so dad could be closer to the hospital."

I am warmed. Yet I keep my distance like a feral cat circling a bonfire. I don't know what else to do.

Clinkety clink. The women mouth conversations over the din, making themselves understood from machine to machine in the same mysterious way my mother and the neighbor ladies converse across several backyards while hanging clothes. The single women yearn for the Right Man to rescue them without seeming to notice the married ones are still here, unrescued. The married ones dream of buying the Right House so they can rescue their marriages and the children. I learn a new vocabulary of failed rescue, of hopes unmet:

"Well, it's not the first time he's been in the clink but he's a straight-john and that's worth something . . . ."

"Of course, there's always pogey . . . ."

"I smelled this disgusting stink. Later I find he spent the whole day in the steam bath getting ready for our date, but he works in a meat-packing plant and he's got the death stink soaked into his skin . . . ."

"So this guy yanked our TV set out of the wall. We were only two payments behind then Joe got canned . . . ."

"My old man says with aluminum doors, sell one and you sell the whole street . . . ."

"I stole twenty bucks out of his pocket and bought this gorgeous nightgown slit up to here. What happened? Absolute zero. He must be screwing at the plant or else he got it cut off . . . ."

". . . so the priest says, 'You got any sins to confess?' I say, 'Yes, Father. I've been using a diaphragm.' He says, 'You know that's a mortal sin.' I say, 'Yes, Father, but you should've seen the way Burt meatballed me when I got knocked up with little Eddie' . . . ."

". . . three years and I still don't know what he makes. I

go through his pants for his pay stubs but he's always clean. Then he wants me to hand over my check every Friday."

"That deadbeat told me he won the car at a Kiwanis raffle, then I discover he forged my name for the payments."

I am so lucky. So magnificently, once-in-a-lifetime lucky. I thought I was alone in the universe, sending futile bleep bleep bleeps into space. I thought I was alone, then someone answered. Tell me, Galileo, given the vastness of space, what are the chances of this?

I am knocked out by the wonder of it all. It sucks my breath away, leaves me dancing in a Technicolor world. Somebody looked deeply into my eyes, saw my turbulence, yet wasn't afraid.

And so the handsome prince kissed the sleeping princess and . . . and . . . .

No, it doesn't quite work that way. This is real life, after all.

Even now, I can't trust.

Even now, I dare not trust.

My other self is still wary, bitter, case-hardened, vengeful, jealous, frightened, furious, egocentric, inventive and sly. She is not going to give up the bones and nettles of her autonomy without a stringent test. Before I am going to be allowed to love anyone, she is going to have to display her entire ragbag of hurts and furies.

We're scarcely into the car before I shriek: "You're late! You said two o'clock, now it's after three!"

His face is expressionless, his voice calm as he maneuvers through the Saturday afternoon traffic. "I had some errands to do. One thing led to another."

"Couldn't you have phoned to say you'd be late?"

"I didn't know that I would be and, besides, I didn't think it was important."

"It is to me!" *I hate staying in that house, my father's house. I can't take this vulnerability, this risk of loss, especially now that I have so much to lose. My emotions are too raw, my happiness too new, my trust too fragile, my terror too real.* "What's the point of going to the beach now? The sky's practically all clouded over."

Words spill out of my mouth—ugly, hysterical, accusing. His jaw is clenched, his hands grip the steering wheel. He's never heard such rage, like a demon vomiting green bile. Neither have I—not outside my father's house. While I cringe in humiliation, somewhere inside me a voice I can't stop spews abuse from my lips. It's a voice I recognize all too well—the same petulance, the same indignant demand for service: "Fetch me! fetch me! fetch me!"

Danny brakes the car, draws to the curb. I think he is going to make me get out. Instead, he asks: "Why are you doing this when you know how much I love you?"

My crazy voice breaks off in mid sentence. Rage falls away like a suit of rusty armor. Relief is real and instantaneous. Here I was, the voice of the Frankenstein monster, insisting that I was human even as I lumbered through the forest murdering things, and I was heard. Now I hear silence ringing in my head. My scream has flown away on the last bat to Transylvania. I am heard!

Danny disarms my parents as he has me. Even my father is cordial. *Like all bullies, he is afraid. He is afraid of Danny. He is afraid of my other self.* Now, instead of demanding, he inquires: "Could I trouble you to pass the bread?"

My mother, having produced the good linen and cooked Danny's favorite foods, flushes under his compliments. I suspect, with both, that their approval carries a large measure of relief. We are like a Norman Rockwell family around the Sunday roast—Helen, now engaged to an accountant, mother, father, Danny and me. Unless you happen to notice that my eyes, as always in my father's house, are as blank as Orphan Annie's.

Afterward my father retires to his sagging throne chair, his left leg propped on a hassock, glad of another pair of ears: "It's an old football injury. I've got what King George had but, of course, the king had all those doctors." He passes around pictures of himself in a Hamilton Rough Rider football uniform. "That was in 1912. I was thinner then. It was giving up cigarettes and football that put on the weight."

Danny and my father play cribbage. When my father asks me to fetch his glasses, his voice is supplicating. It's clear he wishes me to think well of him now that I'm moving out of his jurisdiction. That I should want to perform such small services after his years of hard work also seems reasonable. *The scars my other self bears are not visible so let's let bygones be bygones. No harm done.*

I find his glasses on the old radio console beside the see-hear-speak-no-evil monkeys. By now I'm worldly enough to know the fourth monkey, with hands over its genitals, has been lopped off by the same people who put ruffles on piano legs and bowdlerized Shakespeare. Determinedly neutral, I deliver the glasses, then help my mother and Helen with the dishes. Now that we both have steady boyfriends, our mother confides in us as peers while we exchange occasional conspiratorial glances. "I don't know what gets into Aunt Estelle. She's changed her phone number three times in the past six months. She won't talk to your daddy. He won't talk to her. It doesn't seem right to me—family, after all."

Though I don't recall my mother often touching me as a child, now that I'm almost out the door she can't take her hands off me. Lint on my skirt, a hair on my sweater, a collar to be turned up or down. Her hands flutter flutter as she picks, pats, pets and probes. She is working very hard, as always, to make things come out right, to make things seem right. *My other self shrieks: Too late, too late!*

Out on the back porch to shake the tablecloth, she tells Mrs. Lawrence: "Yes, she'll be going to the University of Western Ontario in London next fall. She's studying Honors English and Philosophy. Helen will be enrolling in teachers' college. Time sure flies."

Mrs. Lawrence can always be counted on: "I guess we know where your girls get their brains, Addy."

Putting her thumbs into her armpits, my mother sticks out her chest the way kids go yeah yeah yeah on the playgrounds. "I don't know about that!" I've seen her do this many times before, always in connection with some accomplishment of mine or Helen's. It's a small gesture, meant to be self-mocking, but it's a lethal one, and deadly serious. Those two thumbs provide the brackets within which she lives her life and expects Helen and me to live ours, patrolled by her pursed lips: "MY girls would never do such a thing!" It's this conviction that keeps her cheerfully at her station day in and year out. By supporting such illusions I work my passage with her.

I dream: *Danny and I make love in the long, sweet grass, swept by the wind. I hear a shivery, rustling hiss. Three matrons, in black gowns and starchy white aprons, advance upon us with measured tread, their hair drawn back in buns, their eyes blanked by steel-rimmed glasses, their lips pursed. I recognize my mother and her neighbor ladies to the right and left, joined by a clothesline. They shake straw whisks inside mixing bowls, swish swish swish swish. The sound is powerful and frightening. Danny and I try to escape, but it pursues us swish swish swish like hornets trapped in the brain.*

Danny and I sit on his bed. His house is empty. His mother has taken his father to a doctor's appointment and his sister is at camp. I start with my legs draped over his lap, playing like a child with the hairs of his chest, just visible in the neck of his sport shirt. *Tinker, tailor, soldier, sailor.* Piece by piece, the clothes come off ... *swish swish swish.*

I sit up, reach for my bra. "It's almost three, Danny. I'd better go home."

He kisses me again.

"Please, Danny." *Swish swish swish.*

Once again, I am lying across his bed, but now my eyes are open. "Please, I have to go." *Swish swish swish.*

"You know I love you."

I reach for my blouse. "Your parents ...."

"We've got lots of time. Dad's appointment wasn't till two-thirty, and he always chats with the doctors on the wards."

"No, I want to go, please." *Swish swish swish.*

His expression is hurt, his voice punitive. "All right, if you say so."

I can't stand Danny's disapproval. "Please, Danny, don't get mad." Soon we are embracing again, but my nerves are edgy, my ears attuned to the slightest sound from outside the window. *Swish swish swish.*

"You'd make love if I wanted to, wouldn't you?"

Unthinkable! *Swish swish swish.* I force out the word: "Yes." I can't believe my tone is convincing, but we've been through this before, and I've learned that my capitulation alone is sufficient.

Now sunny and solicitous, Danny releases me. "Then I think we'd better get you home."

I feel resentful and manipulated, but it's a small price to pay for paradise, isn't it?

Once again I pick fights with Danny—*willful, irrational fights, that indicate my other self is back in charge*. Every bruised expectation, every statement with a possible double meaning is ransacked for its worst intention.

"You promised . . ."

"How come . . ."

I am a fist punching anything that ventures within range: how dare you do this to me? I am a high-voltage fence: touch me and you pay. I am a black widow spider, interpreting tenderness as weakness, fearing love as subjugation, forever threatening to devour my mate.

Danny falls silent, walks away. "If that's the way you feel . . ."

"No, please!" I run after him.

I am terrified he will leave.

I am terrified he will stay.

Go away! No, don't go away. Never darken my door! No,

yes, no . . . please, I can't face a night alone in that house, pacing the floors without hope. Please . . .

Like a bad soprano, I run the same scale, sharp and flat, sweet and strident, hit another piercing note and hold it till everything shatters. *See? Didn't I warn you? Am I still beautiful when I'm screaming? See what power I have to inflict pain? How much of this can you take?* Just as predictably, I am whimpering for forgiveness, taking advantage of our working together to make up before sundown, knowing I don't dare give him a whole night to decide how pleasant life would be without me.

One evening, in the heat of a quarrel about something I later won't even remember, I open the door of Danny's MG and fling myself into darkness. As I tumble down a brambly slope, every bone and sinew shaken by the impact, uncertain as to whether I am going to live or die, I am struck by a blinding flash of the obvious: I am not angry. I never was. I am terrified. I am terrified that when this summer is over I will never see Danny again. I am terrified that I will lose him now that I can no longer live without him. *My other self has spoken: she, too, would sooner be dead.*

By the time Danny finds me in a ditch of rainwater, there is nothing more to argue about. I have found the outer edges of the fear that has been compelling me, and I am grateful to be alive.

Clinkety clink. Paint, gum, urine, turpentine, dead rats—it's amazing what people think to put into empty pop bottles. The stench is nauseating. "Say, what is this?" A bottle, bearing a single daisy, comes up the conveyor belt. Suzie snatches it. "It's for you." The card reads: "Love, Danny. See you for lunch."

"Hey, that's a good one. I gotta remember to tell that to my old man."

We eat our sandwiches in the warehouse, surrounded by cases of orange, lemon, lime, cherry and grape soda pop, mourning the end of summer and our inevitable separation.

"I wish I could go to Western but . . ." I can't study law there.

"I wish I could go to University of Toronto but . . ." My scholarship is for Western.

"I thought I'd be counting the days till college but . . ."

"We'll have Thanksgiving and Christmas but . . ."

"I'll try to drive up to see you for a few weekends but . . ."

On the last Saturday of summer, Danny and I take a picnic lunch to Lake Erie. While we are swimming, a sudden storm lashes the water into frenzied peaks with vast sliding troughs. The lake is a wild thing, manic and wonderful. Lightning cracks the sky. I'm tossed into a foaming curl, then sucked back with a swoosh. Another wave slaps me under. I resurface, gagging. He catches me as I slide under again. Still sputtering, I cling to his back, feel the water slosh around me like whipped cream as he strokes us both to shore.

I cling to him with absolute confidence. We are making it, only a few more yards. Another crack of lightning, another supersonic boom, but farther away now. The dark, hysterical storm has played itself out, the craziness has blown away. It's sort of a miracle, isn't it?

A SEVERED HEAD

My 1957 college yearbook contains a photo of me in a graduate's black cap. From the way the picture is cropped, it looks as if I'm also wearing a black gown. That is an illusion because only my head went to college. My severed head. That was how I rid myself forever of the red-shoed mannequin I invented to hide my other self—I chopped off her head and registered it in Honors English and Philosophy at the University of Western Ontario, eighty miles away.

My incestuous relationship with my father was now over for good, leaving a sooty aftershadow of self-hate which I mistook for the residue of my bad experiences at Hamilton High. Philosophy was my high-minded defense against this legacy. Through rational knowledge I would put together a functional and successful person I could respect. Feelings were on hold. They were irrational, hence dangerous.

The Western campus is as elegant as its brochures proclaim, with gothic gray stone buildings on lawns rolling down to the Thames River. Dubbed the Country Club, it is set amidst rural lanes where horsemen in red riding habits can sometimes be seen cantering. Today, black-gowned professors at tables in front of the administration building answer queries about courses. Undergrads in purple blazers distribute name tags and frosh beanies.

Under a purple-and-white WELCOME FROSH banner, a refreshment booth offers free Cokes and donuts. "Where are you from? What faculty are you in?" Commonality of hometown and courses selected create nuclei around which conversation swirls, while undergrads from other years smile indulgently across the rope barrier. A few try to make contact: "Hey, beautiful. I'll give you a dime for half that Coke. See? I've stolen a straw."

Discovering that our undignified frosh caps are sexual lures, we freshettes become more animated, our laughter higher pitched as we flirt with male seniors by proxy. The freshmen—last year's high-school heroes—skulk around the fringes.

A private estate renovated as a residence for seventy women, Spencer Hall, with its sweeping Gone With the Wind staircase, paneled lounges and squishy carpets, gives me a sense of privilege above my station. Socially, the tone is set by the private-school girls from Toronto with their glossy good looks and self-assured charm. Morally, it is established by the stately, blue-haired housemother who ensures we are inside by 11:15 p.m. with doors bolted.

In the dining hall and at high tea in the lilac lounge, I learn a new upscale vocabulary—Greek house, rushing, pledging, snob appeal, BMOCs, cream of the crop, frat bash, smoothie, prom queen, loaded, curfew, a good catch.

I learn: male students are required to wear school jackets or suitcoats and ties to lectures. Preferred uniform for Western co-eds is a cashmere sweaterset with baroque pearls, box-pleated gray flannel skirt, white bucks and bobby socks.

I learn: party going centers on the fraternities that run weekend open houses in bravely bohemian basements decorated with Chianti bottles. Alcohol, a masculine fringe activity at Hamilton High, is central to campus life.

I learn: though football provides a social focus, as it did at high school, jock is now a derogatory term, as egghead used to be. Athletics for women are infra dig and cheerleading lacks its former luster. Even for boys, sports should be underplayed as one of a portfolio of talents, ideally including good looks, good grooming, good family. All this adds up to: "Oh, he's a living doll!"

I learn: most girls are registered in pass arts and secretarial science—a reflection of the belief that a girl's happiest role is as wife and mother, with typing options. High aspirations are, however, respected. My acknowledgment that I am taking

Honors English and Philosophy usually nets a generous: "Gee, I wish I was that bright."

I learn: the medical faculty has cachet. So does business administration, since its undergrads are often scions being groomed to inherit the family empire. Coincidentally, both faculties are viewed by the women of Spencer Hall as happy hunting grounds for mate selection. As in a Jane Austen novel, a good catch must include guaranteed upper-middle-class income. Everyone at Western is dealing in futures.

I learn: just as skipping ropes and colored pencils reflected a girl's status in primary school, here it is cashmere sweaters and crinolines. While it's déclassé to allude to one's own wealth, loyal roommates are expected to whisper: "Lucinda has forty-three cashmere sweaters." Similarly, even the most boring girl can garner some respect if it is known her pearls are real.

I learn: my new housemates are more sexually competitive than any females I've yet encountered. Having one o'clock late leaves means feeling honor bound to use them. On Saturday nights, a girl without a date should go home for the weekend or die of shame.

For the first few weeks I fill my social calendar as frenetically as everyone else—what Danny and I, with some qualms, agreed we would do. This is old stuff. Knee-jerk reaction. And then. I open the Western Gazette to discover a simpering photo of me taken during orientation week with a provocative caption indicating I am "one of the new crop." Here she is again, the gaudy, hot-footed marionette who danced me *on and ever on, over briars and stubble, for dance she must* . . .

One day I slick back my hair in a bun, because that's easier. Eventually, I stop wearing lipstick. I even buy a pair of horn-rimmed glasses at Woolworth's, which I take off to study. Now that I've dismantled Appearances, I feel like a declawed cat in a den of tigers, all of whom write private-school backhand. Predictably, but charitably, I am labeled a brain and—thanks to a dog-eared fortune-telling book once belonging to Granny Cragg—even an oracle.

I sit cross-legged on my bedroom floor, head wrapped swami-style in a yellow towel—that's not precisely for costume effect since I've just washed it. Eating pizza, the new junk food of choice, I lay out thirty-two cards in four rows. Forehead puckered, I intone: "Your wish is a romantic one." Our wishes always are. "Yes, you will have a date for the Frosh Hop." My client is an attractive girl. No doubt about her prospects.

"Maybe someone in bus ad." Since it's the most populous faculty as well as the most gregarious, statistics favor me.

"There's a young man in Welland." We all have hometown boyfriends, and she's from Welland. "You may go through a breakup there." I'm on pretty firm ground, though it gives me a twinge to recognize that sad fact.

"You've just received a letter with money in it." We all get allowances from home. I embroider: "The money made you angry. It was from a man—your father. Your parents are divorced, aren't they?" Just a shot in the dark, but my client is postively bug-eyed.

"I can hardly believe this!"

"You'll do much better on your exams than you expect." She's too intelligent for pass arts, a snap course. "You may consider doing social work." These privileged daughters of the upper middle classes often confide they want to help people.

"You're also thinking about public-relations work." The new glamor occupation for women.

"This is uncanny!"

"But you'll end up marrying as soon as you graduate." It's inevitable.

I scoop up the cards, feeling fraudulent yet philanthropic, the way I used to feel after pushing around the palette of Arlene's Ouija board.

"How did it go?" asks the girl who is next in line.

"It was wild!" exclaims my satisfied client. "I'm still stunned."

"Please do me next!"

"Sorry, there's a list." The lure of talking about ourselves and our uncertain futures is irresistible. Besides, the price is right. "Maybe next week."

Five other students share my philosophy course, five other talking heads. Together, with the philosopher kings of other years, we sit in the rec hut over black coffee, and these are the things we say:

"Are you implying Thomas Aquinas is absurd?"

"He builds a beautifully coherent system of logic on premises so holey they look like Swiss cheese."

"But if you eliminate God you're left with a solipsism."

"Correction: you don't believe in God. You think He believes in you."

Or: "Determinism seems irrefutable."

"Not when you consider the Doctrine of Chance. Determinism governs reality in an everyday sense, but Chance is the creator of the Universe—or, if you will, of true Reality. Chance is God. We humanize him with white robes and a long beard out of fear."

Or: "Are you actually throwing out objective reality, or merely questioning our knowledge of it? Are you implying every thought is a tiny hammer, and when we do enough pounding in one direction we create a recognizable shape? Then, I suppose, if we get tired of this world we can each imagine another!"

I stare out the train window at the autumn leaves, my stomach in knots, on my way home to Hamilton for Thanksgiving. Danny's letters have been cheerful but noncommittal, as have mine. How many summer romances make it through to winter? I picture Danny at the University of Toronto, surrounded by duplicates of the pretty predators I left behind. What is love, anyway? According to Psychology 20, the meshing of need patterns—a volatile and changing grid.

My train pulls into the grimy TH&B railway station. As I disembark, someone grips my weekend case. I turn, expecting to do battle with a redcap. "Surprise!" A familiar figure in blue-and-white U of T jacket. My response is joy, but so freighted with terror of loss that it feels like pain. Numbly I step into Danny's arms, prepared to fake the grand reunion. At his touch, I collapse, feel my heart pound against his heart, feel tears of relief spill from my eyes. Slowly, ever so slowly, like a deep-sea diver coming out of the bends, I reorient myself in my own emotional universe. I find my head pointed up to the sky where it's supposed to be, my feet planted firmly on the ground.

When I return to Western, I am wearing Danny's Sigma Chi pledge pin, which in campus parlance means I'm engaged.

I burrow into the library stacks for my second term. While my roommates giggle over threatened panty raids, I swing on syllogisms as if they are monkey bars, weave intricate spiderwebs of logic from my own substance to see what they will catch, rub premises together to strike fire, chase down intuitive possibilities as if they are rare butterflies, crack open the bottle of dialectics to let the genie loose.

It comes as a revelation that abstract ideas can dynamically alter my universe. It excites me that people talk with fire in their bellies about God and Reality instead of about who'll be voted homecoming queen.

Steeped with the self-importance that conversion brings, I wrestle with the world's great minds, sometimes imagining in my vanity that it's a fair fight. I dismiss Plato's Realities as Christianity in Greek drag, show Aristotle the error of his metaphysical ways, ponder the existentialist riddle of whether a flower blooms unseen.

Too long hogwashed and hog-tied by Christian "oughts,"

I embrace the pragmatists, the skeptics, the utilitarians and the rationalists. Man is the product of heredity and environment, scratch soul. He is a selfish animal who seeks pleasure and avoids pain, as declared by Thomas Hobbes, with no divine sense of morality. Ethics are a practical response to the problems of group living—freedoms traded off for security. The rules are written by pen on paper, not with fire on stone. I feel exhilarated, freed at last from the burden of inherent sin—of being the bad child born into a nest of saints. We're all self-seekers, make of that what you will!

I am the first kid on my block to give up the ghost—the Holy Ghost. Or to split the hair more finely, to become an agnostic-leaning-toward-atheism since—I hear myself declaim to an interlocutor who bears a striking resemblance to Reverend Thwaite—it's as impossible to prove that God doesn't exist as to prove He does. Should anyone disagree with my flawless reasoning, I breezily resurrect the ontological, tautological, teleological arguments for the existence of God to prove I've given the other side equal time, sucking the five-syllable words like gumdrops because they taste so good.

A bloodless coup? Hell, no. I remember my dizzying gratitude when—after a guilt-ridden battle—I looked down to find God gasping at my feet. He'd been losing blood for quite a while, but it was the skeptic David Hume—a ghost himself for several centuries but very much alive in Philosophy 20—who finally did Him in. Like a public-spirited citizen exposing a fraudulent magician's act, he took right after the three of them—father, son and that pet ghost of theirs—with the long sword of logic. The walk-on-water trick? Collapsible stilts. The miracle of Cana? Jugs with false bottoms. The open grave? So what— Houdini also did a slick trick or two with manacles and an underwater coffin, didn't he?

After that, the dotty old man with the long white beard simply fell on his own sword. It was the only decent thing to do. Hurray, hurray, murder in the cathedral! God, the Son and Holy Ghost have melted like a brick of three-in-one Neapolitan ice cream. Let's bury the remains decently, two yards from Santa Claus and three from the Easter Bunny. I cried when those other two died, but do you have any idea what mischief that religious lot caused in my life?

Now, at last, I have the answer to the Big One:

Q. Who created the world?
A. God created the world.
Q. Who created God?
A. Man did, by choosing to believe He exists.
   I did, to back up my "mind games."
   My mother did, as a witness for her virtue.
   My father did, as a role model in tyranny.
   Reverend Thwaite did, so he could perrrsonally
     create the Devil.

Ergo: life exists to no divine purpose. I've thrown off the shackles of pleasing the Infinite. Man is master of his own fate, and ennobled by that responsibility, not a wheedler at the throne of the Almighty. Thus, the death of God isn't the death of morality, but its enhancement.

When rationality fails, and I find myself plummeting into familiar snake pits, I rescue myself by an old rope, newly woven: the myth of my own specialness. Thus, through the ego needs of my severed head, Descartes's confirmation of existence, "I think, therefore I am," becomes, "I think, therefore I have worth." Verbal cartwheels: the cheerleader as philosopher.

Sometimes my head aches. Sometimes I can't sleep, but when I do I seldom dream. *My other self is bored with my new life. For a time, at least, it's as if the tapes of her adventures have been wiped clean.* These days, when I get angry, it's intellectual rage, so much safer than the real thing.

Dear Danny,

   It really burns me when I think about all that time we spent in high school dissecting frogs and counting metaphors. Everything was analysis, analysis, analysis. No synthesis. No ideas. No awareness of the connectedness of things in time and space. Prissy sonnets about clouds and daffodils because that's what poets wrote in the nineteenth century. Remember the day I asked Mr. Hutton what algebra was used for? His answer is indelibly printed on my mind: "Sit down. You've always been a troublemaker!"

Dear Little Friend,

Yesterday, my MG went missing. I was about to call the police, when they called me. They'd found it hanging by chains from a tree in Queen's Park with a nude mannequin at the wheel. I had no trouble figuring who did it—all I had to do was count the hangovers at the frat. How they did it was another matter. Worse—how to undo it. A lot of advice, no manual labor. This is a long story. I'd better save it till I see you—three weeks, and counting.

In my sophomore year, I join a sorority to offset my loneliness as a severed head. A gabled white frame on a once-fashionable London street, Beta Epsilon houses fifteen sisters and is the headquarters for thirty others. As I carry my suitcase up the walk, two girls rush down the steps to help me. "Hey, that looks heavy!"

Others wave from windows or appear in doorways. The living room is chintzy and cozy. The pledge dorm in the attic, with its bare floors, iron beds and rickety desks, has the sort of ambience I'm used to.

More pledges arrive by car and taxi. Books and boyfriends and trunks pile up untidily on the porch. This is big family stuff as portrayed on "Father Knows Best"—unselfconscious, relaxed, high-spirited. I like it. I'm grateful. I feel safe.

The philosopher kings turn disdainful. No matter how I scourge 338elf after leaving the sorority house, they smell frivolity on me. In truth, the deeper I burrow into the stacks for my sophomore year, the more I begin to prefer the cheerful company of my sorority sisters as a relief from my own dusty ruminations. They are sentimental, well-intentioned, conforming, naive, optimistic, generous, extroverted, poised, polite, spontaneous, gabby, dilettante, charming and utterly likable—everything women are supposed to be.

Current hot topic on the pajama-talk circuit is: can a woman trust a man one hundred per cent? I'm surprised to hear the group come down uncharacteristically on the cynical side: "That's why college guys hang around the nurses' residence. They say nurses are more 'humane'—ho ho ho."

None of us, including myself, suggests a woman might want to be unfaithful. As always, sex has to do with "them," their needs and our reactions. Covertly, I study the group, wondering what each one of us is hiding. I decide: nothing much. Last year in residence several girls undressed all year in the closet so roommates wouldn't see them naked. The cult of the virgin still lies heavily upon us. We have too little to gain and too much to lose.

I know it's winter because when I look at my feet I don't see them for snow. I know it is winter because my nose drips like an icicle, my hands are white snowballs that must be stuffed in pockets. I know it is winter because sounds are muffled, words taste cold, steam hisses out of radiators and light slips off the page of Kant's "Critique of Pure Reason" almost as soon as it arrives. I know it's winter because my mother writes letters that announce: "Yesterday my wash was like boards on the line. I keep asking the new milkman to put the milk between the doors but he doesn't seem to hear and this morning it was half out of the bottle again. Is your laundry getting done?"

I know it's winter because all the evidence a posteriori and a priori points that way, and I am nothing these days if not empirical and rational. It's winter, but it doesn't matter. My life takes place in enclosed spaces: halls, cells, corridors, cubicles. I scratch words on the pulpy lobes of my brain like a medieval monk creating palimpsests. I sweat dust.

*

Dearest Danny,

Yesterday the sun rose, and the sun set, and I barely made it out of the library. Ironically, my essay topic was Humanism. And who is my daily companion? Mr. Plockett. That is what he has asked me to call him. The other four philosophers in my year have either switched or given up. Last to go was a Catholic girl who couldn't take the conflict with her beliefs. She was found in her rooming house going up and down the stairs, trying to land on her right foot.

Beta Epsilon's pink Homecoming dragon was a disaster. The dry ice burned through the throat, and then it rained. We now have about two tons of pink porridge on our front lawn. Miss you miss you miss you!

Dear Little Friend,

I was about to sit down at the bridge table this afternoon when I thought: "Wait a minute, maybe these guys don't have anything better to do, but I have." That's when I cracked my Contracts book. I've declared a four-year moratorium on goofing off—if I can afford it! It's winning at bridge that puts the gas in my car. I did think of selling my blood, which is what the meds guys do when they're cash-short. Some of them are pea green from bloodletting. . . . I like Mr. Plockett. He sounds nonthreatening—to me. Your letters are the nicest part of my day.

Three afternoons a week I work in the library at seventy-five cents an hour, reshelving books according to the Dewey Decimal System. I love the feel, the smell, the sight of the books towering over me, flanking me in orderly rows. Each book is a tiny, vertical grave of some man's thoughts. I am the keeper of the mausoleum, breathing the dust of centuries, a voluntary exile from the sun. I slide out the crypt, play Pick Up Sticks with dead men's bones. A wraith of words curls up from the page, slips through my eye sockets, wraps itself—immortal—around my brain. I return the book but I am still possessed.

I select another teacher—Whitehead, Ayer, Spinoza, follow his chain of reason up a mountain or down a crevasse where light seldom shines. Sometimes I'm left dangling: a scientist with the wisdom of another century or two has cut the rope. Sometimes . . . sometimes . . . I achieve a peak so white, so high, so dazzling that for a few breathless instants I can kiss the sun.

That's how I felt when Henri Bergson's élan vital allowed me to wriggle out of the straitjacket of determinism to embrace free will: through creative evolution, the future is a spontaneous unfolding and hence unknowable. Man is more than the predictable product of his past. Thus, two plus two equals an infinite possibility.

Later, Immanuel Kant provides the definitive loophole through which I shoot from the strictures of the rational into the stars: if time and space are not real in themselves but are merely projections of the human mind then anything is possible—immortality, simultaneous existence of past-present-future, parallel worlds. The universe is clay, awaiting the touch of the human sculptor. Reason remains vital, but as a tool of the intuition: the higher the logical ladder the more glorious the intuitive leap. Thus Hume freed me from God but stole my free will. Bergson freed me from Hume but left me pacing the earth. Kant restored the possibility of immortality by exploding Newton's predictable world of matter moving to immutable laws.

I visit Danny in his Toronto rooming house, reflecting strained finances since his father's stroke. My heart sinks as my feet climb: smell of cauliflower; gardenia freshener to mask WC urine stink; squalling baby. Danny looks all wrong in his room with its one kitchen chair and card-table desk—too spontaneous, too generous, with his head almost scraping the slanted ceiling.

"No wonder you find it hard to study."

He shrugs: "There's an immigrant family in every room. They're here for life. I'm just passing through."

His bed is the only comfortable place to sit—and then, marginally so. Soon we are lying across it, entwined, with radiator hissing and snowflakes dying against the dirty pane. This is why I have come, for this—lying with Danny, holding Danny, being held by Danny, yet even here, with everyone we've ever known a world away, even here I can't take my eye from the dinted doorknob, afraid that it will begin to turn . . . *rattle, rattle as if a hand were still holding on. Slowly, ever so slowly the door opens . . . .*

As we share one pillow, I resurrect what is to me a troubling topic: "Danny, are you sure you don't want children?"

"I don't have any deep biological urge if that's what you mean."

Once again I am blundering into the territory of my other self, producing rationalizations to explain the unexplainable. "I hated my childhood—no reason exactly, but I've got no desire to relive it. I'm not especially ambitious. It's more a matter of curiosity—as if I've gone from A to M in my life, and now I want to push right out to XYZ to see what's there instead of teaching someone else the ABCs."

"You don't have to explain. I'm marrying you because I want you, not to found a dynasty."

"But you come from a close family. I keep thinking what a great father you'd make. I feel that I'd be depriving you."

"What can I say that I haven't already said? There's no problem unless you create it."

I get to the nub of the matter: "I have to admit . . . the idea of pregnancy itself is . . . pretty horrendous to me. It's so . . . parasitic . . . ." *like having daddy's wet-ums inside me for nine months, possessing me, growing larger . . . helpless . . . out of control . . . guilt shame fear fear fear . . . . My other self is quite clear about her warning: If you get pregnant, I won't be able to stand it and you will go stark raving crazy.*

Four years—where have they gone? I've been here four days. I've been here four centuries.

Rain drums on roofs and gushes down eaves troughs. It

pummels crocuses thrusting through the muck and makes early robins wish they'd stayed in Florida. God-who-is-supposed-to-be-dead is peeing on everyone. He has opened his heavenly bladder and let it all come down. The air is murky—urine colored. Mud squishes up through cracks in the ice-heaved pavement like brown turds. Water flows through my soles as if by divine right.

I was kept late at the library and now I must walk to the sorority house because I don't have carfare. Wet on wet. The sort of day in which my mother, up to her neck in mud at a picnic, would exclaim: "Looks like it'll be a nice day tomorrow."

I, however, am existentially tired of the drip drip drip of water on my forehead—the Just-Enough Torture Treatment. Just enough money to make it through the month, if you always walk. Just enough clothes, if you like them well mended. Just enough porridge, if you scrape the pot. Just enough butter, provided you use margarine.

I've never been bitten by a rat.

I've never gone to school hungry.

I've never been thrown onto the street by a bailiff.

I almost wish I had. Then I might feel spurred on to rash deeds: the child with an empty belly who vows to conquer the world. Instead: just enough is the poverty of maximum bearable indignities. The blows of the master's whip are steady, dull and dulling—just enough to keep your head down but not enough to make you rear back and snatch the whip. You turn into a plodder with a blistered heel. You have just enough energy to keep up so you don't give up. Just enough is the feel of gritty pavement through the hole in your shoe and the chafing of a frayed but starchy collar on your stiff neck. It's a mouthful of canker sores you never die of.

Just enough is the poverty of infinitesimal decision, of pinched pennies divided into neat piles. If cabbages cost twenty-five cents and cauliflower twenty, but cabbages go further, which do you buy? If you love the red but the brown goes with more things, which do you buy?

Just enough is the poverty of conventional wisdom and fearful virtue. You're oh-so-boot-licking moral because you have this tiny bit you don't dare risk. You obey all the rules because you're the flea on the tail of the dog, and any change in the system hits you first. If the price of meat goes up, you stop buying it. If the price of milk goes up, you scrap your budget.

You vote Conservative because you have to. The socialists tempt you since a vote for them means you get your teeth fixed free, but it also means other people get their teeth fixed free. The unknown factor: do other people have more cavities than you? That's too big a risk, you have to plump for the status quo.

Just enough is a poverty of the spirit. It breeds pettiness, stinginess, resentment, righteousness. In the impoverished life of just enough these are the virtues needed to survive. I know that I bear the marks of just enough, which is why I'm trudging through the rain. I assume this is a temporary state. For my parents, it was not. It is not difficult at this distance to feel grateful for their sacrifice, to respect them for their doggedness and even . . . to love them.

I mount the sorority steps hearing the throb of Elvis's "Hound Dog." Shaking off water, I open the door and blink. My sisters are running around in white sheets and tinfoil wings with haloes propped overhead on Popsicle sticks. I'd forgotten: our Paradise rushing party.

One of my sisters, in red-flannel devil's outfit, demands: "Where have you been? We couldn't rehearse without you." I am both high and low C in the Coke-bottle orchestra, playing such standards as "White Coral Bells" and "Chopsticks."

"Sorry. I'll just be a jiff." I strip my bed and convert my top sheet—no time for pressing—into standard angel's garb. I am undoing my hair to tie it under my chin as St. Peter's beard when I confront my reflection in a way I have not done since last summer: who is this prim female with scuffed shoes and hair skinned into a bun? The disembodied creature staring back isn't me any more than the gaudy marionette with movie-star pretensions I banished four years back.

In an instant I realize: I'm tired of living in the past and future. I want to live in the present tense. I'm tired of abstract reasoning with its pursuit of false accuracy: since it takes words to describe words, no definition can ever be pure enough. Logic has, for me, become an empty shell from which the sea creature has escaped. The Tower of Babel was no tower—it was an excavation made by philosophers scrambling downward in search of the first premise. My severed head swivels looking for its discarded body.

In the few minutes left, I resurrect glamor and, when our guests arrive, set about with a vengeance to entertain them, ransacking my introverted existence for anecdotes that turn it inside out. "Yesterday when I pulled down two books from the library stacks, Professor Scotty, who teaches Shakespearian drama, was peering through. All I could think of was Pyramus and Thisbe making love through a chink in the wall in Midsummer Night's Dream. I blurted, 'Pyramus, my Pyramus!' He was so flabbergasted he jammed back his books, bringing the whole shelf down. We were buried together under hundreds of books."

As laughter bubbles around me, I feel like a scurvy patient let loose in a bowl of fruit salad. "And then, of course, there's the illicit lovers who go into the dusty stacks to neck. Hey, Dusty Stacks! I think that would make a good name for a stripper, don't you?"

This time, when I come back from seeing Danny in Toronto I am engaged. My roommate shrieks: "Hey, you guys, you gotta see this!" Soon all my sisters are clustered around to view the ring. A couple burst into tears. That's when I start to cry—not tears of joy exactly, more like tears of gratitude at such generosity. How did they get to be so nice? Where can I find the books to teach me that?

Now as I study for my final exams, I catch myself staring

at my hand stretched across a blank page, looking more like an ad in Bride's magazine than something belonging to me. That winking diamond ring, with all its implications, rattles me. Most of my friends back in Hamilton are now married— Arlene to Joe Baker, Lulu to Herb Swamp, Tonya to Iky. I reread a paragraph, underlined, in my biology textbook:

> The life of the burrowing shrimp consists exclusively of burrow digging, extension and maintenance. In the normal course of events, the burrow of one sex is likely to reach that of the other. If neither individual has a mate, a joint burrow is constructed thereafter. The burrowing shrimp, because of restricted habits, mates for life.

Dear Danny,

Yesterday recruiters came around sniffing the new crop of graduates—IBM reps for boys, Bell Telephone reps for girls, just like blue and pink booties. When I told the Bell woman I was graduating in philosophy, her eyes rolled around on their stalks. "Oh, well then, there's nothing we can possibly give you. We need girls who can handle the real world!"

Her disdain would have seemed funnier if I hadn't just had an interview with Professor Wynn from the philosophy department. Chipmunk face wreathed in smiles, he said: "You've been living in a fool's paradise. No one takes a woman scholar seriously, and certainly not in philosophy." Then, offering solace: "Do you type? My niece got a job as a secretary for the president of an oil firm and now she has two girls working for her." The coup de grâce: "You're engaged, aren't you? I always tell my wife the simple example of her sitting before our children reading scholarly material in the original Latin is a better advertisement for a classical education than all my preaching!"

Dear Little Friend,

I've managed to pin down a summer job in a Toronto law office starting in June. The office manager was astonished when I asked if I could have my holidays first thing. Then I told him I was getting married.

I'm on the train back to Hamilton for the last time. I watch duplexes turn into factories and factories into farmhouses with plenty of sticky brown fields between. Fog blots the sun, eliminating light and shadow, flattening the countryside into a medieval painting without perspective. My internal landscape is also without perspective. I try to conjure up the faces of my family and friends and the house where I lived for seventeen years, but the details blur the closer I come in miles.

Again the train huffs into the TH&B station, again it jolts to a stop, its journey back through time completed. Despite the fog, as heavy as slush, I am soon surrounded by familiar landmarks—Eaton's department store, the Tivoli theater, the Pigott building, which, at sixteen stories, I once thought the tallest in the world. As I haul my suitcases up to the Delaware bus, I repeat to myself: I will be calm. I will be civil. Hambone City isn't the center of my universe any more. I'm no longer a pawn in a game in which others hold the power. I'm no longer an extension of someone else's problems. My father's house isn't haunted. I am haunted. I don't see things as they are. I see them tainted by my own humiliations and limitations. I am grateful to my parents for allowing me to escape their lives. It takes a lot of pennies shaved off the price of potatoes to support someone's academic habit. Most working-class kids don't get that chance.

I trudge past St. Cecilia's Infirmary, then around the corner. One house with peeling paint limps forward to greet me. I'm a block away, but already I hear it shriek.

BEIGE WEDDING

Who gives this woman?
I do.

I sit in the gable window of my father's house, watching the sun set on my mother's roses, my father's cabbage patch, the plum tree which I climbed to get closer to the sky. Tomorrow is May 30, 1957. Tomorrow is my wedding day. I touch my diamond ring, trying to imagine myself married. I cannot. I try to imagine not marrying Danny. I cannot. I love, therefore I am human. I love Danny.

What is Danny feeling at this moment? Does he have misgivings? Shivering, I think of my latest recurring nightmare: Danny is fighting against the Nazis. If I stop thinking of him for even a second, he will die.

Who gives this woman?
I do.

I dread the wedding—not the marriage but the ceremony itself. I wish to be married, not to get married. All thoughts of that unhinge me. Something to do with being smothered in middle-class conventions, but also something else, something much darker I can't articulate.

For the wedding cake, I suggest the moldy one from Great Expectations, decorated with mouse droppings the size of jelly beans. For the bridal bouquet, poison ivy. For confetti, we can do no better than rice, cooked to a glutinous consistency.

Danny suggested eloping, but in my mother's circle even a civil ceremony carries a taint. I feel I owe her this wedding as a punctuation of thanks for the education I've received. Not the full-choir treatment with twelve-foot veil and three-tier cake, but at least the church service. Christian with abbreviated rites, like Ophelia's funeral.

Who gives this woman?
I do.

I suspect my anxiety extends beyond the usual girlish jitters. The rehearsal this evening, with an aging Reverend Thwaite still rolling his rrr's like silken yard goods, was bad enough: "Blush here, hold hands there, kiss at the top of page two." Now, picturing myself as the centerpiece in a long line of his and her relatives, smiling for the photographer, gives me goosebumps. Nothing personal—I'm fond of Danny's parents, and grateful for their acceptance. It's the group I fear, the collective. Already I can feel it closing in, asserting its hold on me, anticipating the next generation: gotcha!

I've refused to wear white with virgin's veil. I don't know why, only that I feel fanatical about it—as fanatical as I used to feel about refusing to wear brown stockings. I am mystified.

Who gives this woman?

I do.

The fateful hour, the fateful day. I adjust the sides of my arched mirror so I can see three reflections, not knowing why I do this, just habit I suppose, more ritual for a day of ritual. My wedding dress—beige organdy, with voluminous sleeves and calf-length hem—lies across my bed, awaiting the body to animate it. Actually, it's the other way around. The ceremonial dress will be wearing me.

Since Arlene is in hospital having her second child, Helen is my only attendant, as last year I was hers. Now that we no longer share our father's house, we've begun to discover how much we do share. Helen offered to help me get ready, but I declined. Now is not the time to bridge the years. I prefer to go it alone. Or think I do.

I reach for my wedding gown—remembering, with a most peculiar feeling, the dress I wore for my first date with Danny. Red velvet strapless. Fall Frolic, '52. I laugh about that now: "slightly soiled from use as a demonstrator model." Life does get better—a lot.

Who gives this woman?

I do.

With the fatality of a medieval knight preparing for battle,

I add my dyed-to-match gloves, my picture hat, saying my prayers in my own way: *Danny, I wouldn't marry you if you weren't strong. You know what you're getting into.*

Other Grandmother's ivory garter lies on my bed. Aunt Estelle, now virtually a recluse, sent that over. I pick it up: something old. It wriggles in my fingers. *Kisss Grandmother Pearl good-bye.* I drop it. A garter snake.

Who gives this woman?
   I do.

Carrying an armful of painted daisies, I wait in the vestibule of St. James' Church. My father is there—solemn and neat in three-piece navy suit and gray tie. This church is his territory, no longer mine, the place where he once tramp tramp tramped the collection plate to the altar every Sunday, where Magda and I giggled in the balcony, where I learned in the midst of one of Reverend Thwaite's sermons on adulterrry, where babies come from. *Magda . . .*

"Here comes the bride!" The organist is quite insistent about that. I take my father's arm. With him favoring his "old football injury," we limp together down the aisle toward Danny, freshly scrubbed, at the altar.

Tinker, tailor, soldier, sailor . . .

Did I mention that the sun was shining? It streams through a triple-arched window directly behind me. I see my shadow slide from under my beige satin pumps like an oil slick across the polished floor.

Who gives this woman?
   I do.

A shadow is a funny thing—it's always darkest on the brightest days. As a child my shadow always fascinated me. While passing under streetlights, I would watch it scrunch into a dark dwarf, then stretch into a pale giant, sometimes leading me, sometimes following, sometimes almost disappearing, always separate, but remaining part of me.

And so it is today. As the organ swells, I see my shadow intensify.

That shadow is the last thing I see, for it is not I who arrives at the altar but my other self, fastened to her daddy's arm, dragging her muddy train of memories down the aisle like a cat with dead rats tied to its tail.

"Dearrrly beloved, we are gatherrred in the sight of God and of man . . ."

I will have no memory of the wedding ceremony. It will never be written on my consciousness any more than a hand inscribing water produces a record. If it hadn't been for the photographs, I would never believe I'd been there.

"Who gives this woman?"

"I do."

I will have no memory of the wedding night. Sexual initiation is the territory of my other self. She-who-would-not-wear-white has been summoned to stand fierce guard over her own secrets.

RETREAT

PANDORA'S BOX

Toronto in the late fifties was a stuffy, WASP bastion of one and a half million, with few notable restaurants, no Sunday movies and strict liquor laws, but it was the big time to me. My husband and I furnished our first apartment with Scandinavian teak and began our careers—he as a lawyer with a large firm, I as a journalist for the Star Weekly magazine.

The conservativism of the fifties gave way to the passions of the sixties: peace marches, protests, the sexual revolution, drugs, assassinations, black power, women's liberation. For half a dozen years I crisscrossed the continent with spur line trips to Europe and Africa, interviewing radicals of the left and right, the rich and the poor, kooks, characters, the saintly and the criminal, writing political stories, sports stories, entertainment stories, life-style stories. When anyone asked what I did for a living, I replied with some truth: "I research my fantasies."

By the mid-sixties, my husband and I were living in the Colonnade, a fashionable apartment complex in central Toronto. Scandinavian furniture had been replaced by custom-design and international eclectic. A Grecian urn from a cruise to Rhodes. Religious icons from the Grand Bazaar in Istanbul. Pewter and colored glass from a fishing trip through the Norwegian fjords. A wallhanging from a ski trip to Austria. Seashells from scuba diving off the coast of Mexico. A zebra skin from a safari to Africa.

I loved my husband. I enjoyed my job. We had a marriage brightly woven out of affection, mutual respect, some material wealth, shared memories, good friends. For a dozen years, life was everything I dreamt it could be. I devoured it.

Danny and I are driving across the Saskatchewan prairies to a legal convention in the Rockies on an unruffled fall day in the late sixties. I point to a small gray smudge, hanging like a pocket watch over ripe wheat fields. "What's that?"

"Just a cloud, I guess. Odd in such a blue sky."

I watch it drift toward us, becoming a little larger, a little darker, a little thicker, accompanied by a low growl. Now it looks like a menacing black hand in a pea green sky. Wind whips the wheat fields, sending bits of debris sailing like witches' brooms across the road.

"Looks like we're in for it," says Danny, putting up the hood of our convertible.

Now darkness covers half the sky. Raindrops slash against the windows. The highway is black with water, the ditches a-churn with mud. A small cloud has turned into a major meteorological disturbance. In no time at all it is night.

And so it is with me.

Depression begins seeping like poisonous fog through the cracks in my life. In the past when I was down, I was able to look to specific causes. Now the sun is shining, but I am slipping into the shadows. Increasingly, all I want to do is weep. *I am experiencing the unexpressed sorrow of my other self. Love disarmed her, challenging work kept her at bay, but she still possesses a vital part of me—a part I need to become whole. It is precisely because my life is tranquil that she is staking her emotional claim.*

This pessimism isn't easily acknowledged, articulated or confided. As depression deepens into despair, I become obsessed with the image of a hangman's noose. It's the last thing I see before falling asleep at night, and the first thing on opening my eyes in the morning. It fills my dreams. It hangs before me as I walk down familiar streets, framing everything I see, inviting me to slip my neck inside it, offering relief. *Though I don't yet know it, my maternal grandfather hanged himself, age forty-four, and a maternal aunt soon would.* What I do know is that mental disturbance has staked a claim on both sides of my family. I begin to fear I've inherited depressive genes against which it's useless to struggle.

I dream: *Danny and I are on our way to a feast. A ragamuffin*

with glittering eyes holds up her begging bowl: " Please . . ."
When I try to rush past, she grabs my silk skirt with a filthy
hand. "It's my turn now. MY *turn. Now* ME!*"*

I find myself attracted to my childhood haunts. Lured by
memories, I walk the familiar route to Laura Secord Public
School, my high-heels clicking over sidewalks where my running
shoes used to skip, seeing the scrawled initials that seemed
old when I was young and the cracks that if stepped upon
would "break your mother's back." St. Cecilia's Home for
Cripples and Incurables, where lonely arthritics in wheelchairs
beckoned with their waxy hooks, has now gobbled an entire
block and changed its name to St. Cecilia's Infirmary. Laura
Secord, a red-brick battleship on a heaving sea of asphalt,
flies the Maple Leaf in place of the Union Jack. Our 1940s
baseball diamond is a parking lot now that teachers can afford
cars. The hill where we were forbidden to slide on threat of
the strap has sprouted a kids' geodesic dome.

I walk through the once-forbidden teachers' entrance under
a lintel inscribed "1911." The coronation picture of King
George VI and Queen Elizabeth, donated by the Imperial
Order of the Daughters of the Empire, has been replaced with
a bulletin board showing satellites hurtling through space.
Fountains at which we drank only with permission reach just
to my knees. As I stroll the hall where we marched hup hup
hup in the 1940s military fashion, I remember the teachers
who lurked outside their numbered doors, along with their
trademark eccentricities: "Miss LaStrobe wears glasses on a
chain. Miss Willis spits when she speaks. Miss Macintosh has
a red slip that shows."

My old neighborhood is still working-class, though no longer
white, Anglo-Saxon Protestant. Fewer trees line the streets
because of successive road widenings. More frame houses
have been stuccoed or insul-bricked to cut down on their
upkeep. Women still hang out their clothes, but the breadman
no longer makes deliveries in his horse wagon and most of
the old neighbor ladies are dead or in nursing homes—nosy

Mrs. Newton who spied through her venetian blinds, crabby Mrs. Dicey who guarded her chestnut tree with a broom, crazy Mrs. Spittal who collected manure from the delivery horses for her roses. "Yeah, yeah, Lucy, your mother eats horse balls!"

The asparagus patch where I used to rescue ladybugs is now a junk heap. Barker's corner grocery is Speedy's Dry Cleaners and the butcher store is a pinball arcade ("no swearing, no loitering, no horseplay"). The haunted house, once a target for Halloween pranks, is a nursery school. The Candy Factory where ten cents bought enough blackballs to bulge the pockets has become the parking lot for a McDonald's restaurant. The three-hundred-foot Mountain is diminished by the highrise buildings along its brow.

Still with a sense of mission, I sort through cubbyholes and closets in the attic of my father's house. In a trunk with a broken lock I find photos of the Golden Amazons, a Western yearbook, dance favors, basketball crests . . . a fairytale coloring book. Flipping through neatly crayoned pictures of the Seven Dwarfs and Cinderella, I find . . . Rapunzel, letting down her golden hair with ME ME ME scratched across her. The queen in Snow White is so badly slashed only her red apple remains. Sleeping Beauty's body has been heavily outlined with black, including a now pregnant belly. Her father is plastered with swastikas. On a blank page, I find crude pictures of Teddy Umcline, also with an enormous belly. It explodes. Out pops a devil with a forked tail.

The violence of the drawings shocks me. Although I've always prided myself on my detailed memory of the past, I have no recall of anything like this. What could have been on my mind?

Back in Toronto, I now frequently catch myself doodling— during editorial meetings, on the phone, at my typewriter. When I look down, I discover Teddy Umcline with a pregnant belly. His jaunty tie eventually transmogrifies into a hangman's noose. Full circle.

*

In the fall of 1968, the magazine for which I worked eleven years ceases publication. While my colleagues seek job interviews, I go into an empty office where I can peck aimlessly at my typewriter, and close the door. Though the phrase "women's liberation" has yet to be coined, the powerful polemic that will lay the foundation of the feminist movement is beginning to appear. Casting back over my years at Hamilton High through this new perspective, I decide to attempt a feminist novel covering forty years in a woman's life.

Writing has never come easily to me but now that the words have taken a highly personal turn, my fingers fly. *My other self has learned to type. She presses my keys, throwing up masses of defiant memories—stream-of-consciousness stuff without punctuation, semi-sentences and then whole paragraphs scrolling out of my typewriter.* Days melt into weeks. Weeks slide into months. Fall hardens into winter then lightens into spring.

The deeper I delve through my time warp into the past, the more vivid it grows at the expense of the present-day world. It's as if I have fallen down the Alice-in-Wonderland hole into that detailed child's universe below an adult's kneecaps where getting poop on my shoes and burs in my hair are serious worries, where I know every anthill in the backyard, the location of every chestnut tree. In school, the rows of desks are like streets and houses in a village. Time is also child-scaled. Recess lasts only fifteen minutes, yet whole playground societies, based on a tennis ball or a skipping rope, rise and fall. The struggle for identity, for recognition, seems as intense as in any boardroom. Colored pencils and gum cards and marbles change hands as collateral, conferring the same sense of property and status as stocks and bonds. Sometimes I feel as if I'm losing my adult marbles when the sun rises and sets and Danny returns home from the office to find me still pondering the political subtleties of a Red Rover game.

It's a classic catharsis—I'm not just recalling the past but reliving it with an appropriate accompaniment of grief, pain, relief, some laughter, even exhilaration. *My other self leads me to the edge of her secret world, offering up murky clues without taking me over.* Nightmares about the Nazis tug at my mind—something about having my head shaved as a collaborator. Other memories I can't quite get hold of—vague recollections about wetting my pants, of having fits or temper tantrums, of hiding my brown stockings.

As I write, the world inside my head becomes more real than the physical world; feelings more real than facts; thoughts more real than spoken words; my unconscious mind more real than my conscious mind; the visionary world of dreams more real than the waking world. Now, as I let go of the habits and rituals that anchor me to the here-and-now to explore the lost landscape of my childhood, I feel as if I've jumped off a cliff and am flapping my arms trying to learn to fly before crashing. Sometimes I do catch an updraft. Then I soar, producing twenty-five pages in a day. At other times I find myself struggling out of a mud hole—the worm's-eye view of art and life. Sometimes the interval between Danny's leaving for the office and his return seems lonely and forever; at other times it seems annoyingly short with the breakfast dishes still in the sink as if I were a harried mother of ten.

Someone taps me on the shoulder. I jump up, clutching my throat as if expecting a wolf pack. It's Danny, of course. "I asked you a question—I asked it three times. Do you want to eat on the patio tonight?" A wry smile: "Six months ago if I asked on a Monday, you'd answer on Tuesday. Now I have to wait till Wednesday or Thursday. You don't seem to notice time has passed."

We barbecue filets, cut up beefsteak tomatoes, open a bottle of champagne. I notice our willow tree has lost half its yellow leaves. The fuchsia petunias have grown leggy. Our goldfish pond needs cleaning. It's the end of a wonderful fall day, perhaps the last of the season, and I've scarcely noticed. Already the air is nippy. Soon it will be winter—my third in the same damned room, neglecting Danny, neglecting my friends, forgetting the amenities of life, and for what?

As the sky reddens behind the Toronto skyline, I try to explain. "When I started out, I couldn't imagine where I'd get enough words to fill three hundred pages. Now I have a manuscript over two thousand pages written in the first person hysterical. It's like a gush of primordial pain from a part of me I never knew existed. I've tried walking away from it, but it sticks to my shoes. Every time I start back at the beginning, the bloody thing lengthens like Plastic Man. Page ten becomes page twenty-one and so on. I haven't been able to talk about it because I haven't known what's happening. I still don't. Believe me, I know what a drag all this must be for you."

"When you were a journalist you were away part of the time, but we had lots to talk about," replies Danny. "Now you seem to be away all of the time. I haven't wanted to interfere because I could see it was important to you."

"It's weird. Everyone thought I'd miss the exotic assignments but what I really miss are all those people sitting at their desks whom I might or might not talk to. I don't even bother calling anyone any more. I'm so used to writing both sides of a dialogue that by the time the phone is answered I've already had the conversation in my head. So you see, fella, you're my only contact with the human race. You're all I've got!"

Next day I receive a bouquet of red roses: "To my Lady of Shalott, weaving her endless tapestries from shadows in mirrors. Love, Danny."

The truth of that image shocks me into making a radical decision: I am not writing about forty years in a woman's life. I am writing about eight years in a child's life.

One day in 1971, the book that never would be finished is finished. At 255 pages, it exists as an entity separate from me, with the circumstance of its creation still more or less a mystery to me. I title it *Pandora* after the mortal who, in classical mythology, was created by Zeus as the first woman. Like the biblical Eve, Pandora unlooses a plague of ills by touching the forbidden—by opening a box.

Pandora is published in Canada in 1972, and in the United States the following year. My mother is upset by the content of the book, but mollified by good reviews. Though too impatient to read any book, my father seems proud of it as an accomplishment. Picking up the jargon of television, he comments: "I guess some families do have generation gaps."

Certain things about the book puzzle me: Why did I give my fictional father a hooked arm? Such an obvious phallic symbol now seems melodramatic. Why did I suggest incest in my father's family? Why did I stud our family history with suicide? Why did I portray my father as threatening the life of my cat, and why does the thought of old Smoky, even today, reduce me to tears?

Nevertheless, the ground feels solid under my feet. The sky is clear for as far as I can see.

TRIANGLES

It seems to be a law of human nature, as compelling as Newton's, that whatever is hidden in the psyche will struggle to reveal itself. Through Pandora, my other self had acquired a voice. When I tried to continue her story in a sequel covering my teenage years, I blocked. That period was too volatile to probe without grave risk of remembering. That I was not yet prepared to do. But neither could I force my other self back into her dungeon. In the ensuing power struggle, I lost. As in high school, I became a zombie while her needs, her goals, her secret agenda once again took over my life.

And what was that agenda? Nostalgia for her first love. She wanted to reunite with daddy.

Fairytales endure because they spell out our hidden desires and our hopeful solutions. Their kings and queens and witches and ogres represent our mommies and daddies with their ultimate power to nurture or destroy us. I had already lived one fairytale in which a prince rescued me from a daddy-monster. Now my other self wanted to rescue her daddy-king from mommy so they could live happily ever after.

Though my father was still alive, there was no question of reengaging with him. Morality made that repellent. Besides, I hated him. My other self required a daddy substitute, attractive to me as well as to her. The man she chose was, like most kings, married. This was not incidental. A triangle allowed her to hate his queen as a projection of the jealous fury she felt for the mother-rival who failed to protect her.

Adultery is a large word beginning with a scarlet letter. In fifteen years of marriage, I had never considered it. The marriage I had was romantic, fun and even glamorous. My mate was my best friend. We were affectionate rather than passionate lovers—a lot of holding, of stroking, of cuddling. Often we were children together. As far as I was concerned, passion was the stuff of my mother's purloined novels—unrequited yearning in which bosoms heaved across unbridgeable gulfs. He was a wealthy plantation owner and she a slave girl; she was a lady and he a faithless gambler. I'm not sure I believed in it.

When the time came to burst out of my marriage, it wasn't so much passion that tempted me but compulsion that drove her. Like a sleepwalker I watched askance while someone who looked like me cast aside everything I valued to recreate an infantile world in which no will or desire existed outside of the illicit affair.

Does this mean my other self had secretly enjoyed her incestuous affair with daddy? I don't know. I do believe the relationship began in tenderness and even innocence, and that those feelings had powerfully imprinted. Perhaps, in retrospect, the undercurrents of secrecy, of power, of naughtiness and of danger became enticing. Perhaps, like old veterans sitting around the Legion Hall, she grew to romanticize trench warfare.

Once I had a husband.
Once I had a lover. The lover had a wife.
Once I had a magic cat . . .

It's the last stop on my book-promotion tour—station CHCN-TV, owned by Paul Lawson, my friend Lulu's father. The reception area is plushly decorated and dramatically underlighted. Stars glitter from a simulated sky. A frieze of photos advertises CHCN's own stars, including Gerald Nash, also from my Hamilton High days. Despite retouching, Gerald's reddish hair looks thinner and his jowls fatter than when I knew him as Joker, the class cutup.

"Makeup's down that corridor," directs the receptionist. "Tell Maggie you're on 'The Nashery.' "

Maggie is coiffing a man who claims he can talk to snakes. "During the Korean War we had to wade through a swamp infested with them. We could hear them rattling all around us. I don't know what prompted me—maybe it was the Lord.

I started hissing and rattling right back till there was silence. It was then I knew I had the gift."

As Maggie dabs beige foundation on my forehead, Gerald pokes his head in the door, his own face already white-powdered to disguise a florid complexion. "Hi. Welcome back to Hamilton." Holding up Pandora, he exclaims: "Wonderful stuff. Couldn't put it down. I've been looking forward to this interview." He gives me the thumbs-up signal.

I'm taken to a lounge with a TV monitor. ". . . or maybe it was the Lord. I started hissing and rattling right back till there was silence." As Gerald struggles to conceal his distaste, two rattlesnakes are released onto his coffee table, one wearing a skirt, the other a bow tie. The trainer emits tiny whistles. They sway in unison. "That's the waltz. Now here's the tango . . . ."

I'm escorted onto the set. As a microphone is slipped around my neck during a commercial, Gerald again effuses: "I'm really looking forward to this." Smiling, he holds up my book for the camera. "Perhaps some of you have noticed this novel in the stores. Interviewing this author gives me particular pleasure since we shared so many happy memories at Hamilton High." He turns to me. "The realistic detail in your book astounds me. How can you remember so many things when I can barely remember the names of my teachers?"

"Well, Gerald, I'm just as surprised that you can forget."

"Fair enough! But isn't there something off base about your recollections?"

"What do you mean?"

"Take the scene where Pandora gets into the breadman's horse wagon. Here, let me read a bit.

"Do you want to take the reins?" asks the breadman.

"Sure!" Pandora moves between the breadman's knees. She feels Molly's slow, grumbling rhythm pass up through her flanks and along the reins. The breadman lays his whip on Molly's withers. She plunges forward. Clippetty cloppetty. Pandora loses her balance. The breadman presses her body between his knees. Pandora doesn't like to be squeezed. She calls: "Whoooh!" and tries to wriggle free.

The breadman tugs the reins. "Hooo-back!" They are in a stand of slippery elms. "What's the matter? Can't you take a little excitement?"

The breadman has pointy teeth like the whale that swallowed Pinocchio. Pandora can smell his breath. She puts her hands against his chest, and pushes. She remembers her manners. She drops her hands. "I had a good time, Mister Breadman, but I guess I'll go. My mother is calling me."

"That's a real shame. I thought we'd have a picnic." The breadman pulls down a box of cherry tarts. He slides his finger through the cellophane.

"Well . . . " Pandora hesitates, one Sisman scamper on the steel step. She moves back inside the wagon. "Maybe if I'm not too long."

Pandora sits primly on the leather seat. She takes the nearest cherry tart, which is also the biggest. They munch companionably. Juice sticks to the breadman's moustache. Pandora averts her eyes knowing it's not polite to stare when people are chewing.

The breadman laughs: "Your old man got a moustache?"

"No."

"Does your boyfriend have a moustache?"

"I don't have a boyfriend!"

"A cute girl like you? Ahhh, I bet you do! I bet he's got a moustache."

"I don't know anybody with a moustache except Hitler."

The breadman laughs: "That's rich!" He licks cherry juice from his moustache. "Ever been kissed by a guy with a moustache?"

Pandora ducks her head.

"Know what it feels like?"

The breadman swings Pandora up on the seat and runs his moustache against her cheek. "See? It tickles!" He runs his fingers up and down her arm. He tickles her neck. He sticks his fingers into her bellybutton. He thrusts his hand up her skirt and yanks at her button pants.

Pandora punches the breadman with both fists. He slaps her. She sucks in her breath to scream. The breadman claps his hand over her mouth, jamming the scream back into her body. She convulses. The breadman sees three railwaymen down the tracks on a jigger. He snarls. "Shut up, and maybe I'll let you go."

Pandora forces herself to calm down. The breadman takes his hand from her mouth. He yanks her head back by the hair. "If I let you go, what are you going to say?"

"Th-thank you?"

"No! What are you going to tell your old man?"

"N-nothing."

"You better not," hisses the breadman. "Because if you're lying, I'm coming to get you!" He pulls Pandora's hair tighter. Her eyes water. He reaches for his whip. "See this? You tell one word and . . ." The breadman takes his hands from Pandora's body. She jumps past him, down the steps and out of the wagon.

Joker confronts me: "Did such an incident ever happen to you?"

"As a child I was sometimes approached by men at the movies or in Gage Park, as kids so often are. I combined all those fears into one incident."

"But doesn't that sort of sexual assault go beyond most kids' experience?"

"Not the attempt at assault. I didn't allow the breadman to succeed with his attack because I wouldn't know how to write about a kid as emotionally damaged as that."

"Speaking for myself," he smiles confidently into the camera, "and, I suspect, a lot of viewers, I don't believe that incident for one minute. First you weave a false web of innocence around childhood and then you want us to believe—"

"But I didn't weave a false web of innocence. Pandora was tempted by the cherry tarts, that was partly why she got into trouble. That kind of detail is the strength of the book, as many reviewers have pointed out."

Joker gives a pointy-toothed grin. "Reviewers more gullible than I, if you'll forgive me for remarking. For such a sexual assault to take place, we must look to the conduct of the child. Why would she get into the breadman's wagon in the first place? Some little girls can be seductive at an early age. I think your book is typical of the kind of hysterical imaginings we're seeing too much of these days. According to you feminists, we men are always the enemy."

Joker is breathing deeply, almost heaving. *So is my other self.* I can smell his breath—sour with a sweetish overlay of mints. *So can my other self.* His once-florid complexion is now so pasty he looks cadaverous. I try to protest, but the hysteria in my chest leaves me helpless and humiliated.

Joker signals for another commercial. "Whew, I think it went rather well, don't you? Hope you don't mind a little probing. Would you autograph this for me?" Again he gives me the thumbs-up signal. "What a super book!"

As I walk to the lobby, I'm still fuming, *my other self is still trembling.* If Joker didn't like my novel, why not be honest enough to say so instead of all that false fawning?

The receptionist smiles. "That must be some book you've written. Want me to call you a cab?"

"Please." I pace the lobby, struggling against tears, startled both at the depth of my fury and of my vulnerability.

A gray-haired man is striding toward me, the confidence of his bearing compensating for a slight limp. I step out of his way. He stops, beams. "What good timing!" Paul Lawson clasps my hand in both of his, steadying me, *steadying my other self*. "You did a fine job of putting Nash in his place. I don't know what got into that bastard! He's usually so unctuous."

These reassurances, so unexpected, so wholehearted and from such an impeccable source, spawn my instantaneous and overwhelming gratitude: "Thank you, Mr. Lawson!"

He throws his camel coat over his shoulders. "Can I give you a lift somewhere? I'm headed uptown."

"I'm meeting a reporter at six at the Royal Connaught, but I've already ordered a cab."

"That's easily fixed. Judy, cancel that, will you? I've got to stop by the house—on Delaware, remember? I'll get you to your appointment on time, guaranteed."

He ushers me into his white Cadillac convertible, brought to the front by the valet. "By the way, the name's Paul. That Mr. Lawson stuff makes me feel a thousand years old. Of course I am, but flatter me, please."

As he waves to the gate man, I study the elegant profile, now slightly fudged, and the youthfully cropped gray hair, remembering the naval officer's picture on Lulu's dresser. How distant and glamorous he seemed, just like a movie star. I'm amused to find I'm still a little awestruck.

He turns, catches me watching him and winks. "I hope you know I'm one of your biggest fans. Of all the girls Lulu brought around, you were the one I had my eye on. I might say I've followed your career with a good deal of fatherly pride."

Again, I feel gratified: "How is Lulu these days?"

"Well enough, I guess. You heard, I suppose, that she and Herb moved to New York?"

"Yes, she sent me a change of address scrawled on the back of a program for the Met."

"That's my girl! Sure wish she'd give television a try. I've offered her every lure but only the 'legitimate' stage will do. I suspect she caught that from her grandmother. She's doing

Ibsen's Doll's House for the Hamilton Players next spring. You'll have to give her a call."

As we turn west onto Lawrence Road, avoiding the season's first patches of ice, we chat about the changes in Hamilton since I left fifteen years ago. "Actually, I'm more surprised at how many things have stayed the same."

"Well, you're lucky you got out. I'm belatedly working on that myself—we'll see."

He parks in the driveway of his Delaware graystone. Gone is the look of times past, of neglect and decay. The roof and porch have been replaced, the trim freshly painted. The hedges seem crisp, even on this dingy November day.

Paul picks up my thoughts. "It was about time, wasn't it? Millicent was too embarrassed to have her ladies' gangs over. She was right, of course. I had the world's best childhood, and I guess I was trying to preserve it." Another grin. "Still am." He starts up the walk, then turns. "Why not come in for a few minutes? I may have to make a phone call, too."

"Sure. I'll say hello to Miss Mildon."

"Sorry, but the old girl passed away last July. Just stopped breathing. She was eighty-one. Worked right up to the end on her own insistence. I hope that's the way they carry me off."

He unlocks the door. "Make yourself comfortable in the solarium. You can help yourself to Miss Mildon's grape cordial—or something stronger. We've got enough of that to last another eighty-one years."

I explore the Lawson solarium—the same ferns a few fronds taller, the same aquarium with the same trapped princess in the tower. As I flip through the issues of Fortune and Financial Post that have replaced Lulu's Photoplay and Silver Screen, I hear Paul on the phone. "Where's your optimism, Bud? It's not as if you're down to your last yacht. Not bloody well yet."

Paul Lawson comes whistling into the room, then stops. "Do you have any idea how attractive you look sitting there in my mother's rocker?" Cupping my chin, he kisses me on the forehead. "I wish I was your age. I'd know what to do with a moment like this." He draws back. "Good God! You're a friend of my daughter's."

During the ride uptown, he is chatty, avuncular and very correct. He lets me out at the Royal Connaught at precisely 5:59. "By the way, we're starting a late-night journal at CHCN. Strikes me, after seeing the Nash interview, that you'd be good for the critic's job—reviews of restaurants, plays, things like that. I'll call you. It won't be for a few months. We'd have to start with a pilot."

My other self paces her underground prison, trailing cob- webs like a rotting bridal veil, remembering that she was once a princess. She telephones, jarring me from a sound sleep: "I'm coming up."

Paul Lawson phones early in March, as he promised. We lunch at Winston's, in downtown Toronto. I order a sweet- bread hors d'oeuvre: he follows suit. He orders filet mignon, rare: I follow suit.

"Perfect compatibility. I would have guessed as much." He lifts his Scotch. "You choose our toast."

So far this has not felt like a business luncheon, though that is how it was billed: too much eye contact, too many significant pauses, too much hearty laughter offset by my own flirtatious giggles. It's flattering, it's fun. Since my journalistic days, I've rarely spoken to an attractive man whose wife was not five yards away. I steer us back on course: "To an amiable working arrangement."

Paul puts down his Scotch. "Enough is enough. The tele- vision job was just a transparent blind to see you again. Didn't you guess that? If you want it, you can have it. I'll get my producer to call you to negotiate." He jiggles the ice in his Scotch. "The truth is, I haven't been able to get you off my mind. How do you feel about that? The father of your high- school chum . . . a dirty old man."

Disarmed by his frankness, I hear myself blurt: "I've been thinking about you, too." As soon as I say it, I realize it's true.

"You have? Now that's worth drinking to!" He sips his Scotch, then impulsively puts his hand over mine. "You're very lovely, you know—especially sitting across from me, smiling at me. Are you happy?"

I stare at our linked hands. *So does my other self.* "Over the past dozen years, I would have said yes. Lately, I've been discovering life is more complicated than I suspected."

"Good grief!" He withdraws his hand. "I didn't mean to ask whether your life was happy. I only meant here, having lunch with me. See what a superficial person I am? I've never known happiness for more than a few minutes at a time. I wouldn't dare look deeper than that."

"I thought you told me that you had an idyllic childhood?"

"True. My mother spoiled me rotten, and I loved it. Though I'm ashamed to admit it, I also loved the war. I had a lark all the time the world was blowing up." He rubs his gimpy leg. "Even while I was blowing up. All that just seemed a game—an adventure."

"Then what is real to you?"

He gestures toward four men in pinstripe suits, engrossed in a financial report. "Those bastards and what they represent—unfortunately."

"They don't look real to me. They all look the same. Eeeny, Meeny, Miny and there's Mo on the end."

"I'm an ambitious man. When I decide to go for something, I push hard and I push to win. Mind you, I don't always like the result, since I also hate responsibility. What do you as a journalist make of that combination?" He grins. "Perhaps my real problem is my lack of a personal life. Am I being entirely absurd, or do you suppose we could have an affair?"

I await the ironic disclaimer. When there is none, I reply rather starchily: "I've never been unfaithful to Danny. Never even thought of it."

"What—never? Hm, I guess that puts me in my place. I

just assumed . . . I don't know what I assumed, maybe that
everyone's marriage is like mine. Millicent doesn't mind so
long as I don't publicly embarrass her—the kind of thing
where everyone knows but her."

I conjure up Millicent Lawson, bitter lines radiating from
eyes and mouth like high-impact marks on the moon. "Are
you sure?"

"What a peculiar question. I've never thought about it for
so many years that . . . No, I don't suppose I am. I've never
been in love—not with her or anyone else. I'm probably in-
capable of it. If she's jealous she doesn't bother me about it,
but then I don't make demands on her either. She's as free
as I am."

"Invisible ropes are often the tightest."

He laughs mirthlessly. "If I'm tied, it's to a system. But
that happened before I was born. Look, this is depressing.
I've admitted my personal life is a wasteland. Let's change
the subject. Tell me about you. All those wonderful globe-
trotting assignments—God, how I envy your freedom!"

*My other self, disguised as a princess, enters a maze of mir-
rors. In the inner court, a king sits on his throne, holding his
bleeding heart in his hands, weeping. Though the way is
strewn with nettles and scorpions, she is feckless and impatient. To her, as to any child, the delay of a minute is like an
hour, an hour a day, a day a year . . . .*

I stare moodily out my apartment window at the storm clouds
collecting around Toronto's Parliament Buildings, still thinking about my lunch with Paul Lawson five hours earlier.
Danny's key clicks in the lock, followed by a cheery greeting.
Tossing several travel brochures on the bed beside me, he
asks: "How about a week in Bermuda or Mexico? There are
some terrific package deals. Look at these—"

I pick up a folder. "What gives?"

"My bank trial should be over by the weekend. I just
thought it was time for a vacation." Sitting on the bed, he

reaches out a hand. "I've missed you. I thought things would change after you finished your book, but you're still in your own private world."

The invitation is obvious and intimate. I push aside the brochures and curl up beside him. "I've missed you, too."

"Good. I was feeling like a groundhog who had waited for his mate with a bouquet, only to find she'd come up at a different hole."

As Danny's arms enclose me, I feel myself grow resistant, then force myself to relax. *Am I being entirely absurd or do you suppose we could have an affair?*

Danny's head is on my breast, his face streaked with sweat, his hair unruly. "That was nice. For the first time in a long while I felt you were really here." He picks up a travel brochure. "Is there anything that would make you happy?"

Happy. That word again. I remember how glibly I used it as a journalist: are you happy with your new contract? Are you happy living in New York? Are you happy? All Danny wants is a simple answer so he can prepare for tomorrow's court appearance undisturbed. Instead, I parry a question with a question: "What would make you happy, Danny?"

"You know the answer to that. If you're happy then I'm happy."

Once that graceful response would have flattered me. Now it frustrates. "But what do you want for yourself? Sometimes I can't be happy for one, let alone for two. We always talk about my needs and problems as if you didn't have any."

"I don't."

"None that you acknowledge. Maybe that's the problem." Now this topic is launched, however inadvertently, I realize it's a good one. "If you don't keep track of what you want, apart from what I want, or what we want, then you're going to lose track of yourself."

His voice is tight, but controlled: "I don't have the slightest idea what you're talking about."

"I'll give you an example. If we're having dinner with other people, you never ask for the butter for yourself. You always ask for it to be passed to me, then afterward you help yourself."

"Would you prefer me to forage for myself and forget about you?"

"We're not talking about butter. We're talking about your acknowledging what you need and want."

"I'm supposed to ask directly, is that it?"

"Yes."

"All right. What I want is for this conversation to end so I can prepare my case for tomorrow."

"Danny, this is important."

"So is my case. Very."

"You say I'm off in my own little world but when I try to talk—"

"Shout. And at the wrong time."

"You don't listen!"

"I'm listening, all right. You said this was to be about my needs. I've told you what they are." Putting on his bathrobe, he strides into the den and very, very softly closes the door. When he emerges four hours later, he is still locked in his shell of silence. We get into either side of our king-size bed, then turn out the light.

When I try to put on my golden coat, I encounter resistance. Danny's arms are already in the sleeves. They embrace me, clasping me tighter. I find it hard to breathe.

I choose the window seat at Miller's Malt Shop so that I can look out at the gusty April day. Since it's Saturday, the restaurant, with its fifties-style chrome stools and Formica counter, is almost deserted. So is Hamilton High across the street. As I study the redstone with its imposing Roman portal, I once again see myself standing outside, in sloppy-joe sweater and one of those pencil-slim skirts that were so effective in shortening our stride. Tonya, Arlene, Babs, Cooky . . .

Lulu slides into the seat opposite me, wearing a red slicker over a black body stocking, her taffy hair bound with a gold scarf. "Sorry to suggest this old dive but it's so close to my rehearsal hall I couldn't resist. How did you know I was back from New York? Don't tell me the Hamilton Players' publicity department actually managed to get us a mention somewhere!"

"Your father told me."

"He did? Where did you see Paul?"

"I bumped into him last fall after a TV interview I did with Joker Nash."

"Oh, yeah, I heard about that stinker! So much for old friends. What do you think about him and Babs finally getting together? Imagine, after all the years she spent panting after him at Hamilton High!"

"Joker's a hard one to read."

"He phoned a month after her divorce and whammo."

"Well, he accidentally did me a favor. After my interview on "The Nashery," your father offered me a job on CHCN's new late-night magazine. We shot a pilot this morning, which is why I'm in Hamilton."

"I'm not surprised. Paul always used to ask after you—when he was speaking to me, that is. Now he's sulking. He disapproved of Herb and me moving to New York, and now he disapproves of my leaving Herb and the kids there to commute. After the life he's led, the bounder! Name it, and he's done it."

"I've sometimes wondered—how does your mother feel?"

"That's the funny part. She's on my side now. It's the two of us against Paul for a change."

"No, I mean how does your mother feel about your father's philandering?"

"Oh, that. It depends. She stamps her foot and screams. She wrings her hands a lot. She does the charity number. She ignores it. She drinks. She traipses off to the Golden Door every spring to recoup—which, incidentally, is where she is right now. She's of the old school. You hang in till one of you croaks—preferably the other one."

I struggle to make my voice casual. "How do you feel—as his daughter, I mean?"

"I used to be jealous. Now I think c'est la vie. It gives me an example to aim for. Hey, what is this? Is Danny having an affair or something?"

"No, of course not."

"Good. As far as I'm concerned you've got the perfect marriage." She sighs theatrically. "The love of my life was my drama coach, Boris Wayne. Remember Romeo and Juliet?"

"Of course, 'Boris says' . . ."

She picks up a knife from the table:

"O happy dagger! [Stabs self.]
There rust and let me die . . ."

The light dawns. Lulu's pregnancy. Boris says . . .

She tosses away the knife. "Don't look so startled. I thought you guessed. He panicked. I panicked. Herb offered to marry me and I accepted. Herb's been fair, too—never thrown it up to me, not once. We're good friends and I think we're good parents."

"What happened to Boris?"

"Nothing at all. Nothing ever does to those guys. He's still with his wife and still madly in love—with yet another protégée. I'm his confidante these days. It's funny seeing the whole thing replayed without being part of it—like munching popcorn, watching a familiar schlock movie and knowing you'll spend the evening happily washing your hair. Actually, I'm grateful to Boris. My shrink says he helped get my father out of my system—you know, the old Freudian knot. By the way, how are your folks?"

"Oh, my mother keeps busy with her church work. My father doesn't get out of bed much anymore. Partly it's senility. Partly it's just irascibility—it's hard to tell the difference. He's in St. Cecilia's Infirmary. I have to visit him this afternoon."

"It's peculiar, isn't it? I mean, the aging process. My dad

bought CHCN-TV for his fiftieth birthday and now, three years later, all he can think of is buying a dozen more. Hell, you'd think those TV towers were dinky toys."

We both dive for the bill. "Let me," insists Lulu. "I want to suck up to you for when you write about the Golden Amazons."

"At the rate I'm going, it'll be an historical drama."

Lulu is dashing across the street, collar turned up against an April shower, when I notice her scarf on the seat. I start after her, then remember: her house is only a few blocks from the infirmary. *My mother traipses off to the Golden Door every spring.* I'll deliver it myself.

Though St. Cecilia's Infirmary is twice as big as it used to be, some things haven't changed—the spike fence where I dragged Popsicle sticks as I ran to school, the bridal-wreath bushes that ate up foul balls. As a child I was chased away from the grounds so often that I still feel like a trespasser entering the front door.

The gleaming halls, smelling of disinfectant, look like those of an ordinary hospital where people do get well and not "for Cripples and Incurables," as its black-and-gold sign once baldly stated. Through doorways I glimpse white stick-people, surrounded by the paraphernalia of sickness and old age, their vital organs hung in glass bottles for the world to see. I count the numbered doors: 206, 207, 208.

My father lies spread-eagled across his starchy bed, a mound of bloated flesh, with the left leg bound and propped. My mother is already here, and Helen. "Hi, we wondered where you were."

I join them around the bed, posting myself as close to the door as I can while still remaining in the room. Helen's three children are now in Laura Secord Public School and her husband has just started his own accountancy firm. "On Saturday Jeff didn't get home till ten. For us, spring means income tax, not robins."

My mother shows us the afghan she is knitting for a church

raffle. "Remember this blue wool? I made both of you mittens on strings."

As far as I'm concerned, this is just another duty visit, like a dozen others, arranged like stepping stones through time so my mother can drop into conversation with her church friends: "Oh, yes, both the girls were home just last week." Though my father's in his eighties, the doctor says he could last another ten years. His heart is strong despite the excess flesh it's always carried, the care at St. Cecilia's is indulgent, his day's expenditure of energy slight. As we chat in hushed hospital tones, he passes in and out of consciousness like a child playing in a revolving door. What breath he has, he still uses to hector: "Addy, where's my water? Not this stuff! It's lukewarm."

I check my watch. Another half hour before I can dash. I think of Lulu's scarf in my bag then discipline myself: no, absolutely not.

So far, my father hasn't recognized Helen or me. That sometimes happens. As I stare hypnotically at his heaving belly, recording its breathy discharges, I find myself remembering our Sunday visits to Other Grandmother's—the same tense vigil as he and Aunt Estelle snapped like scrappy dogs over the shreds and bones of Other Grandmother's love.

Aunt Estelle. I haven't thought of her in a decade. She and my father haven't spoken in thirty years, not since Other Grandmother died. Aunt Estelle, still a prisoner in her natal home, threading her way through ever-narrowing lanes of National Geographics and inherited antiques. Aunt Estelle, who feeds the neighborhood cats instead of herself. Aunt Estelle, who indulges in shopping binges in which she buys only hats. Aunt Estelle, who places Kleenex over doorknobs because of the germy things people do with their hands. Aunt Estelle, with her musty cellar full of dead fruit like babies in glass jars. My Aunt Estelle . . .

Suddenly, I find myself gripped by a vivid sense of identification. Aunt Estelle was born on March 5. I was born on March 8. We are both Pisces. We share the bloodstone.

I am baffled. I almost laugh aloud. Why am I thinking such stupid thoughts? Astrology doesn't mean anything to me. It never has. Yet now it seems to offer some compelling point of recognition. My head feels ready to explode with the significance of it all. *Aunt Estelle who . . . Aunt Estelle who . . .*

My mother announces with a hint of relief: "Three o'clock. I suppose we should go." She, my sister and I file up to my father's bed. My sister kisses him. I suppose my mother does, too. *Kiss Grandmother Pearl good-bye.* Almost shuddering, I do the minimum, touch my flesh to his, finger to back of hand as if forced to touch fire, or ice. My father opens his blue eyes, vivid against the whiteness of hair, of skin, of sheet. For the first time that afternoon, he looks directly into my face. He says: "Thanks for coming, Estelle."

My other self shrieks: it's not Aunt Estelle. It's me! I make my excuses to my mother and sister. *My other self bolts from the hospital, with the smell of sickness, of death, of the undigested past thick in her nostrils. Aunt Estelle Aunt Estelle Aunt Estelle . . .*

I catch the Delaware bus. Once again the sun is shining. I'm startled by the vibrancy of yellow and purple crocuses against wet loam. I see several beds of tulips, a forsythia tree in bloom.

I jump off the bus.

Down down down the stairs I go, scraping my running shoes on each step, dragging Teddy Umcline by an ear.

Halfway up to the door my nerve gives out. I steady myself against a budding maple, reminding myself that I've walked this path a thousand times before. Besides—Lulu's scarf slithers like a silken snake through my fingers—I have a reason.

The Lawsons' antique door knocker looks like one on which the ghost of Marley would be happy to appear. I lift it, let it fall, hear it echo.

I hang outside my daddy's door in the sunsuit my granny made for me—just like the one she made for Teddy Umcline.

When no one answers I feel relief, then disappointment. I turn to go, then notice a newly installed buzzer. Pressing that,

I hear it ring—not chimes but a rasping, old-fashioned bzzz like a dentist's drill.

Hitching at the strap of my sunsuit, I scrape my foot back and forth over the metal band marking the threshold of my daddy's room . . .

I ring once more, wait ten seconds. Again I'm turning toward the steps when a male voice barks through the door: "I'm coming. Hold your horses." Paul opens it, wearing a white terry bathrobe, his gray hair wet and tufted as if from the shower.

My daddy sits on his bed in his undershirt . . .

We stare at each other. I start to babble: "I had lunch with Lulu today. She left her scarf—"

Before I can blunder through the rest of my speech, he pulls me inside, closes the door, embraces me.

I'm my daddy's favorite . . .

We maneuver the distance between hall and solarium. As we fall to our knees on the carpet, I think giddily of the lump concealing the bell that fetches Miss Mildew for afternoon tea.

My daddy squeezes my bare legs between his thighs. His flesh is soft and moist and smells of talcum from his bath . . .

Paul's flesh is moist and smells of talcum from his bath. I find myself staring backward through jungly growth into the aquarium with its castle containing the trapped princess, watching goldfish dart and weave among its slimy turrets.

Now I am lying facedown on my daddy's bed. The scroll on the headboard looks like my mother's pursed lips. My daddy rubs up against me: "Whose little girl are you?"

Gazing into my eyes, Paul announces: "Amazing! Wasn't that amazing? I haven't done anything quite so impulsive since I was seventeen."

My daddy and I share secrets.

He slumps onto the couch, gently pushing me to the rocker. "No, sit there. I want to look at you. I want to savor this."

I yearn to sit on his lap, to touch, to caress, to keep contact, eager to protect my fragile mood of well-being.

Tinker, tailor, soldier, sailor.

"Amazing!" he repeats. "I still feel shaky. Would you like some brandy?"

With childish bravado I insist: "I'd like some of Miss Mildon's grape cordial. Why spoil a tradition?"

He pours a glass, then reaches for a cigar. "Mind if I smoke this?"

I take the cigar from his hand, peel it, trim it, roll it in my mouth, light it the way I remember seeing Lulu light it.

"You do that very well."

"Not, I can assure you, from experience. I'm a novice at this." The wider implication of that statement catches up to me.

"I'm sorry I jumped you as you came through the door. In fact, as I recollect, I pulled you in. You've been on my mind so intensely that I never questioned what you were doing here." He gives a little laugh that catches in his throat. "For the record, why did you come?"

I begin my covering statement, then break off, gesturing toward him, still feeling on a high, but knowing there will be a terrible downslide. "For this."

"I'm glad. I feel so joyful." He laughs. "And so gauche. You know, this place does have a bedroom and I'm a blissful weekend bachelor." He holds out his hand, his face in a boyish grin. "Do you have time?"

"Not long." Danny . . .

Offering me his arm, he leads me up the curving mahogany staircase. I slide my fingers up the railing, expecting it to break, dashing me to the tiles below. We stop outside Laura Lawson's room, full of Egyptian treasures. "Your mother's . . .?"

"Well, it's not a shrine, you know. The spare room. It's a bit musty. Here, I'll open the window. Unless that's too windy?"

The breeze through the window smells of lilacs. It blows the curtains inward like Rapunzel's golden hair, giving me goose bumps.

"No, I like the wind."

His eyes seem large and childlike; the sad, deep vertical lines from cheekbone to chin have all but disappeared. As Paul wraps his arms around me, I close my eyes, feeling the arms in the naval portrait by Lulu's bed reaching out to embrace me, reciting the titles of the novels on my mother's bedside shelf as if they were a mantra: This Night Above All, Dark Waters, Interlude, There Came A Stranger . . . Passion.

He insists on driving me back to Toronto. "Believe me, you're saving me from a truly boring dinner party, one of Millicent's friends conscripted to keep an eye on me." As he ushers me into his convertible, he offers: "I'll put up the top so you won't muss your hair."

I think of Millicent Lawson with every lacquered strand in place, and repeat: "No. I love the wind."

He seems relieved. "So do I. It blows the tensions away." A boyish grin. "Not that I have any left. Here's a blanket. I'll blast up the heat."

In suede jacket and open shirt, he still seems familiar and intimate, though he's wearing nothing more nor less than he would to play golf. As we break from the city onto the Queen Elizabeth Way at eighty miles an hour, he explains in an enthusiastic rush: "I expect to be spending a lot more time in Toronto. Things are really popping for me along the line of acquisitions. It's too soon to talk but—what the hell, why be coy? I trust you not to blab. I'm trying to buy Toronto's CKMO-TV."

For forty minutes, he talks about his hopes and dreams, driving swiftly with one finger on the wheel. It's flattering and thrilling, like seeing very far from very high up. As we turn off the Gardiner Expressway onto Spadina Avenue, he declares: "I want to see a lot more of you. If things work out with CKMO, I'm also going to buy a condo along the lakeshore. Maybe you can help me pick it out." He screws up his face like a kid taking medicine. "Of course, Millicent will want to use it for ballets and stuff at the O'Keefe Centre, but—hell!—you can't have everything." Another grin: "At least, not all at once."

Turning onto Bloor Street, Paul slams on his brakes. "What an idiot! Why did I drive so quickly?" He gestures toward the Park Plaza. "Do you have time for a drink?"

I check my watch—7:17—then shake my head. "I'm already late for dinner." Danny . . .

"I was afraid you'd say something like that." He kisses me lightly on the forehead. "I want you to know you're responsible for one of the most remarkable days of my life. I feel like a young buck again." Walking around the front of the car, he opens my door. "I'm going to watch you go into your building and imagine you're coming the other way."

It is now 7:22. As I stand in the lobby, pretending to wait for the elevator whose button I haven't pressed, I announce to Burt, the doorman, as if in sudden inspiration: "Oh, I forgot. Danny likes the late edition!" Then I rush out onto Bloor Street.

The white convertible is two blocks away, just turning onto Bay Street. Paralyzed, I watch it go. Then I run in the same direction, around my apartment building, once, twice, three times, staring up at our twelve lighted windows the way I used to stare at the get-in-here lamp in my parents' window, knowing Danny will be on the patio with the late edition already spread around him, perhaps with the barbecue glowing for steaks.

I return to the lobby, preparing my mood and my story like an actress boning up for her next performance, hating the deceit as much as the infidelity, understanding, suddenly, that the marriage which once made me feel so authentic has now become the place where I playact while the real drama goes on somewhere down the street.

By the time I step off the elevator, I'm feeling more defiant than guilty. After checking myself in a wall mirror for telltale signs, like blue fangs, I yank open the door. It's locked. I'm still fumbling for my key when Danny opens it, martini in hand. He kisses me on the forehead, exactly where Paul just pressed his lips, one more of the perverse and persistent echoes reverberating through my life.

Taking my hand, Danny leads me out to the patio. Here is everything as I imagined it—the scattered newspaper, the glowing coals, the steaks rubbed with garlic, a bottle of wine. I feel shaky and very very distant, as if I were looking at my life through the wrong end of the binoculars.

Danny is regarding me expectantly. "Well?" I glance around more carefully, see a flash of white on a patio chair. It jumps, falls backward as it chases its tail.

"It's adorable!" I scoop it up. "Where did you get it? Whose is it?"

Of course, I know the answer.

"It's yours. Happy sixteenth anniversary."

I panic. "But that's not till next month!"

"I know, but I've been passing this pet shop every day, and I've been watching this little thing. I picked it out right away. I knew it was the one you'd want."

He's studying me with the joy of anticipation, and yet with that nervous edge I've seen a lot of lately. The kitten purrs against my chest. Of course, I love it. It breaks my heart. I gag out the words: "Thank you, Danny, it's perfect." Like you.

Before retiring, we make a bed for the kitten in the bathroom. I lie very still, waiting for Danny to drift off. Then I sneak into the bathroom, place the warm body on my chest and cry myself to sleep.

A tornado sends me tumbling head over heels down a football field. "Cartwheels! C'mon, girlie, give us crotch." I try to catch myself on the goalpost, but I can't stop tumbling. My hecklers toss apple cores, dung, mud, powdery corsages, old love letters. A dart strikes me, leaving a scarlet A carved in my forehead.

From the applause all around me at Hamilton Place, I assume Lulu must have been wonderful. I am unable to concentrate—

at least, not on the play. Paul is first-row center with Millicent. I see their heads in the glow from the stage, in partial profile, like the heads of royalty on a gold coin. An elegant couple, it hurts me to admit. Her gray-streaked hair is drawn back in black wings from a widow's peak. Diamond earrings drip to an emerald dress and mink stole. Herb Swamp sits to the left of Paul. The oldest Swamp boy, now nineteen, to the right of Millicent, with three other kids in descending size. Then there's an aunt or two, also in satin and furs. It makes for a formidable first row.

As the applause from a half-dozen curtain calls fades, I delay Danny long enough to allow the Lawson entourage to make its way up the aisle. It's a slow progression, with Paul and Millicent pausing to accept the plaudits of well-wishers. Just before reaching the lobby, Paul turns and looks directly at me, as if he had been watching me all along through the back of his head. That smile is like sunshine breaking through clouds. Anxiety melts. I feel my face glow, then recompose it, fearing Danny's scrutiny.

"There's Herb Swamp and Paul Lawson," announces Danny, without inflection. "You'll want to speak to them."

We are now even with the Lawsons. Millicent is putting on her white kid gloves, finger by finger. Is it my guilty imagination or does she flick her eyes my way?

Arlene and Joe Baker call to us from the lobby. We are joined by Tonya and Iky. "Isn't it great that all the old gang could come?" exclaims Arlene.

"Thanks to you," says Tonya. "You flushed us all out."

Babs arrives, tugging Joker by the hand as if afraid he might fly away. Indeed, he does look pumped full of helium. He fondles my arm in greeting. "The famous authoress." He is sweating profusely. I remember his sour smell at the time of our interview and wonder: does he have a drinking problem? He is still patting my arm. I don't like the feel of that. I edge away.

Paul and Millicent are surrounded by congratulatory friends. As I watch, pretending not to, Paul glad-hands toward me.

In sudden animation I re-enter our conversation. Arlene is saying: "If you don't mind a few blackflies, the July First weekend would be fine." She turns to me. "How's that for you?"

The cottage? The weekend? "Dandy, I think."

"Just imagine, it'll be the first time we hens have had a pajama party since primary school."

Paul joins our circle. Casually throwing his arm around me, he asks with pride: "What do you think of my girl this evening?"

A chorus: "Terrific! Lulu really has talent."

"You can bet your boots she has!"

Unselfconsciously he tightens his arm around me, drawing me from the group. "I've had a devil of a time getting to you. The Toronto deal is really flying. You look beautiful, as usual. When can we get together?"

"Danny's used to me going to Hamilton on Thursdays for tapings."

"Good. I'll meet you in the lobby of the Royal Connaught at seven." He smiles boyishly. "No, let's make it six. That's an hour sooner."

Before I can reply, Millicent grasps Paul's arm and pulls like a kid retrieving a skipping rope. Her smile is tight and twitchy. "How nice to see so many of Lulu's school chums. Wasn't the production splendid?"

She runs on and on, never pausing for answers—inconsequential things, strung together at random—the way Danny and I now sometimes talk. Paul looks forbearing then irritated then bored. Just as Millicent falters, Lulu and the cast make an entrance. "Look, Paul, we'll be needed for photos!" Millicent tugs him away. He mouths over his shoulder: "I'll call."

I dream: *Guarding the throne room is the black queen, sitting in the center of a sticky golden spiderweb. Her lips are pursed, her black wire hair is pulled back from a widow's peak, her eyes are folded ravens' wings. Around her waist she wears keys and padlocks to which are attached four squabbling monkeys—one blind, one deaf, one with its tongue cut out, one that's castrated.*

To get to the king it is necessary to pluck out the blind, all-seeing eye that the queen wears like a ruby diadem in the center of her forehead. That blind eye is the source of the queen's power . . . .

I'm lying on the wharf at Arlene's Lake Simcoe cottage, watching Tonya's snorkel bob around some lily pads. Arlene is lying beside me, freckled face shaded by a straw hat. Though she's talking to me, she too is watching Tonya, trying to get in as many words as possible before she surfaces.

"I finally told Joe, 'All right, it's Elvira or me and the kids.' He broke down, sobbed in my arms. 'It's you,' he said, 'but I've got to win this election and she's my manager. Will you see me through?' Naturally, I said yes, and then IT started all over again. Elvira this, Elvira that. 'Elvira says I should grow a mustache. Elvira says I should put a pot of geraniums on my head and hop down the street with a bone in my mouth!' He's only an alderman who wants to be a councillor, for gosh sake! He's not running for prime minister, but she's got her talons into him and now he can't buy a tie without asking her. He's even talking about 'strategizing' for mayor. Honestly, I didn't know it was possible to hate another person so much. I certainly didn't know I was capable of it. One morning, after seeing their heads together over a speech, I reached into the closet for my jacket and got hers by mistake. I knew it was hers because of the Chloe perfume. I took a pair of scissors and started slashing and cutting until—"

Arlene breaks off. Tonya is emerging from the lake in mask and flippers. Shaking off water, she joins us. "Why so quiet? Am I interrupting something?"

"Well, uh, no," stammers Arlene. "Just the usual—love and marriage."

Tonya snorts: "A great institution for men but it sucks for women."

I pick up Tonya's snorkel. "Maybe I'll try this after all."

I paddle out from the wharf, intending to stay in only as long as it takes to detach myself from the conversation. I see a school of minnows and chase them to an inlet where the water is shallower and soupier. Through a tangle of lily pads I see a pop bottle, a rubber tire, some rusty cans, a submerged log. A carp darts from a rock crevice, through seaweed flowing like green hair, followed by another and another. I remember the aquarium in the Lawson solarium with the princess imprisoned in her tower. Involuntarily, my legs, my whole body begin to thrash. The more my anxiety builds, the harder my limbs work and the more rhythmic my breathing becomes till I feel as if I were a single-celled organism whose only reason for existence is rage—mostly at myself.

With a tremendous splash, I leap from the water.

"Good God," exclaims Babs. "It's a bird, it's a plane, it's superfish!"

The whole gang is on the wharf. "We were getting worried," says Tonya. "I thought you were only going in for a few minutes."

"What time is it?"

"4:15."

"It can't be." I pick up my watch: 4:16. "That's two hours, but I was gone only about twenty minutes."

"The hell you were. I thought about yanking you out, but we had no trouble seeing where you were."

My skin is puckered and blue. "It can't be!" Excusing myself, I run back to the cottage. I lock myself in the bathroom and am sick in the toilet bowl. Afterward, I lie on the floor, feeling the tiles tilt under me, realizing that I am losing control, that something irrational is taking over my life. I try to conjure up Danny in our apartment, furnished with the mementos of our life, but I can barely remember what he, or anything I once valued, looks like. Nothing matters to me any more but seeing Paul, touching Paul, being touched by Paul. I know that this weekend he is opening his Lake Rosseau cottage with Millicent and the grandchildren. I am so consumed by venomous jealousy that my heart actually aches—

jealousy of his wife and of his family, of his sailboat and his motor launch, of his television stations, of everything that keeps him from me, of everything that he enjoys without me. It's a feeling so murderous and so bottomless and so pointless and so disgusting that all I can do is despise myself more.

Crawling to the room I am sharing with Arlene, holding my guts like someone eviscerated in battle, I fumble through my suitcase till I find my date book. I flip at random to October 31, 1973, still four months away, across a sea of blank squares, each representing an unused day in my life. Halloween, the festival of cats and witches—why not? With black pen, I scratch it out, vowing that will be the last day I'll remain on planet Earth in the anguished and humiliating state in which I now find myself.

Back and forth the princess paces, tearing her blond hair out by its roots. Wearing Arlene's scornful expression, the queen draws her scissors from her bodice. "I didn't know it was possible to hate another person so much."

I sit at my desk, staring out at the illuminated Toronto skyline, still struggling to write the sequel to Pandora, trying to take my heroine through her high-school years, but producing only fossilized polemic—from my head and not from my gut, now otherwise engaged. Usually I don't work in the evening but tonight I'm expecting a call from Paul, which I want to answer in the privacy of the den. I stare malevolently at the silent white instrument as if I might possess magical powers—the same delusion that helped me through Hamilton High when I was just as crazy. It rings. I snatch it.

"Hello?"

A male voice, but the wrong one. For Danny.

Struggling to control disappointment, I call to him as he reads his newspaper in the living room. Then I try to return to my typewriter, but the false hope offered by that ringing phone has unleashed all my insecurities. My suitcase is packed for tomorrow's trip with Paul. My lies are all in place—a reading from my novel at a library in Ottawa on September 3.

Ever since I presented this fictitious weekend engagement to Danny, with my sentences too well rehearsed, no eye contact and too many unscheduled pauses, the silence between us has been intense and the loneliness unending. How much does he suspect? I have no way of gauging. We've never met this situation before, never even come close.

As yet, no accusations have been made. We're both too terrified to crack the veneer of our perfect marriage for fear that, once pronounced imperfect, we'll never get it shiny again. These are the days of eggshell silences. No words said that we might wish unsaid—just private misery during which we watch our kitten at play while issuing comments on the Grade One reading level. "Oh, look, see what Ting-Ling has done. Run, Ting-Ling, run." Each evening, Danny spends longer in the bath. I watch TV shows I never see. We both drink too much.

Now I hear Danny's voice rising and falling in false joviality: "Ha ha ha."

I watch the clock—9:05 . . . 9:15. If Paul phones and the line is busy, will he wait until tomorrow? My irritation converts into what it really is—desperation. Please, get off the phone!

9:23. With Paul no news is bad news. Dare I phone him? I picture him at his desk in his bathrobe, a cigar in one hand, a brandy in the other, waiting for Danny to get off the line. No voices. Can it be? I pick up the phone, hear the dial tone, replace it, leaving sweaty fingerprints. Ring, damn you!

9:31. The walls of the den are closing in. If only I could have gone for a walk this afternoon, but the bloody phone kept me attached to it like a hopeful adolescent in crinolines and waistcincher.

10:00. Too late. Paul won't call now. I go into the other room, relieved at least to give up the vigil. To know the worst.

Danny looks up from his paper. He studies my face. "What's the matter?" His voice is genuinely concerned. "Are you ill?"

For a crazy moment I feel the urge to confide. Whatever

else, Danny's still my best friend. Instead, I mumble: "I guess it's just the curry I had at noon."

"Want a drink?"

"Please. I'd love one."

"What were you doing when I was on the phone?" He hands me a gin and tonic. "I could hear you pacing in the den."

"Really? Sometimes I do that when I can't get a scene right—which is most of the time these days."

I put the icy drink to my forehead.

The phone rings. Danny reaches for it. I know instantly from his forced tone that it's Paul. "No, no. That's okay. We were just sitting here. I'll put her on." Sounding both kind and wretched at the same time, he asks me: "Is this what you were waiting for?" Am I that transparent?

Gratitude overcomes guilt as I accept the receiver. "Hello. Oh hi!"

"Sorry I didn't get to you sooner."

"Fine."

"How are you feeling?"

"Fine."

"That's good because I want you to know I have no control over what's happened."

"Yes?"

"Millicent came back from the cottage today."

"What does that mean?"

"Well, we can't go."

"Why?"

"We can't, that's all."

I steal a look at Danny, head cocked in my direction but pretending not to listen—the ruse of the outsider, the child, the servant, the wronged mate. Voice flat, I risk another round of cryptics: "I don't see the connection."

"She'd smell a rat."

"That's just something else to be dealt with."

"There's more. It's too complicated to explain."

"It's necessary."

"I see. You're going to be difficult." His voice becomes petulant. "It's a family matter. She's planned a party for Lulu and the kids. Before they return to school in New York. I can't skip it—our grandchildren, after all." He adds placatingly: "Look, I know this must be difficult for you. I'll call you tomorrow."

"But—"

"Believe me, I'm as disappointed as you, but I've had this sprung on me." His voice turns steely. "I'd hoped you'd understand."

I hold the receiver long after the click, trying to compose myself while slipping down the slimy slope into hysteria, murmuring an occasional phrase, pretending Paul and I are still talking, frantically trying to invent more lies to get me out of the first set. Danny is still pretending to read his paper, but his hands are shaking—as much as mine.

I put down the phone. He puts down his paper. All I want is private space in which to explode, but I don't dare leave the room.

Danny hands me my abandoned drink. "I think you need this."

It's something to hold. The kitten is playing with her tail, her paws loud in the awful silence. Danny makes a compassionate move toward me as if to comfort me. Involuntarily, I raise my free hand like a traffic cop: no! He recoils. More silence. It piles around us like snow in winter.

Snap. Danny's fingers break the stem of his martini glass. Blood spurts from his palm. I move toward him. He raises his bloodied hand: stop! He rushes toward the bathroom. I suspect he's going to be sick. I rush to the kitchen. I soak up the spilled martini with paper towels. The kitten is zigzagging across the room, chasing the olive. When Danny returns, his hand is wrapped with gauze through which blood seeps. Summing up six months of misery, he asks: "What's been happening to us? This is no marriage."

He waits for the denial. Words stick like ice cubes in my throat.

He pushes forward, testing: "Do you want me to leave? Is that it?"

He's taking the traditional stance—the husband goes, the wife stays. It's the position of gallantry, for which I'm grateful, but also of control, so that he'll know exactly where I am. Here it is, the great divide. We've passed all the old warning signs and rushed headlong to the precipice without so much as one relevant quarrel. I want to offer reassurances. I listen, horrified, to my own silence.

Danny's voice is in the lowest of registers: "Well?"

It's only now I realize how bad things really are. I am a rocket set in a trajectory. No sad or bitter consequence has any reality for me. A voice I don't recognize answers: "Yes. If you don't mind, Danny. Please."

We stare at each other, amazed the question has been asked and even more stunned by the answer.

"Well, then." Pride will not allow him to back down. He's taken his gamble and he's lost. Already I'm feeling profoundly sorry for him, for me, for us. "I guess I'd better pack."

He heads for the bedroom. I trail after him, then sit helplessly on the bed, eyes rolled back in my head, hands folded, as he opens drawers—slowly at first, like a kid who's threatened to leave home, confident he'll be called back. His actions grow more purposeful, more hostile, more polite. "Have you seen my blue socks? I have an early meeting tomorrow. Do you mind if I take the toothpaste?" He's holding his left arm like a broken wing, the way his father did after his stroke. He's done that a lot lately. Oh my God, oh: "Danny—"

Of course, he turns. Of course, he drops the blue socks. "What's that?"

I bite my lip, sorry to have offered false hope. "Nothing."

We chat on and on, our voices hollow. Nothing. "I'll have to come back for the shirts in the laundry." Nothing. "I'll check into the Park Plaza. It's closest." Nothing. The kitten plays with one of Danny's ties, pulling it from his suitcase. Nothing. "Well, then." Nothing. He closes the suitcase with a final snap, picks it up with his right hand, feels the bandage, then switches it to the left. Nothing. "Well, then." He chucks Ting-Ling under the chin. "I guess you're on your own, little girl." Nothing.

Danny walks stiffly to the door. I follow, making no attempt to close the distance, afraid to let his shadow fall upon me, afraid even that will have the power to collapse me, knowing that whatever lies ahead is better than the festering untruths, the screaming hurts, the split inside me—half a heart, one lung, torn and bleeding viscera. Already, at least, I feel the relief of that.

The door clicks open. Danny crosses the threshold. I suspect even now he believes he'll soon be returning, that this is a fluke to be ironed out, the kind of thing one ruefully recalls on a fiftieth wedding anniversary. "Remember, dear, when . . ." I doubt he has any idea what is happening. Neither do I, but in these vivid moments of special insight I have a vision of our future, and it is very, very bleak.

The door closes. The lock snaps. So do I. I fall to the floor as if my spine had broken.

I remember . . . the first time Danny and I saw Paris. We arrived on a balmy, rain-washed spring evening when everything smelled of blossoms and wet loam. From the window of our pensione we see it framed in blowing lace: the Eiffel Tower, illuminated like a lighthouse over a sea of tiled roofs. Abandoning our bags, we slide down the creaky elevator, leave our key with the henna-haired concierge, then start toward it through a lane of boarded-up shops, down glistening cobbled streets that zig in one direction then zag in another so the tower disappears on our left only to pop up on our right. The faster and farther we walk, the more it seems to elude us.

Now we are following the Seine as it laps its sinuous way through the city—under arches, past boarded bookstalls, down boulevards that open like flowers into parks and palaces, seeing the whole of Paris stretched out as if in our palms, but running now, hypnotized, toward the lighted tower, so compelling that we have ceased to notice the rest.

At last . . . we stand at the base of the Eiffel Tower and look up: this is no postcard, this is real. Still holding hands, we admire its reflection in the water, its girders like a glowing spiderweb. We turn back to the tower itself: it is gone. We spin around to the reflection: gone.

Someone had turned out the lights.

And so it was with our marriage. One moment it was the centerpiece for which the rest of our lives existed. The next it was not. Someone—myself?—had turned out the lights.

CATS

O nce I had a lover. The lover had a wife.
   Once I had a magic cat . . .

On a foggy day in late September, I move my personal effects in green garbage bags to a duplex in an older section of Toronto called the Annex. "Personal effects"—that which accompanies a corpse. Helen inches along the slippery streets in her station wagon. A hostile Ting-Ling digs her claws into my flesh as impersonally as into green plastic.

I am trying to explain the unexplainable. "In some ways a good marriage is more vulnerable than a bad one because the expectations are so high. It becomes its own yardstick, and you never want to settle for less."

Helen doesn't respond. I try again. "Danny and I have always done everything together. Anything one of us didn't like, we ended up not doing. Now it seems we've both chopped off big hunks of ourselves—like Cinderella's ugly sister hacking off toes to get into the glass slipper."

Helen still hasn't responded. I give it my last shot. "Danny saved my life by giving me unconditional love, the way a good parent does. Now I sense that I have to leave the nest and get on with my journey. He feels terrible, so do I, but men get a second chance that women don't get. He'll probably marry a younger woman and have a family—I hope he does, he'd make a wonderful father. Very few men are as capable of love. I still love him, I always will, but he deserves more than I can give him."

Helen slides into my new driveway, slick with rain. "I see. You left Danny for no reason. I suppose that's why most of us do the important things in our lives."

I start to explain once again then break off: I left because I left.

*

Even in drizzle, with soggy brown leaves piling up in the gutters, my new neighborhood has an authenticity which, in any season, is charm. I thought I preferred high-rise, but now I'm delighted by how comfortable I feel with my feet on the ground amidst sagging board fences, howling cats and curbside garbage cans.

I buy secondhand furniture from Crippled Civilians. In the past I've liked my environment lean and sleek. Now I find myself putting ruffles on things. My single bed (half the king-size I left behind) is a cascade of white frills. In the shank of morning, I sew gingham pillows—the first time I've done such a preposterous thing since Grade Eight home economics when I made a pincushion. The tiny stitches steady my nerves. Now the room looks like that of an indulged fifties teenager with ponytail and a charm bracelet—the Debbie Reynolds that in high school I refused to be while secretly yearning to be. A white princess phone completes the illusion. Though it looks pretty, it causes me no less trouble than the one I left behind. It doesn't ring when it's supposed to. When it does, I often don't like what it says.

I've never lived by myself before. Sometimes I eat breakfast at 4:00 a.m. and sometimes at noon. Often I feel excitement as if I've picked up the threads of my own story after a long sleep. Often I feel drugged. I lose weight no matter what I eat. My greatest luxury is an emotional one—a time and a place to weep. Inside these walls I don't have to pretend anything to anyone any more. Sometimes I weep for Danny, and sometimes for myself, and sometimes I weep old and desperate tears for reasons unknown to me. Then I sleep.

Danny and I have dates—evenings full of dashed hopes and ragged silences with the conversation doubling back to the same thing.

"When are you coming home?"

"Danny. You promised."

"But what else is there to talk about? I want you to know how I feel—how I'll always feel."

Silence.

He manages to grin. "See? I told you there was nothing else to talk about. How's Ting-Ling?"

"Terrific! She loves having a garden." I stop: to imply either one of us is happier without Danny is cruel; to imply we're not gives false hope. "How are you?"

"Miserable. I hate living in our apartment by myself. All the plants are dying."

"You're probably watering them too much, feeding them too much."

A wry smile. "That sounds like me."

He takes a deep breath, more like a gulp. "There's something I have to ask. Is there someone else?"

Staring at the white knuckles wrapped around his drink, I reply: "No."

An exhalation of air as his chest relaxes, his fingers loosen. Instinctively, I understand my answer was the right one. He had to ask but didn't want to know. I also sense it is a true one. By now I'm sure I had to leave Danny anyway, though I don't understand why. Why? It makes no sense. Only that I am compelled. Why?

Danny parks our little red Jaguar in front of my first-floor duplex, walks me to my door. "I don't want to come in. I don't want to see how you live without me." Sliding his hands into his pockets, he straightens his shoulders with a jerky motion, then saunters down the path like a kid kicking dirt and whistling. I watch him leave, sensing that I won't be seeing him for a long time. The stage has been cleared—but for what?

I sit at my desk looking into a backyard tangled with pumpkin vines, red sumach and wild roses. Ting-Ling plays with my paper-clips, with my fingers on my typewriter keys, with her own shadow. A cat was my first friend. I love cats. I trust them. Often I dream I am this cat. As she settles on my lap, I pull a page from my typewriter and I read:

There are many ways to tell a love story. You
can tell it from the viewpoint of each of the lovers;
you can tell it through the eyes of a partial or
impartial observer; you can tell it omnisciently as if
through the mind of God; you can study it
anthropologically with regard to evolution or
species survival; you can interpret it sociologically
in terms of the mating habits of a particular culture
at a particular time; you can analyze it
psychologically from the premises of any number of
a dozen schools of thought. All these approaches
produce their own truths, even though some may
seem contradictory. Each version becomes a lie only
when it masquerades as the only way of telling the
story, the only truth.

A polished paragraph but bloodless, its emotion killed
by analysis. My eyes drift to a copy of Pandora. I can
barely remember writing it. Where did that gush of pain come
from?

On my desk is a photo of Paul in his naval uniform—the
one Lulu and I used to swoon over, smuggled to me by Paul
as a joke. Stuck in the frame is an invitation shaped like a
black cat. Looping Ting-Ling's leash, I frame the picture in
a noose:

CKMO-TV
invites you to attend
a Halloween celebration
at Hadwin Inn
October 31, 8:00 p.m.
Come as your happiest fantasy.

The invitation is from Paul, now majority shareholder of
station CKMO-TV. There is also a condominium on the water-
front, though I have yet to see it. Laying the cornerstone of
his ambitions has not been without personal sacrifice—mine.

The phone rings. I'm expecting Paul, but it is my mother, calling from St. Cecilia's Infirmary where my father is a permanent resident. "Since you're heading out west tomorrow I knew you'd want the latest report." The tone of her voice tells me that I should want it.

"Yes, I was going to phone." My voice is tinged with resentment. "How is father?"

"About the same." A heavy sigh. "Yesterday I was knitting by his bed when he began to sob in a heartbroken child's voice: 'Daddy's dead, daddy's dead.' He seemed to be reliving his own father's death when he was six. What sort of a life is it when he doesn't know where he is half the time?"

"He's probably better off reliving the past than fretting about the hospital food. It's unfinished business—what he needs to do."

"Do you think so? I've never looked at it that way."

As she speaks, I find myself staring at the photo of Paul with my father's image in mind. The broad cheekbones, the intense blue eyes, the vertical lines bracketing the mouth are very much the same, now that my father's lost so much weight. Automatically, I add the injured left leg, so long propped on a hassock, thinking of Paul's limp. Why didn't I notice these things before? I'm still giddily absorbing all this as my mother continues: "When are you coming back from Banff?"

Banff? "Ah, in three weeks." I rattle on, still staring at the photo, feeling very strange. "The first week is vacation." With Paul. "Then I'm teaching at a writers' workshop."

"Let me know your phone number. I always like to have it in case of an emergency."

It's four-thirty when I hang up. For several seconds I continue to stare at Paul's photo. *Aunt Estelle. Aunt Estelle. We share the bloodstone.* I don't like the constriction in my throat or the nausea in my belly. I lie down on my ruffled bed. Ting-Ling curls at my feet. I fall into a sleep so deep it's like a swoon.

I am a princess lying on a bier in the forest, my hands folded over a jeweled gown. Aunt Estelle cuts a swatch of

*my hair and presents it to my father. Now I am standing by
the bier, holding the blond hair, looking at the princess. Through
the glass floor of the forest I see a ticktacktoe game marked
with Xs and Os. Pointing to the princess, Aunt Estelle announces: "She's not dead yet, but she is dying."*

I come to slowly, overpowered by an awesome sense of
loss, of death. *I am a princess lying on a bier in the forest . . .
She's not dead yet, but she is dying.* I feel the need to hold
onto this dream, to try to understand it, but the phone is
ringing, erasing the images as if from a tape. I fumble for the
receiver.

A cheerful baritone: "Hi! Are you packed?"

I strive to match Paul's lighthearted tone. "Mostly."

"Good, I don't know when I've looked forward to something so much. Five days in the Rockies—what a bonanza!
I'm really ready for this."

"Me, too."

"When I packed Millicent and her sister off for New York
you could have heard my sigh all the way to Rockefeller
Center. I'll pick you up at ten. Usually I board as the plane's
leaving the runway, but this time I'm not taking any chances."

"Wonderful!"

We chat some more—a luxury with Paul, who specializes
in three-minute phone calls. As the conversation winds down,
I reassure myself: "See you this evening?"

"Of course, but don't be upset if I don't have much time.
I'll be tied up with the press—a promotional party, after all."

"I understand. How will I recognize you?"

"That's easy. I'm going as the King of Hearts—don't you
think that's perfect typecasting? Actually, it's my secretary's
idea. I sent her to the prop department and that's what she
came back with."

"Swell. I'm going as a cat. A black cat." Also perfect
typecasting.

I put down the phone in gratitude. No conditionals, no
loose ends, no last-minute changes. Returning to my desk, I
write a note to the student who is feeding Ting-Ling while

I'm gone, then check over the seminar I've prepared for my writing workshop.

At seven-thirty I climb into the tub. As usual, Ting-Ling follows me from boudoir to bathroom, rolling my lipstick from the mirrored counter, playing with her reflection as well as mine. I put on a long-sleeved, black velvet formal, add a white fox ski helmet, to which I've sewn felt ears, and a white muff into which I can retract red claws. Last of all, I draw charcoal whiskers, using Ting-Ling as a life model.

At nine o'clock, I take a taxi to Hadwin Inn, located in a crisscross of expressways in Toronto's Don River valley. The ceiling of the ballroom is hung with swirling mirrored balls that send splintered light slithering over the guests. I look for Paul. There he is, the King of Hearts, resting his gimpy left leg against the bandstand. I start toward him, intending to make brief contact, then freeze. Beside him, matching him satin heart for satin heart and crown for crown, is Millicent, the Queen of Hearts. Together, they hold court.

As I veer away Paul looks up, catches my eye. Shrugging, he rolls his eyes to the ceiling. For the next hour I zigzag from friend to acquaintance, like a character trapped in a fun-house maze, getting back distorted images of myself every time I confront yet another pair of mirror eyes. There's Joker Nash, dressed as a magician. ("But why would Pandora get into the breadman's wagon?") And Babs Bertoli, now his fiancée, dressed as a cancan girl. ("A guy comes into this psychiatrist's office wearing a fried egg sunnyside up on his head and three strips of bacon dangling from each ear.") There's the staff of "Late Night," the TV-journal for which I'm a critic. ("The television job was just a transparent blind to see you again. Didn't you guess that?") There's Herb Swamp, newly appointed advertising director of Paul J. Lawson Productions, dressed as a pirate. ("There rust and let me die.") I'm amazed at how effortless I can make it all seem, how serenely I smile through my whiskers as I carry on conversations I can no longer hear, drinking glass after glass of champagne, feeling myself rise toward the twirling baubles on the ceiling.

Now the King of Hearts is at my sleeve, the red-satin heart on his chest beating. "Aren't you going to say anything?"

Champagne in one hand, the other buried in my white muff, I inquire: "How bad is it?"

"The worst. I can't go with you tomorrow."

"How come?"

"Millicent arrived back from New York today. Her sister had an abscessed tooth, and then there was something wrong with their reservations at the Waldorf."

"How does that affect our trip?"

"She wants to go to Vancouver with me."

"Vancouver?"

"That's where I'm supposed to be. I could hardly say I was goofing off on a holiday to the mountains without her. I told her I was working on another acquisition in Vancouver—that was my cover. Now she wants to go with me and visit friends. What a mess! I could end up with a bloody TV station in Vancouver just to appease her." He seems to think that's a merry joke, or else he's as giddy as I am. He laughs long and loud, his red-satin heart pulsing. "I had Miss Phipps working for hours, canceling my reservations and getting us into the Bayshore."

"Canceling our reservations, yours and mine."

"No, you can still take the holiday. I'll look after all that, but I had to cancel my part."

"Why didn't you just tell Millicent she couldn't go with you?"

"She's my wife, damn it!"

"Precisely."

Now when my daddy plays with me I feel smothered, as if I'm drowning. My head grows dizzy with fatigue.

"Look, can't we talk about this later? Everyone's watching."

I struggle to separate myself from that which possesses me.

"Where? At my place?"

"Hardly. God, how should I know? You have no idea what I've been through. I'll call you tomorrow."

Shut up! Do you hear me? What will the neighbors think?

"Aren't I leaving for the Rockies tomorrow?"

"Oh yeah. I'm not seeing straight. Please, be reasonable. Everyone's looking at us. Lower your voice. We'll sort it out somehow, but frankly all that's on my mind right now is getting this show on the road. You'll have to live with that."

If you don't shut up, I'll send you to the place where all bad children go when their parents don't want them any more—an orphanage where they lock up bad children.

"I can't live with it."

"You're not going to hold a gun to my head. I take that very badly."

Desperation makes me bold.

"Millicent has a gun to your head and it seems to work very well."

"That's just part of the package. Hell, I'm too old for this. Will you get out of my way? I've got work to do."

At last I say the won't-love-me words:

"No, I won't. I have to settle it this evening."

"Be quiet! Everyone is looking."

I don't care! I don't care! I don't care!

"Then let's give everyone something to look at."

She smashes her left fist into her daddy's belly. "Touch me again, and I'll kill you!" He doesn't resist. He doesn't fight back. So that is all it took, would have taken.

I strike Paul in the satin heart with my left fist, breaking my champagne glass. Dragging a bloody palm across his chest, *I leave my king with a bleeding heart.*

Costumed party goers are still arriving as I depart. "Which way is downtown Toronto?"

Several arms point in the same direction.

"Thanks." I start down the highway.

"Hey, you're not going to walk, are you? It's six miles."

Not I really, but my other self, now in full control of my mind and body.

I'm amazed how easily the yards click by. It's as if I were running barefoot on grass instead of striding in three-inch heels on cinders. Despite the chill in the air, I'm confident my decision to walk is the right one. Everything is falling into place. *Mostly I'm just holding my breath, feeling dizzy, like when the big boys push you too high on a swing.*

I have a plan—a plan I've been hatching for a long time, perhaps all my life. I even know the tree—a dying red maple, conveniently placed in a cemetery, right on my route. My head feels clear. All these thoughts seem perfectly logical, perfectly reasonable as I click click along the Don Valley Parkway toward central Toronto. For years the image of the noose has hung tantalizingly overhead. *My grandfather, my aunt* . . . Now that I've made up my mind to accept its invitation, relief is instantaneous and palpable. *She's not dead yet, but she is dying.*

I'm glad the night is clear, though I'm not sure why that matters. The stars are as bright as they can be when competing with the lights of Toronto and several lines of traffic. I suppose I should be walking against the cars but the highway's shoulder is a broad one. When they swing close they catch me in their headlights. Most slow down, no doubt surprised to see a woman dressed as a cat walking along an unlit highway, but I refuse to look their way, to slacken my pace or otherwise show uncertainty that might invite anyone into my life.

Now I'm passing a viaduct. The light from a three-quarter moon slickers a pond thirty feet below. It vaguely occurs to me that I could jump off the viaduct, thus saving myself the walk, but I seem unable to stop the click click click of my feet moving without fatigue and of their own volition.

Another sweep of headlights. Again, my shadow shoots in front of me. Behind me cinders crunch, wheels brake. Determinedly, I stride forward. A male voice calls my name. I turn. Not Paul. Three people in a car—Herb Swamp, Babs and Joker. Herb opens the door, enticing me. "Come on, get in."

Joker grins through a window, in whiteface and top hat. "We'll give you a ride."

I smile, absolutely calm, entirely self-possessed. "No thank you. I'm fine. Really, I want to walk. I need the fresh air."

Herb hesitates. My deportment is flawless—except I happen to be strolling along an expressway, dressed as a cat. But then Herb is dressed as a pirate. Joker is a magician. Babs is a cancan girl. It's a crazy night.

"Are you sure?"

It's clear I'm not going to get into the car unless forced. They're afraid to go that far, to break through the usual adult courtesies of choice and privacy. In other words, to declare me mentally incompetent. With great reluctance, Herb closes the door.

"Be careful," calls Babs as the car edges away, no doubt with many backward glances and much debate.

That same scene is repeated with other friends, other strangers. My trump card is my steely, smiling, touch-me-not calm. Like a cat, I'm protecting home territory—in this case, my definition of myself.

By the time I get to the turnoff for the cemetery, I've failed to resolve the basic problem involved in a suicide by hanging—where to get a rope and how to string it. I'm forced to admit my hanging fantasy is too complicated for spontaneous—ha ha—execution. I check my resolve, much like one checks a pulse, to see if it has weakened. Certainly, the civilizing effect of familiar streets and buildings, as opposed to the featureless highway, has taken a toll of my single-minded goal, but when I go back to first principles, I'm faced with my inability to imagine myself without my relationship with Paul to focus me. The rest of my personality has disintegrated. I have no other life but *daddy won't love me love me love me*.

I draw up a second plan, centered on the sleeping pills in my medicine cabinet. I'll collect those pills then check into a hotel. That way friends won't be forced to deal with the body. Again, I'm proud of my logic, of my cool decision-making abilities, like a cancer patient choosing her own cemetery plot, arranging for the church, selecting the hymns.

It's almost 3:00 a.m. when I arrive at my flat. Even as I'm opening the door, my phone is ringing. Like Pavlov's dog trained to its bone, I run to snatch it. A male voice: "Thank

God! Are you okay?" Not Paul. Herb Swamp, wanting reassurances.

"Yes, I'm fine. Honest."

I've barely hung up when the phone rings again. This time it's Babs. "Yes, really, I'm all right. I guess I had too much to drink."

Another call and another and another, each flinging a rope across the void through which I have been tumbling, weaving a safety net. I'm touched by the intense concern and the lack of censure. I'm also startled to learn how conspicuous my actions have been. I hadn't intended to make such a public statement. *If you tell* . . .

Exhausted, I lie down on my bed where Ting-Ling is curled. Again, I don't so much fall asleep as pass out. Again, my dream is intense:

I am curled in a tight ball, still wearing my cat costume. Everything is very dark, very still, as if I were in a cellar.

When I awake the sun is streaming through my window. My first response is joy. Here is the day I didn't expect to see. Then I look at my packed suitcase, remember the plane I've missed and, with a fist to the stomach, everything else. Unable to drag myself from bed, I plunge back into sleep, *back into the cellar. Now I am a cat with a red leash wound like an umbilical cord around my neck. Someone is yanking it. I'm looking down a long dark tunnel, and I'm choking. An alarm goes off. I count the rings: thirteen . . . fourteen . . . fifteen . . .* The phone is ringing. I know before I answer who this will be.

"Hello."

A long silence. He is breathing heavily on the other end. "I guess you realize you've destroyed everything between us, don't you? After last night I could never trust you again. I'm surprised you didn't just phone the newspapers and give them the story. Millicent is hysterical. I've been up all night. She's been threatening God knows what."

Paul's voice slows down, becomes as exhausted as I feel. He waits for a response. When there is none, he plunges on.

"I suppose you won't believe this after all that's happened, but I hoped, more than anything else in my life, that we could work something out. I guess we're just two kinds of people, that's all. We'd better call a halt before we kill each other."

I stick my head under the covers. Sometime after noon I get up. As I scrub off the remains of the cat whiskers, I remember I haven't seen Ting-Ling since . . . when?

My back door is ajar on its night chain. Apparently I forgot to close it. Going into the yard, I call: "Here, puss puss puss." Still dressed in slippers and housecoat, I continue into the alley, calling: "Here, puss puss puss." *If you tell . . .*

I explore the entire block, at first in haste and then with diligence—behind bushes, under cars and verandas, through leaf piles. I ask everyone I meet: "Have you seen a big white cat?" *I've looked under the back stoop by the pail where I am hatching pollywogs for a frog circus. I've knocked on every door in the block and ransacked every garbage pail from the railway tracks clear through to the setting sun, sometimes crawling on all fours to get the proper perspective.* As far as I know, Ting-Ling has been gone since nine o'clock this morning, perhaps since four or five a.m. *If you tell . . . If you tell . . . If you tell . . .* Now, the sun is setting. *If you tell . . .*

I spend that evening and the next day calling animal shelters and visiting a couple of them. I find another very friendly white cat but not Ting-Ling.

For the next three days I advertise on trees and in newspapers, and solicit the help of neighborhood kids. *I know if my cat is dead it must be my fault, but I can't remember telling anything unless I've accidentally whispered it at night to the monster in the dark.*

When I'm not out searching for Ting-Ling, I'm in my ruffled bed with the covers over my head. I mourn my lover. I mourn my husband. I mourn my cat. Lost husband, lost lover, lost cat—everything is mixed together, everything is loss loss loss, impossible to unweave.

*

A week later, I'm once again packing to take the plane west to Banff—clothes, notebooks all in a who-cares jumble. The doorbell rings. A workman in thick boots and a floppy hat stands outside my door. He leans against a pitchfork, his manner apologetic. "Are you the lady who lost the cat?" He removes his floppy hat. "I was cleaning leaves from the cellar drain next door and . . ."

I follow him to my neighbor's on the left, down three steps, then through a broken door into a cellar tunnel. I find Ting-Ling, her body frozen in an antic position like a Halloween cat electrified against the moon. *My red leash is wound like an umbilical cord around my neck. Someone is yanking on it. I'm looking down a long dark tunnel, and choking . . .*

The workman points to a puddle of foam by her open jaws, like a cartoon speech balloon with nothing in it. "That's vomiting. She choked somehow—maybe poisoned herself."

I remove the red collar from around my pale white cat, then I wrap her in a pillowcase embroidered in daisies. Using his pitchfork, the workman digs a grave in my garden. I am devastated, and yet grateful. In a strange way that I don't understand, I know a scapegoat has been found. I know that now I'm not going to have to kill myself. *Till death do us part.*

MY FATHER'S HOUSE

Once I had a husband.
    Once I had a lover. The lover had a wife.
Once I had a magic cat.
Once . . .

I am floating in a hot mineral pool, my hands folded across my chest, my hair fanned like seaweed. Halfway down the valley, set in pine forest, is the Banff Centre, where I am teaching creative writing. Beyond that are the snow-peaked Rockies tipped in morning sunlight. Whenever I can, I spend an early hour here. For many months now I haven't recognized myself, or understood myself, or liked myself. The womb-temperature sulfur water soothes.

Someone is calling—one of my teaching colleagues, waving her arms on the pool deck. I swim over. "Your mother phoned. She wants you to call right back."

"Did she say what it was about?"

"No, but she was at a hospital. Here's the number."

I look at the torn envelope. St. Cecilia's Infirmary . . . *for Cripples and Incurables.*

"I'll use the pay phone inside."

Shivering despite my towel, I dial the infirmary number. First the long-distance operator, then a switchboard operator, then a nurse. "Yes, your mother's here. I'll call her."

My mother's voice is careful but controlled: "Hello?"

"I got your message. What's wrong?"

"The doctor says daddy can't last the night. It's pneumonia. He's having a hard time catching his breath."

My father opens his blue eyes, vivid against the whiteness of hair, of skin, of sheet.

"I'm not sure how fast I can get a plane."

"He was asking for you."

"Thanks for coming, Estelle."

*

It's after ten by the time I get back to my room at the Banff Centre. My hands are shaking so hard it's difficult to open drawers.

A knock on my door—three teaching colleagues, faces somber. One has an Air Canada flight schedule: "A plane leaves Calgary at 4:30. We've made a reservation for you. I'll drive you to the airport."

The second assures me: "I'll cancel your student appointments."

And the third: "I'll take your afternoon seminar."

They're doing all the thoughtful things friends do yet . . . *too soon, too soon.* "Please, don't make me get on that plane," I plead like a child. "Please, please don't make me. I can't get on that plane."

They stare in bewilderment, then in rueful compassion. "I nearly missed my father's funeral," one admits. "I was drunk. My sister didn't speak to me for a year."

"My mother's in a nursing home. I often have to force myself to visit her," another confesses.

"A plane leaves Calgary tomorrow morning at 9:50. It gets into Toronto airport at 3:20 Eastern Time—that's a three-and-a-half-hour flight with a two-hour time change."

The doctor says daddy can't last the night.

"I'll take that."

Like a sleepwalker I float through the next few hours, compelled by the clock from one rendezvous to another, mouthing teacher-student advice that manages to sound relevant, my guilt at not having rushed to my father's death-side overcome by an almost pathetic gratitude at my reprieve.

I return to my room. It's 2:45. My body feels heavy, my head light. I lie down on my bed, *my eyes closed, my hands folded across my jeweled gown* . . . I've just dozed off when an unearthly shriek awakens me. I stare out my window to the mountains. Was that sound real, or just inside my head? I look at my watch. Exactly three. I think: my father could be dying at this very moment and I wouldn't even know it.

At five o'clock that evening, I again phone home—the dutiful daughter, delayed by circumstances beyond her control, checking in. My mother's line is busy. Ten minutes later, it's still busy. It stays that way till nearly six.

By the time I hear my mother's voice, I've already read the signs. She confirms: "Daddy passed away at five o'clock." She continues, as if supplying vital information: "I know it was exactly five because I looked at my watch."

I put down the phone, relieved to know I couldn't have reached my father's deathbed even if I had tried, yet puzzled: five o'clock? Did my father die as I was phoning home? How unlike my mother not to be at the hospital.

I go to bed that night with my suitcase packed, content to be taking the morning plane. Midnight. Two o'clock. Three. I jolt awake. Again I've heard that sound like a rusty nail dragged across a blackboard sky. This time I recognize it. It's the whistle of a train, but weirdly amplified—one drawn-out shriek shattering the glassy air, the same sound I might have heard a dozen times a day but chose to notice only twice: now and at three this afternoon. That was three o'clock Mountain Time, meaning five o'clock Eastern Time. I make the connection I previously blocked. My father had died at precisely the time both I and my mother had looked at our watches. For whom the bell tolls? It tolls for me.

A colleague drives me to Calgary airport next morning. I board the 9:50 plane to Toronto feeling diffuse, disconnected. Over the prairies, I cry a little, still more from shock than grief. That may, or may not, come later. Certainly guilt. Guilt is the legacy I expect from my father's death, fair payment for the hate with which I shared my father's house, fair payment for the coldness with which I slammed his door.

As the limousine from Toronto airport speeds southwest along the Queen Elizabeth Way, I stare at subdivisions unsoftened by foliage, the barren remains of woodlots and a frozen orchard or two. And then Hamilton, dominated by the smokestacks of the Steel Company of Canada. We traverse the city through its downtown core, past the new civic buildings sleekly arising from the old, to a familiar tree-lined street under the Mountain brow.

Carrying my suitcase, I walk up the steps of my natal home, my father's house. I reach for the doorknob, polished shiny by many hands. Resigned to staying overnight for the first time in sixteen years, I step across the threshold.

I feel ... *strange*, in suspension, as if my father's house and not I were holding its breath. I feel—groping now for the elusive definition. I feel ... *not-terror*. Startled, I realize I've never before crossed this threshold without becoming paralyzed with fear. It's a feeling so deeply connected with this house that I can experience it only in its absence. Now I feel *not-terror*—a positive state. My father's house is just a house. Here, then, is my father's legacy: not guilt but relief—exaltation!

My mother greets me at the door with a tearful hug. "I haven't heard from Helen. She and Jeff left for Florida two days ago. If only she would call in!" A role reversal. The bad daughter is home, the reliable one is missing.

I comfort my mother by telling her about the train whistle and the clock. "The world's a stranger place than we sometimes realize. I believe Helen will understand that she must call home. She will get here for the funeral."

My mother is grateful. The longer I have stayed away the greater my credibility. "I remember how you used to sit beside Granny Cragg when she read teacups. Granny used to say, 'That child knows things!' "

I am deeply touched. My maternal grandmother's little kitchen on the second floor was the heart of the house. It radiated warmth into which you could creep. I am also resentful: Why didn't you ever tell me that before? When my grandmother's blessing would have meant so much to me. When I was the bad child. Why tell me now?

As I struggle against tears, my mother leaves the kitchen. She returns with a blond curl wrapped around her ring finger. Rubbing it to demonstrate its silkiness, she announces: "This was daddy's hair when he was seven."

As I stare at that swatch of hair, I grow dizzy, remembering how often my father claimed my blond curls came from him, but also remembering the princess dream I had ten days before, still vivid, still haunting.

I am a princess lying on a bier in the forest. Aunt Estelle cuts a swatch of my hair and presents it to my father. Now I am standing beside the bier, holding the blond hair, looking at the princess. Through the glass floor of the forest I see a ticktacktoe game, marked with Xs and Os. Pointing to the princess, Aunt Estelle announces: "She is not dead yet, but she is dying."

I stare queasily at the flaxen curl, feeling some connection between it and the swatch of hair in the dream, but not sure what that could be or why or how, overwhelmed by a sense of mystery, of crucial things too long forgotten. Again my mother leaves the room. This time she brings me a cardboard shirt box. "Your daddy kept this under his bed."

I open the box. I find dozens of pictures of myself that disappeared over the years, mostly those recording a tarty adolescence—myself in skimpy bathing suit, in a strapless gown, in basketball trunks, in cheerleading outfit, my mouth a too-red slash, my hair too blond, my stance too provocative, the poor man's Marilyn Monroe.

One picture is of my father—neatly dressed, as always, in shiny navy suit, the day he received the Steel Company's gold pin for forty years' faithful service.

My feeling of the uncanny is now so overpowering I must struggle to breathe. Though I don't understand, I sense that I hold in my hands a cardboard coffin in which I am imprisoned, from which I must seek release. *I am a princess lying on a bier in the forest . . . She is not dead yet, but she is dying.*

*

My father's body is laid out in Truscott Brothers' funeral home, no longer in the parlor as in the old days, the proper separation of life from death, its skillful anesthetization, discreet, dignified—a guest book, thick rugs, candelabra, middle-class respectability on loan for the cost of the funeral. How fragile he looks in his navy suit, his hands folded over his vest—this man who once weighed 350 pounds, or maybe even 400, a man for whom my mother bought extra-large shirts then added triangle inserts under the arms. On his finger he wears his Rough Rider football ring; his gray tie is neatly knotted.

My daddy's shirt buttons are pearly in the light. There's not much room on my daddy's lap because of his big fat tummy. His tummy feels warm against my cheek.

Visitors come and visitors go. Mostly acquaintances from St. James' Church, where my mother is still active, several neighbors, one or two men from the the Steel Company—all elderly, all in rehearsal for their own deaths a curve or two down the river. I playact my older sister's role, being good and being overpraised for it, mother's little helper, feeling fraudulent but not unhappy, like a child parading in someone else's clothes. Discovering exactly where, and how much, that shoe pinches.

In the pregnant space between death and burial, I wander through our three-story house, from room to room to room, seeing it as it used to be—the patch-on-patch chintz sofa iced with doilies; the walnut dining suite with twenty-four gargoyle legs to be dusted; my father's sagging fetch-me chair; the bowdlerized see-no-evil, hear-no-evil, speak-no-evil monkeys on the radio console. My father's bedroom, my father's bed with the inlay scroll . . . *my mother's disapproving lips.*

On impulse I board one of the trolley buses, which replaced the belt-line streetcars that once circled Hamilton. I travel past the Palace Theater, where we lined up to see Alan Ladd and Betty Grable and Esther Williams and Tyrone Power, past the no-frills Pagoda restaurant, which was my mother's version of dining out, to that skinny Victorian house where it all began, the house where my father was born.

Architecturally, it was a house of secrets, with its trapdoor leading through the kitchen linoleum into the cellar, an attic reached by a hole in the ceiling, a bedroom hidden behind a curtained closet, a bathroom ventilator from which you could spy on the kitchen, a potbellied parlor stove with black arms stretching upward as if in supplication. Now it is a red-brick real-estate office, its iron trim painted gaudy green, its torn lace curtains replaced by venetian blinds.

My father lifts me up so I can see a brown photo of a sailing ship in a gold frame. "Grandpa Jonah was a translator on that ship. Your grandfather died when I was your age. He spoke fourteen languages."

"Where did the sailing ship go?"

"From San Francisco to Japan. He was in the U.S. Navy."

"Did Grandmother Pearl sail with him?"

"No, grandpa met grandma in Germany, where she was born. He had his own import business by then. He shipped the finest china from Bavaria, the finest silk from Japan—stuff so beautiful it would knock out your eye."

I peer around the gloomy parlor, draped in dust. "Where is it now?"

My father's voice flattens like the boards of the incline. "In the depression . . ."

Helen does call home. She does arrive in time for the funeral. In the parlor chapel an elderly Reverend Thwaite speaks of "this tenderrr husband, this loving fatherrr, this gentle Christian, this fine example to us all."

My mother is nodding at each new platitude, apparently glad of this judicious whitewash, already believing it to be the truth: this man who quit school in Grade Eight to support his ailing mother, who didn't smoke or drink, who played no card games beyond cribbage or solitaire, who never took the Lord's name in vain; this good neighbor who tipped his hat on Sundays and commented Monday to Friday on the weather, who kept his snow shoveled and his leaves raked, paid his bills and never appeared on the front veranda in his undershirt.

My agitation builds. I'm surprised at my passion—not anger but indignation. Indignation for my father, for this lack of recognition during this, his last star turn. He had been a man stuffed full of rage. That was his truth and his tragedy. Aren't we even going to bury the right man?

The modest cortege threads around Hamilton Harbor, following a smudgy trail of smoke from the Steel Company. We bury my father's body in Woodlawn Cemetery, "At rest, 1891–1973," this man whom I hated and still can't remember why. As his coffin is lowered on creaky chains, I look at my watch—three o'clock—then I start to cry. *Daddy's dead, daddy's dead, daddy, daddy, daddy . . .*

REVELATION

SATAN'S CHILD

When my father died, he came alive for me. A door had opened, like a hole cut in air. It yawned before me, offering release—from what to where?

Before I could pass through it to wholeness and health, my other self would have to give up her secrets. Was she willing to be dragged from her closet into the klieg lights? Exposure meant the death of her dreams as well as her fears, of the princess as well as the guilty child. It meant dying as a separate personality. As for myself, did I truly wish to open the Pandora's box under my father's bed? How would I feel to discover that the prize, after four decades of tracing clues and solving riddles, was knowledge that my father had sexually abused me? Could I reconcile myself without bitterness to the amount of my life's energy that had gone into the cover-up of a crime?

Resolving that conflict took another ten years. During that time I lived an increasingly contented life within a network of close friends and wrote four novels, each rife with sexual violence that offended some critics and puzzled me. Where did this harsh impulse come from? I didn't know. Like the thirsty Tantalus floating in water he couldn't drink, I was compelled by an inner vision I couldn't see. From each book I learned something about myself that was of value, but I knew I was writing below my capabilities and that frustrated me.

I also felt drawn to read about, and to experiment with, various psychological disciplines. Through Freudian and Jungian analysis, I learned how to interpret dreams as messages from my unconscious. Through primal and massage therapy, rolfing, bioenergetics, yoga, meditation, I grew more in touch with my body and my emotions. Each discipline raised questions about my real past. Why had I been such an angry child? Why did I hate my father? What was the source of the icy terror I now sensed under that anger and hatred?

Unbeknownst to me, I was approaching a time when I

would remember. The obsession of a lifetime was drawing to a close. My path of revelation was to be the path of dreams— dreams triggered by physical shock.

I believe many unexpected deaths occur when a person finishes one phase of life and must become a different sort of person in order to continue. The phoenix goes down into the fire with the best intention of rising, then falters on the upswing. And so it was with me. At the point of transition, I came close to dying along with my other self.

I have a pain in my womb. It doesn't go away. Two doctors say I must have a hysterectomy. My response is stoical, but I have bad dreams.

I ride the incline up the Mountain. As I fumble for my fare, my purse plummets into dense undergrowth. I scramble barefoot through brambles under the incline, begging everyone I meet: "Have you seen my purse?"

I find a cleft in rock. A voice intones: "This is where the evil comes from." A child's hand reaches out. It's covered in slime and blood.

I check into Women's College Hospital in downtown Toronto one blustery day in February 1983. My operation is scheduled for the next morning. As an orderly wheels me into the corridor, my anesthetist clasps my hand. "Nothing to worry about. We'll be going in soon."

I climb down the perilous passage into the cave. A blond child is curled like a cat around her swollen belly. A demon-monster raped her here many years ago by stuffing a giant white larva down her throat. Now it has lodged in her womb, threatening her life. I fetch a priest. Dressed in white robes and mask, he raises his silver dagger with both hands, then plunges it into the girl's abdomen.

My mind awakens from the anesthetic but my body does not. It refuses to do what I request it to do, what it has always done. Nurses hook it up to machines, which perform its functions, duly recorded by numbers on dials. Nature, it seems, abhors a vacuum. Where once I nursed fibroids the size of a five-month fetus, now I nurture a virulent infection.

Another operation is scheduled and performed. This time I awake in a private room, very weak and still attached to my machines. The body, whose goodwill I once took for granted, still refuses to function. Friends drop by with flowers and kind words. I see them indistinctly. Nurses hover. The dials on my machines still do not say the right things. Another doctor joins the team. I hear talk of a third operation.

Inside the blond girl's womb the priest finds a fetus, half-human, half-animal. He holds it up by one cleft foot. "See Satan's child."

Since this blond girl produced it, she is responsible for it, even though she claims to have been under a powerful spell. A computer photo of the monster-father is released to the press. It is apelike, about three times human size and covered in shaggy fur. Its face is a devil's mask with holes for mouth and eyes. I am present as a reporter. I have an uneasy sense that I've seen this monster before, but how could that be?

The demon-monster lives on a grassy island. I cross the muddy channel, hand over hand, on a rope. It's even uglier than I thought, with scarlet mouth and bright green dangling warts. As I struggle back to the mainland, the monster comes shrieking in lust after me. Close up, he's more like an ordinary ape, but very savage, with vivid blue eyes and slathering razor teeth. He overtakes me when I'm still dangling over muddy water. I scream. The blond girl recalls him to the island, but not before he scrapes me with his filthy coat, leaving his rank smell on me.

Eventually my body does kick in, its function does become normal. The numbers on my machines stabilize, and the machines are removed. I'm dismissed from hospital. Yet, even back in my own bed, my dreaming mind continues its serialized hallucinations.

I am with my mother and sister in a shadowy garden in

the woods. Snakes, the exact shade of the barky earth, lurk everywhere, and sometimes they strike. A huge, oily, black serpent menaces me from a tree.

The garden opens onto a beach. As I stare at an imprint in the sand, a frightening thought strikes me. "Imagine if this mark and the one a mile away are part of the same footprint. Imagine how big the monster that left it would have to be!" And that is how it turns out. An enormous black thing lurches up up up up up up out of a rocky passageway until it is the height of a tall building. It is smooth and rubbery like the snake on the tree, but in the shape of a hulking black man. Does it have a face? It's too dark to tell.

I awaken overwhelmed by the size of this unknown thing confronting me. Believing myself to be on the murky path to revelation, I conjure up the same black snake man before falling asleep the next night. I ask myself: what does this mean? What am I afraid of?

The black shape transforms into a castle, highly polished and carved out of a single piece of ebony, like a chess piece. It is without doors or windows—an impenetrable fortress. I have a feeling that something evil happened in this place, or maybe in another place still too dark to see.

On subsequent nights the castle becomes a Victorian house—Other Grandmother's house.

Aunt Estelle sits on the porch, her waist strung with chains and padlocks, guarding the door. She looks like the black queen, except her blind eye has been plucked from her forehead, leaving a nasty hole. The dead carcasses of her four monkeys lie strewn at her feet—see-no-evil, hear-no-evil, speak-no-evil and the fourth with mutilated genitals.

I am a child of about eight. I go around and around the house with a flashlight looking for an opening. Though everything seems tightly boarded, I know I'll be able to sneak in through the cellar. In some way I already understand what is going to happen, but I must take this journey anyway. This house is just a starting place. I'm anxious to begin.

My dreams intensify, grow more specific.

I am outside my father's house. A lawn sign reads: "Home Truths." A man perches on the porch rail, dressed in whiteface, top hat and tails. There's something tricky about this man, like the joker in a deck of cards. Beckoning me onto the porch, he says: "When people are blind, they have the death smell."

"What do you mean?"

"A blind person knows when someone is going to die. They can smell it. It's the death smell."

"Maybe that's because a blind person's other senses become stronger."

"Don't play stupid. Blind persons aren't those who can't see, but those who can't be seen. Like duck hunters, they duck behind a blind." He laughs, revealing pointy teeth. "Someone who is hiding behind a blind is going to die, and someone who is blind will see. They are one and the same. YOU *will see."*

By now I have advanced onto the porch of my father's house. The door is ajar, the Joker is beckoning me through, but I am afraid. I know all the electrical wires have been cut, the phone has been disconnected and the stove yanked from the wall. No communication exists between my father's house and the outside world.

I awake with a heavy sense of impending doom. I can't shake the feeling that I, or someone close to me, is about to die. Throughout the day, my stomach seizes every time the phone rings, as if I were anticipating bad news.

After a week in which I sleep heavily with no recall, I again awaken in the grip of a terror that doesn't dissipate. Again I have had a compelling dream about death, which I scramble to remember. All I know for sure is that I am repeating with great urgency: "THE PRINCESS WHO IS A PISCES IS TO BE KILLED." Tossing between consciousness and sleep, I piece together the rest of the dream as best I can.

I'm not exactly a child, but neither am I an adult. I have to break the news of the princess's death to both my parents, but especially to my mother. I shout my message over and over, not only to convince my parents but also to awaken myself so I'll hear it too. Finally I get the message across to my father. He ushers me in to my mother as if to say, "I think you'd better listen to this." Both my parents are very grave. I absolutely and completely have their attention about something I want to say more than anything before in my life. I shout: "THE PRINCESS WHO IS A PISCES IS TO BE KILLED."

And that is when I awaken, lying on my back with my hands clasped over my midriff as if on a bier. My breathing is sharp and shallow, and I'm crying tears of relief at finally having been understood. I sense something real and important has happened that goes beyond any dream. A song from The Wizard of Oz bubbles through my mind: "Hi ho, the witch is dead, the wicked witch is dead."

I have one more dream that seems connected by emotion, though not by imagery, to the rest:

My mother is setting a table in the basement. She directs me to a seat beside my father where the tablecloth is stained with broken eggs. I break a goblet. When I try to hide it, I find a shelf of broken goblets with sharp V clefts, all crudely mended.

After recording this, I scrawl a footnote. "The worst part about this dream with its obvious sexual imagery is the sickening way it makes me feel—nauseated, right down into my gut." A second even shakier footnote: "I seem to be on the verge of remembering something sexual having to do with my father."

I now suspected I'd forgotten much that was vital about my earliest years. I also suspected something terribly wrong might have taken place, but I couldn't leap from suspicion to accusation, even in my own mind. I was never going to believe anything I dreamed to have literal truth, no matter how persuasive. *My insight and intuition could only prepare me to remember. They were my detectives who could uncover clues, but who couldn't deliver a confession. That had to come from my other self.* Yet, in getting rid of the gnarled tissue in my womb, I couldn't shake the disconcerting belief that I had aborted Satan's child.

THE JOKER

The memories of my other self are difficult to recapture because they are so fragmentary. Even in my father's house she remained hidden in her closet for months, even years, till daddy again beckoned her out. Her separate life was largely confined to a single room with a window that might suggest the season and time of day, but rarely the year or even her age. The deeds that involved only her were confusing, repetitive, shameful and mysterious—she had much to fear. Like a small child playing hide-and-seek, she often tried to conceal herself by closing her eyes so that visual memories were sometimes not recorded.

For more than forty years the memories of my other self lay deeply buried in jagged pieces inside me—smashed hieroglyphic tablets from another time and another place. When finally I began excavation, I brought these pieces to the surface in random order, to be fitted into patterns and dated. However, the story of my other self—as I came to know it—started in a blaze of discovery that April afternoon in 1983 when I first learned of her existence. The setting was banal, the circumstances unlikely for the revelation of dark secrets, but the time had come. I was ready.

Tonya and Arlene drive from Hamilton to shop for furniture for Arlene's new house. We lunch at the Courtyard, a glass-roofed restaurant in midtown Toronto. Still convalescing from my hysterectomy, still more at home in the world of dreams than in the real world, my mind drifts lazily in and out of the conversation—about Tonya's new job, about Arlene's new house.

"Naturally Babs is heartsick but she's always been a survivor."

Their hushed tone catches my attention. "What's wrong with Babs?"

They look at me in surprise. "About Joker—uh, Gerald. Haven't you heard?"

"About 'The Nashery'? Has it been canceled?"

"Jeez, no. Sorry, I thought you knew."

"It's so ghastly everybody's just sick about it."

"Gerald tried to sexually molest Babs's daughter. She's still not sure how far he went. The kid was hysterical. Babs didn't believe it at first but she confronted him and he broke down."

Let's take the part where the child is sexually assaulted by the breadman. Frankly, I don't believe for one minute that—

Feeling a snub-nosed bullet explode in my chest, I pick up a dinner knife with my left hand and stab the table. "I want to kill that bastard!" Dropping the knife, I apologize in the language of the eighties. "I guess I'm overreacting."

"No, I feel the same."

"Everybody does."

My chest continues to explode as the conversation flows around me.

For such a sexual assault to take place, we must look to the conduct of the child. Some little girls can be seductive at an early age.

I get up from the table, almost upsetting my water glass. "Excuse me."

Did such an incident ever happen to you?

No, I wouldn't know how to write about a child as emotionally damaged as that.

"What's the matter?" asks Arlene. "You look terrible."

I try to protest, but hysteria in my chest leaves me helpless and humiliated. Joker is breathing deeply, almost heaving. His once-florid complexion is now so pasty he looks cadaverous.

"Where are you going?"

My lips expand in a beatific smile. "I'm going crazy."

I walk toward the restaurant door. Tonya blocks my path. "What's wrong?"

"I think my father raped me."

"Is that supposed to be a joke?"

"I didn't know what I was going to say till I heard myself. Now I think it's true."

"Don't go. Let's talk."

"I can't. I have to go home."

"We'll walk with you."

"No. I have to be alone."

I walk out of the restaurant in a state of heightened consciousness, seeing the sky more luminous than ever before, the buildings a dazzling white, the people cut out of glass and edged in light, feeling the sidewalk slide in a carpet of hysteria under my feet . . . I think my father raped me.

Inside my apartment, I throw down my keys, lie on my bed, close my eyes, fold my hands, *the princess on her bier* . . . waiting. Spasms pass through me, powerful, involuntary— my pelvis contracts leaving my legs limp. My shoulders scrunch up to my ears, my arms press against my sides with the wrists flung out like chicken wings, my head bends back so far I fear my neck will snap, my jaws open wider than possible and I start to gag and sob, unable to close my mouth—lockjaw in reverse. These spasms do not feel random. They are the convulsions of a child being raped through the mouth.

I am sobbing, my lips pressed in a downward bow like a child refusing food. I am trying to shriek NO! but without daring to open my mouth for that is the new organ of assault. My father's house is empty so what does it matter if I scream? For all my protests I'm afraid to strike my daddy with my fists. I'm still afraid of my daddy. I'm still afraid daddy daddy daddy won't love me love me love me. My arms are glued to my sides as he forces me back against his bed so that my knees buckle. The edge of the bed cuts into me. My daddy is pressing his belly against me. I can't breathe. My daddy is forcing his wet-ums into my mouth. I gag. I'm smothering. Help me! I scrunch my eyes so I can't see. My daddy is pulling my body over him like mommy pulls a holey sock over a darning egg. Filthy filthy don't ever let me catch you shame shame filthy daddy won't love me love me dirty filthy love him hate him fear don't ever let me catch you catch you dirty dirty love hate guilt shame fear fear *fear fear fear fear fear fear* . . .

I recapture that moment precisely when my helplessness is so bottomless that anything is preferable. Thus, I unscrew my head from my body as if it were the lid of a pickle jar. From then on I would have two selves—the child who knows, with guilty body possessed by daddy, and the child who dares not know any longer, with innocent head attuned to mommy.

The episode ends. My head snaps forward. My jaws close. My arms unglue from my torso. My breathing deepens, opening a cavity in my chest. I return to the present, to my adult self, to my own Toronto bedroom. I return from time travel into my past to an April day in 1983, but I am no longer the same. One startling piece of information has been fed into my head like a microchip into a computer: I KNOW my father raped me. My brain is alive with new memories, with shocking insights. In seconds, my history as I have known it undergoes a drastic shift.

Joker Nash, dressed as a magician in whiteface, top hat and tails, perches on the railing of my father's house. A lawn sign reads: "Home Truths." Beckoning me onto the porch, he says: "Someone who is hiding behind a blind is going to die, and someone who is blind will see. They are one and the same. YOU will see."

The Joker on my father's porch has at last delivered. And the true villain of the piece? Not the breadman, as I wrote in Pandora, but the breadwinner with the devil's hooked hand.

Deeply shaken, I phone my sister, needing to make contact but not sure what I'll say or even if I'll say. I don't get beyond the hellos before someone else seems to grab the receiver—

my tongueless other self, at last finding the words and will to speak: "Daddy daddy daddy daddy daddy daddy daddy raped me."

My sister, herself a mother with a long history of sorting out a day's small tragedies with the dirty socks, struggles to separate the words. "Tell me that again."

Her corroboration—thank God!—is instantaneous. "I always felt something strange was going on." And then, with the same speed by which I made unthinkable connections: "Remember your convulsions? You used to hold your breath and gag and turn blue. I was supposed to run and get mother."

Ah yes, my famous fits. The bad child. As my mother later explained: "She would fall on the ground, screaming and choking and vomiting, unable to catch her breath. We were afraid she would swallow her tongue."

In gratitude I assure my sister: "I know I wasn't the only victim. I know you suffered as much as I, but in a different way." The rejected child, rejected from she-knew-not-what.

Now hers is the baby voice, managing through the cryptics of pain to condense her life story into a single sentence. "Yes. That's why I got fat."

I put down the receiver, still assuming that what happened between my father and me had occurred only once. Humane considerations aside, who could risk doing that over and over to a screaming child and expect to get away with it? Yet, the following week is full of other revelations, counterpointing my childhood memories of Sunday drives to the Stoney Creek Dairy for double-scoop cones and report cards with gold stars. I have more convulsions as my body acts out other scenarios, sometimes springing from nightmares, leaving my throat ulcerated and my stomach nauseated. So powerful are these contractions that sometimes I feel as if I were struggling for breath against a slimy lichen clinging to my chest, invoking thoughts of the incubus who, in medieval folklore, raped sleeping women who then gave birth to demons. Similarly, as my bed shakes with the violence of my fits, I recall the child Regan in the movie The Exorcist, riding her bed like a brass bronco, in the throes of demon possession. In a more superstitious society, I might have been diagnosed as a child possessed by the devil. What, in fact, I had been possessed by was daddy's forked instrument—the devil in man.

Though I maintain phone contact with my sister during this period of first impact, I choose to be alone. Already two people occupy my bedroom—my adult self and my child self, whom I name the Child Who Knows. Though my restored memories come wrapped in terror, it is a child's terror that I realize I must feel in order to expel. Thus, the adult me comforts the child, holds her hand, pities her suffering, forgives her for her complicity, assuages her guilt. She has carried the burden until I was prepared to remember our joint history without bitterness. I feel only relief, release, compassion, even elation. The mysteries of a lifetime, shadowy deeds dimly suspected, have been clarified.

Now I understand my hatred of my father, rooted so far back I couldn't guess the cause. Now I understand my childhood revulsion at sitting on his lap, coupled with a dim recollection that I had once enjoyed it. Now I understand the agitated child's drawings I found in a trunk. Now I understand my fear of pregnancy which, to my child's self, would have seemed like yet another physical invasion—a nine-month rape. Now I understand the obsessional affair in which I relived my relationship with daddy. Now I understand the fear of confession that kept me from my father's deathbed. Now I understand the powerful psychic connection I felt at his death, though I had shunned him for twenty years. Now I understand the exorcised house where I felt not-terror. Now I understand my sexually violent novels. Now I understand my strange yet purposeful dreams and my feeling that I had aborted Satan's child.

I am surprised to discover that I feel no anger toward my father. Little boys are taught to convert fear into rage or bravado. Little girls, to convert anger into fear. I was a hostile little girl, a furious teenager and a frequently bad-tempered adult. Anger was my salvation, the way I survived in my father's house, but it became my prison, blocking softer emotions. Now, as that tough shell cracks, a more vulnerable self is released.

Exactly a week after the first revelations, I go to bed with a feeling that the past has been placed in decent perspective and that it's time to get on with the present. That night, I have another provocative dream:

I am trapped with Aunt Estelle in the cellar of Other Grandmother's house. I am about seven. The cellar is wriggling with slimy, luminous worms that fall down our necks and squeeze up through the floor while we frantically and futilely swat at them.

I awake shivering with goose bumps and repeating: "Aunt Estelle, Aunt Estelle, Aunt Estelle."

Though I have no proof, I now possess one more conviction of the Child Who Knows: Aunt Estelle and my father had once been lovers. In the twilight world of illicit passion in which that other part of me so intensely dwelled, this union was taken for granted in the same way as the wedlock of my father and mother was a fixture of the ordinary world of hymns and grocery stores.

My Aunt Estelle who shares the bloodstone. Aunt Estelle who is also a Pisces. "Thanks for coming, Estelle."

MIRROR, MIRROR

A tinted photograph of my sister and of me hangs on the bedroom door of my Toronto duplex. I put it there soon after I remembered my father had sexually abused me. Helen, age eight, and I, age four, are at Winona beach, where St. James' Church once had a camp. Both of us are in mother-knit bathing suits. I am standing in front, my blond hair tied with a pink bow, and wearing a big grin, with my eyes scrunched against the sun. She's standing behind, her auburn hair pulled behind her ears, her freckled face clouded by a frown.

A photograph album repeats these images—always the discomfited older child is behind the younger, who grins for the camera, her clothes exhibiting what might be called seductive details: an off-the-shoulder neckline, a jaunty ribbon, a trailing slip, the lace edge of a pair of panties. From time to time, I find myself staring into that cherubic face in the photograph. "Tell me, little girl, what do you still know that I don't know?"

I consult Dr. Steven, a Toronto hypnotherapist. "I believe my father sexually abused me as a child. So far most of my regurgitated memories are physical and emotional rather than verbal or visual. They're very vivid, everything fits, but even now the whole idea is so shocking that I ask myself: did this really happen?"

Dr. Steven directs me to an armchair then instructs me to stare fixedly at a tinfoil pyramid. "Your eyes are closing. You are perfectly relaxed, perfectly at ease. Now, tell me, what do you see?"

After several false starts, I begin: "I am a child in my father's house. My father sits on his bed in his underwear. I'm hanging around outside his door, scuffing my foot back and forth across the threshold. There's something coy about my behavior. Part of me wants to go in, part holds back.

What lures me is a confused mixture of mystery, adventure and, most especially, the desire for attention . . . Now I'm sitting on my daddy's lap. I don't know whether I was invited in or whether I went in on my own. He's squeezing my legs between his thighs. I giggle, feeling giddy. He distracts me with nickels, or maybe it's with chocolate-chip cookies . . . It's hard to recapture a single story line—one similar incident seems superimposed on another like a double or triple exposure. Now I'm lying face down on my daddy's bed. He's rubbing against me in a strange way that confuses me. I seem to feel that if I don't look it isn't really happening. Instead I'm staring at the scrollwork on the headboard of my father's bed. I seem to be counting things, concentrating on that—sometimes it's the bites in the chocolate-chip cookie, sometimes I'm counting pennies. The scrollwork reminds me of my mother's lips saying "dirty dirty." I'm rather enjoying that—defying her. It's fear and pleasure mixed, like playing with fire. Mostly my feelings can't be classified because I have no framework of experience in which to place them or to judge them. I don't seem to be unhappy, but that's partly because I hold my breath a lot and that makes me dizzy, or light-headed, as if I were swaying in a hammock outside time and space."

On subsequent visits to Dr. Steven's office I produce other childhood memories in which I express a growing sense of panic and of wrongdoing, and then of abject helplessness. When I block, he suggests: "Try moving the image of yourself away from your house to some imaginary place that's safer."

"All right. I'm in a forest. I'm looking up through oak leaves into blue sky. The images no longer seem real—as if I'm in a fairytale forest. My mother is dressed like the witch in Snow White. She's dipping apples, or maybe it's tomatoes, into a steaming cauldron—something to do with her canning on our kitchen table, combined with jars of fruit in Other Grandmother's cellar. All this is very confused."

"Then take a different path."

"All right. It's growing darker. It's very dark. I seem to be lost ... lost and miserable. I'm walking with my hands held out in front of me, like Frankenstein. They strike something solid—some kind of barrier. It feels shiny, like a mirror. Yes, it's a mirror, an oval mirror—again, it's like the queen's mirror in Snow White—'Mirror, mirror, on the wall.' I see it in the moonlight, but I can't see what the child sees because now I seem to be the reflection in that mirror looking out at her ... that is, at myself. Wait a minute." Agitation jolts me out of hypnosis. "Something doesn't jibe. The child's too old—maybe eleven or even twelve."

"What's wrong with that?"

"My father didn't abuse me after I started school."

"How do you know?"

"Because as soon as I begin school my memories are very clear and detailed even now. I remember everything—all my teachers, what kids were in my Grade One class and where they sat, what kids were in the school plays including the understudies. I'm lethal to have at a school reunion."

Dr. Steven is cautionary: "Are you sure you want to keep stirring up these old memories? Why not rest it a bit? Maybe you've had enough."

Reluctantly, I leave his office, but I don't wish to rest it. I've rested it for too many years. Taking a blanket, I lie down under the oak tree in my backyard. Overhead I see a complex tracing of copper-leafed branches—the same ones I conjured up in Dr. Steven's office as my dream forest. I concentrate on them, spontaneously moving back into that other forest ...

I'm a child alone. It's very dark. Again I am walking with my arms outstretched. Again, my hands strike something solid—another mirror, except this time it's the mirror from my attic bedroom with two sides that tilt inward to create a multiple reflection. The central glass is cloudy with smoke. Gradually, it clears. I see a five-year-old child with matted hair and blue fangs staring back at me. Around her throat is the bloody mark of a broken leash. She lays her outstretched palms against mine. They fit mine exactly. We are one. She says: "I love my daddy."

Before my eyes, the child grows older. Now she is eight, nine, ten, eleven. Now I am in Miss Buchanan's room. Now I'm in Miss Sissons's room ... now ... now ... now ... I see a gaudy cheerleader with brassy hair. She, too, wears the bloodmark of her daddy's leash. I try to pull my palms away to blind my eyes but they're stuck to hers. She says: "I love my daddy." She too is I, and I am she. All three of us—my adult self, the blue-fanged child, the gaudy teenager—are reflected in the triple mirror.

For a long, long time I lie on the ground staring up into the oak branches, trying to assimilate what I have just seen. I now know why the image of the abused child that I've carried in my mind over the past couple of months frequently seemed too old. I now know that my incestuous relationship with my father went on far longer than I had first grasped—all through a time when I remembered everything else but ...

Imagine this: imagine you discover that for many years another person intimately shared your life without your knowing it. Oh, you had your suspicions—the indented pillow beside you, the toothpaste with a thumbprint that wasn't yours. Now it all fits, you know it's true, but during all that time you never actually saw this person.

And so it was with me. She was my shadow-self, unknown to me. She knew passion where I knew only inhibition, then grief where I knew guilt, then terror where I knew anger. She monitored my every thought, manipulated my actions, aided my survival and sabotaged my dreams, for she was I and I was she.

RESOLUTION

MY MOTHER

When I first discovered the truth about my past the last thing I could imagine was telling my mother. However, as the days and weeks and months passed, I came to feel a powerful need to do so—not I, but the damaged child in me. Her last act: the need to tell mommy. I ignored this impulse as long as I could. Logic and humanity demanded it. What did an eighty-three-year-old woman need with such desperate information?

Yet the desire to confide would not leave me. A scream of grief had lodged permanently in my chest. It expanded inside me with the insistence of hemorrhaging blood. It was sorrow, anger, love, perversity, vindication, helplessness, guilt, anguish, confrontation, love, despair—everything. Gradually, these feelings articulated themselves into an internal gush of words:

"Mother, why didn't you protect me? The walls of my father's house were thin. A cardboard house. A house of cards. As soon as he put his foot over the threshold I could feel it tremble, become unsafe. How could you not know?

"I became the other woman before I was five. The one who shared his bed. Did my child's willfulness contain the arrogance of that? Did some of the wronged and jealous wife in you respond to the gall of that? I suspect far more than esthetics was at stake in those pitched battles we waged over my flaxen curls, my main claim to princess status. How you yanked at them, taking control of them, insisting on the braids that I hated, threatening me with the scissors. When I, as a child of five, saw the queen in Snow White turn into the wicked witch, I feared what I was seeing—your other self, the witch in you, the Witch Who Knew.

"Since my father was an obvious and dangerous villain it was necessary for me to believe you were a saint, even if that meant blackening my own character to keep that myth going.

It was safer to be a bad child with a perfect mother whom I failed to please, than to be a frightened child with a flawed mother who failed to protect me. And yet, and yet, now that I have rescinded the legend of your saintliness, you too are released to become more human, to be worthy of understanding and love.

"You were born at the turn of the century, when girls who did not marry were dismissed as spinsters. War and depression had delayed courtship for you, as it had for so many others. My father had what passed for a good job and a stable future. Through such conventions you acquired your lot in life. Your philosophy was to make the best of things, whether it be leftover potatoes, a hand-me-down coat or a troubled marriage. I saw only the fossilized remains of that—a petulant father who shouted all the time and a forbearing mother who savored romantic novels, escaped to church where she found joy in service, who endured her days in my father's house by keeping busy busy busy. Still, you were a mother who was always cheerful, who sang hymns as you hung sheets on the line, who never allowed yourself a day of illness, who shouldered more than your fair share of community responsibility, who delighted in telling Sunday school stories to children. You were then, as you are now, the first to phone a sick friend or take a tray of cookies to a grieving neighbor, the first to volunteer for a difficult or tedious job both inside and outside my father's house.

"Divorce was a religious and a moral matter, as well as an economic one—the subject of horrified whispers. You had a strong need to do the right thing, and to be seen to do the right thing. Your oft-stated concern: what will the neighbors think? Not what is, but what is seen to be. Thus you elected to stay at your post, to refuse to see what was there to be seen and yet to pave my yellow-brick road to a better life with dollars saved on the price of eggs. Your best for my sister and for me.

"I suppose you felt powerless—not just in this one thing but from the beginning of time. A family of four girls, with you in the middle. Serious illness as a child. Immigration from an English mining town to North America. A father defrauded of his savings, depression in a strange land and no jobs to be had. Tragedy in your family—one sister and then another dead from diseases no one dies from today until you, with your bookkeeping job, were the sole support of your family. And then, that final death.

"Your mother says: 'He must be down in the garage feeding the pigeons.' You go down to the garage. You open the door and, yes, your father is there—hanging from the rafters, his feet twisting a foot off the floor, his forty-four-year-old face a strangulated mask never to be erased from your dreams. After seeing that, how many other things would you not want to see?

"Grandma clung to this shred: 'There must be a note.' Together you pulled the house apart slat by slat. Nothing. Only silence from that early grave.

"Yes, mother, you had much in your life you dared not see. So it comes to this: can I blame you for choosing selective sight, the same method of survival that I, your daughter, would choose? If some part of you knows, or suspects, the story I have to tell, then some voice inside you, too, must scream for release. Just as I have been split all these years, so have you. Knowledge is your karma, as well as mine—the natural, inevitable result of all your actions as well as mine. Finally, truth is the only thing worth saying, but even if that proves too harsh, I confess that I am bloody-minded enough to take that responsibility onto myself. I need a chance to heal, to be free. I've earned that right. Forty-seven years is long enough for the working out of any curse. The Child Who Knows-and-is-tired-of-knowing is about to have her cri de coeur."

I walk the familiar streets past Laura Secord Public School and St. Cecilia's Infirmary and the Goodfellows' little bungalow, now lawn-paved and insul-bricked. Green shoots glisten against decaying snow and oozy mud, ripe with promise. Lawns are fuzzy green and the forsythia bushes are golden. Always my mother's first words of spring, more reliable than the robin: "I cut some forsythia today."

I am returning to the scene of the crime: home for Easter, the chosen time. I'm glad my natal home is still standing, still inhabited, the rooms still intact—the corpus delicti that the prosecuting attorney is keen on seeing before he'll believe there's been a crime. Although I suspect the door key is in the same place, I ring the bell, a visitor now.

My mother embraces me. "Good! You're early." As always she is overly glad to see me—overly glad in that her welcome outstrips anything I can muster. "Yes, I had a good trip. Yes, the weather is lovely. Yes, it's wonderful to see the crocuses and tulips. Yes, you've cut some forsythia today."

Now that my father's house has given up its secrets it has become an old friend, each room a scrapbook of my past, little changed but the flowers on the wallpaper—from roses, to lilacs, then back to roses. Once again I invent excuses to rove from room to room, almost a ritual now, wishing to repossess the territory of the child that was, to see it from her eyes, three feet up from the carpet, feeling an overriding curiosity. Will things look different now that I know, and know that I know? I, an opener of boxes, of closed doors, of secret compartments, of everything labeled DON'T, NO or POISON, am turning into Pandora, my fictional name.

Here it is again, the attic where my bedroom used to be— the iron cot by the lace-curtain window; the arched mirror; the frog's eye gable, now without its patchwork toadstool. In the cubbyholes are trunks for woolens laced in mothballs, card tables for ladies' teas and all those other accessories I, as a child, thought no one ever lived without, now permanent castoffs even in my mother's house.

Down down down I go to hang outside my father's bedroom —unoccupied now, like most of the house; a graduation picture of myself on one dresser, my sister on the other; the bed the same, with the same scrolled headboard—my mother's pursed lips.

She is calling up the stairs with the lilt and heft she used to fetch me from the street: "Time for church!" Church with my mother—something I haven't done for many years. The church where I was christened, the altar where I was married.

"Who gives this woman?"

"I do."

Here's the aisle my father strode with the collection plate, tramp tramp tramp as he and the other elders marched in twos. A big congregation then, now mostly widows with young marrieds drifting back with their children. Even female elders now, chalk one up for necessity and the women's movement. Even here things do change.

"It was sad when they cru-ci-fied my Lord . . ."

I remember when it seemed a confession of poverty to attend Easter service without a new spring outfit. Now only a few have made the effort—old faces under new hats. I see Mrs. Lunt and think of Magda—a single parent long before it became fashionable and now a doting grandmother.

"He arose. He arose. Hal-le-lu-jah, Christ arose!"

Afterward my mother parades me among her peers, proud of the rare opportunity to display a daughter home from foreign battlefields, from larger wars. I cringe, feeling like Judas with thirty pieces of silver lining my pockets, but also knowing I will carry through. I believe in my truth, in the need to speak. I believe in the power of truth to heal both ways.

Home again. I set the table, finding everything exactly where it used to be, where it always has been—the same worn silver, same plates, same cups, same pans, all glued and taped and soldered and wired. Opening a cupboard is like participating in an archeological dig.

Mother has cooked a ham, though there's only two of us. I try to carry on a normal conversation—whose gall bladder is acting up and what cousin's daughter has just married or had another baby—struggling to keep the names straight while my mother jumps up every few seconds to fetch something to the table.

As it happens we are still having tea, the last mouthful of apple pie still on the fork, the plates unstacked, when I blurt the unavoidable bad dialogue. "Mother, there's something I have to tell you ... something terrible." I offer the only reassurance I can. "Something that happened a very long time ago."

My mother puts down her teacup: "What is it?"

Forty years are swept away. I'm crying now, abandoned by my adult self when I need her most. "This will hurt you. It will hurt you a lot."

"What is it? Tell me. You must tell me."

"This will take all of your strength as a Christian."

She is full of concern, clear and firm. "Don't worry about me, just tell me."

I get up from the table. "Please, come into the living room." My mother follows. We sit on the same chintz couch I remember as a child, reupholstered by her after a high-school night course, then resuscitated with mock-leather paint, now also wearing thin. "You're going to be asked to forgive someone, someone I've already forgiven. I don't want to pass this on to you as a burden. I want us to dispel it together."

"Yes. You must tell me."

I deliver the rest of my speech, rehearsed but sincere. "If you're bitter then I was wrong to tell you. It will be my burden again."

My mother takes my nail-bitten hands in her gnarled ones. "Just tell me."

Despite my adult words it's clear I am the child here. At last my other self has a mother after four decades of wandering in the wilderness. Mother ...

My mother still holds my hand. "You must tell me. It's all right. Tell me."

*I'm not exactly a child, but neither am I an adult. I have
to tell both parents, but especially my mother. Both are very
grave. I absolutely and completely have their attention about
something that I want to say more than anything before in
my life . . .*

"Remember those convulsions I used to have as a kid?"

She frowns. "Why, yes, you had trouble catching your
breath. We were afraid you'd swallow your tongue."

Now I sound like a textbook: "Some psychiatrists see
childhood convulsions as a sign of sexual abuse." I pause for
this to sink in. "I was sexually abused as a baby."

My mother scarcely reacts. I wonder if she has heard, if
she has allowed herself to hear. My other self is crying, I am
crying as we await the inevitable next question.

At last she asks: "But who?"

"Who had access?"

"I don't know."

I press: "Who?"

Indignantly: "There wasn't anyone."

"Someone did. Who?"

"Well, I don't know. There was just your father."

"Yes!"

She is looking into the distance, still holding my hands,
squeezing them.

I babble: "He was affectionate at first. It wasn't just once.
It went on a long time."

"Well!" My mother is near tears but not crying. I am
sobbing. We fall into each other's arms, comforting each
other. I feel overwhelmed with gratitude and hence with love.
I am believed! Again I am babbling: "Thank you, mother.
Thank you for believing me." For accepting both of us—me
and my other self.

My mother's body feels birdlike but strong. "Of course, I
believe you. You're my daughter!"

She is still staring off into space, quietly picking up the
pieces of her life as if it were another plate to be mended:

"Your daddy and I . . . I don't suppose we ever talked. Many's the time I was tempted to leave, but whenever I was most exasperated your daddy would turn around and do something really nice." She sighs: "I don't suppose I could forgive him if he were alive, but now . . ."

MY FATHER

I take out Pandora's box once more—ivory, the color of dead corsages, of old bones, the box that once lay under my father's bed. Again I rifle through the pictures—myself in velvet formal, in cheerleading outfit, in bathing suit. At the bottom of that box lies one more picture—of my father receiving the Steel Company's gold pin for forty years' faithful service. He stands in semiprofile, eyes lowered, his expression one of modesty mixed with pride. In his view, he has accomplished something.

My father had other moments of pride—as a player on the Hamilton Rough Riders football team when it won a national championship in 1912, as a lieutenant during the First World War—yet it is in this gold pin photo that he comes closest to smiling for posterity. For forty-three years he put on his navy suit, white shirt and tie, then drove his second-hand car to his seven-to-three, three-to-eleven, eleven-to-seven inspector's job at the Steel Company. That gold pin is a medal for some kind of gallantry, I know that now. The platitudes offered up at my father's funeral held their own truth—this Christian man who didn't smoke or drink, who played no card games beyond cribbage or solitaire, who helped with the grocery shopping, who never took the Lord's name in vain; this good neighbor who tipped his hat on Sunday, who commented Monday to Friday on the weather, who kept his snow shoveled, his leaves raked and his bills paid. Is it fair to dismiss all this as hypocrisy? Was this not a second reality, offsetting the pictures that do not appear in the box?

My father's rage was an impotent rage. He shouted and waved his fists like a child in a high chair. I know that now. He demanded and he was obeyed, but he was never heard. I know that now. The weaker he became, the less I was able to justify my rage toward him and the guiltier I grew. But my rage did not diminish. Our secret lived between us. It tainted every sentence we spoke. I couldn't share my father's house and function as anything but a zombie. I couldn't share the same room and breathe normally. I couldn't sit at his table without choking. Any fumbling attempt he made at rapport was turned aside with contempt. How much I made him suffer I have no way of knowing. Perhaps his hide was thick enough to withstand my condemnation. Perhaps his internal problems were so acute I could scarcely make a difference. I suspect he paid as dearly as I for the amnesia that was once his salvation. As in the child's game of statues, we remained frozen at our darkest hour, with no possibility of forgiveness or compassion or redemption while he lived. I know that now.

My sister remembers hikes with my father and picnics. I do not. Any normal pleasures have long since been blotted out by the ink stain our relationship became. My father had no friends except those he met at church. He was estranged from his relatives, and belonged only to groups to which my mother gained him entrance. Once ensconced in a chair beside a set of ears, he offered little beyond a parade of his ailments. He had no hobbies other than stamp collecting and perusing the newspaper for bargains. I can't even imagine the loneliness of such an existence. I can't imagine the frustration that caused him to do what he did or the agony that must have resulted. Did he pretend I was a willing victim? Did he think he had the right? Did he do to me what had been done to him? Did he know that I couldn't remember what we did in secret? Was he as profoundly split as I? Was there a Daddy Who Knew and a Daddy Who Did Not Know?

I ask questions of the past but I don't expect answers. Though I shared a house and a crime with my father, I scarcely knew the man. Mine is not a story of the boot, but of the imprint of that boot on flesh: imprinting.

This I do know: my father was not a monster. His life was a bud that never opened, blighted by the first frost. His crime became his prison, his guilt his bars. He served his sentence as I have served mine, but his was for life, whereas I got off after forty-seven years for reasonably good behavior.

In my earliest memory I am an infant lying on my father's bed, being sexually fondled but blissfully unaware of any deception. Then I was treated with tenderness. That was my Garden of Eden. As in Genesis, pain came with knowledge and expulsion. Yet some remembrance of happiness remained. I felt I was special, the chosen child, the princess. That lie had some truth. That lie was a blessing as well as a curse. I know that now.

The force with which I came to hate my father was a measure of the love I and my other self once bore him. I know that now. Inarticulate with pain, my father expressed his love in a perverted way which was all he could manage. I know that now. I was a stand-in for a mother and a sister, but we are all each other's surrogates. All of us are born into the second act of a tragedy-in-progress, then spend the rest of our lives trying to figure out what went wrong in the first act. I know that now.

When I look at the picture of my father receiving his gold pin, I think of the blinkered donkeys who ground grain: around and around and around, dragging their millstones till they dropped in a grave carved by their own hooves. Though I don't understand him, I can pity him and forgive him. I forgive my father so I can forgive myself, so I can embrace with compassion that fierce and grieving child who held her tongue to save her cat and that frenetic and gaudy teenager who danced in the red shoes and the willful princess who betrayed the white knight who saved her. I also forgive my father because I love him. That is the biggest shock of all. Not only that I once loved him but that I love him even now. So that is the last winged creature to fly out of my Pandora's box. For hope, read love. I love my daddy, I know that now.

I am walking through a forest wearing a sky-blue dress. I come upon a ragamuffin in a tattered sunsuit, hiding behind a tree. I extend my hand. Wiping sticky fingers on her sunsuit, she accepts it. Together we walk deeper into the forest.

We come to a clearing. My father is lying on a bier, hands folded across his navy vest. Through the glass floor of the forest I see the Xs and Os of a ticktacktoe game. I lift up the child to say goodbye to her daddy. With her finger, she makes Xs and Os on the side of her daddy's coffin—hugs and kisses, good-bye, good-bye. Hugging the child, I assure her she has done her best, that she's a good child, a wise child, as all children are . . . . I feel her melt into my chest.

Now I close my father's coffin. I wave good-bye with a handkerchief. The handkerchief turns into a white bird, which grows larger and larger till I feel myself becoming that bird. Now I am flying, my wings strong and sure as they beat the air—a seabird on its way to the ocean. In my mouth I have a quill to be dipped into the sun, a quill to write with fire before plunging into the ocean.

So that is it. My other self is dead. My father is dead. The king is dead. The princess is dead. "Hi ho, the wicked witch is dead." I have been released from the monster that never was. Now I can close the coffin, truly close it.

X X X X

O O O O O

Good-bye, good-bye.

POSTSCRIPT

My husband's way of surviving our marital breakup was to cut off the past. Because our divorce was uncontested, involved no children and no alimony, it was handled by mail in 1977 on the grounds of my desertion. I thereafter respected his wish for total privacy, though that seemed more like an amputation than a parting.

Only once did I glimpse Danny during the next ten years. One sunny Friday in 1978 I was shopping near our former apartment when I saw him park "our" red Jaguar, filled to bursting with white chrysanthemums. I had been told, several weeks before, that he was remarrying soon. Instinctively I knew he was festooning our former apartment with flowers for his wedding. My first impulse was to rush over to wish him well, but a wiser part of me held back, knowing I must not allow my shadow to fall across his wedding day.

That poignant image of the little red car, abloom with white flowers, stayed with me for a long time.

Frequently, over the next few years I dreamed about Danny. Not as he was, but as he had been—a mate and a trusted friend. This did not indicate to me any longing for the past in reality, only the honoring of our inner bond. On those rare occasions when I did dream of him as he was now—a man married to someone else—we would hug each other, weep with pleasure at our reunion, then go our separate ways.

My separate way included the revelations in this book. Three years ago, toward the end of 1984, I decided to retreat to a place where I could heal and integrate, and perhaps write a book. Before leaving, I had a strong desire to see Danny. I wanted him to know that he had been the best mate anyone could ever want; that I had been compelled to leave him to struggle with demons far nastier than we could have guessed; that he had made survival possible by giving me faith in myself.

We met at a downtown Toronto restaurant, full of dark paneling and good leather, one stormy afternoon in late November. He looked the same as always—handsome with an affable, almost cherubic smile, his light brown hair only slightly grayer and thinner. One thing was different and I noticed it immediately—a gold wedding band.

Danny's first question—"Do you still write?"—indicated this might not be the easy meeting I had hoped for. My career was a noisy one, spawned in the same city. Such detachment seemed unnatural. When I offered him a copy of my latest novel, he politely declined with the reminder that we now lived separate lives. His avuncular stance was the sort used to humor a difficult client who insists on special attention. It seemed impenetrable.

I struggled to stick to my agenda. Eight months had gone by since my past had exploded into my present. I thought I had been over this ground often enough, with enough people, to be dispassionate—even clinical. However, this special telling, with this special person, touched on a level of grief so deep I found myself unable to speak without the certainty of breaking. Fumbling in my purse for a purple felt pen, I began writing on cocktail napkins in block letters: I HAVE SOMETHING STRANGE TO TELL YOU. Eventually, in this peculiar way, my story was related.

Afterward, in a wet courtyard, just receiving the afternoon's first murky rays of sunlight, he held me tightly for several seconds. Then he touched my shoulder bag with a whimsical smile. "Thanks for my book."

Two years later, while I was preparing this manuscript for publication, an announcement appeared in a Toronto paper, making this day tragically different from any other: "Suddenly, on Tuesday, January 6, 1987 . . . Loving husband of . . . Dear father of . . ." Danny—my Danny for twenty years—had died of a ruptured heart at age fifty-five.

Oh, Danny, now I know the meaning of the verb to keen— to wail, to lament. A friend had phoned me to spare me a colder shock. A quarter into a newsbox brings my confirmation. How important that quarter seemed as I fumbled it into its slot—twenty-five cents to purchase official word of a husband's death.

I pick flowers for you at the florist's—painted daisies, the same as I carried in my bridal bouquet. It seemed important to choose each one myself, then to circle our former apartment block, looking up at our twelve lighted windows.

The newspaper says your family is receiving at the funeral home from 2:00 to 4:00 p.m. and from 7:00 to 9:00 p.m. I arrange to be there at 5:00, supported by a mutual friend, who knew us as a couple, who even shared our wedding anniversary. No one else is in your lying-in room—a small chapel set with an elegant mahogany casket. At first, I think I've stumbled into the wrong place, the wrong life, the wrong death. I do not recognize the corpse in the coffin. Not even after staring. An old man with gray flesh lies in your place. Not one recognizable feature has made it through death and the cosmetician's art. How can this be? You looked yourself when I saw you two years ago.

I touch your hand. Your flesh is cool and dense. Dead, really dead. No comfort there. And yet, as I examine this mock-up of you, I realize your corpse is the best advertisement for "something more" that I have ever seen. Since my college days I have acquired far more patience with the mysterious, more reverence for the unknown. "He is not here. He has risen." You are not here. That I know for sure. I am looking at your remains—that which is leftover. Dead and *gone*.

I grieve over what you have left for us. I speak to your corpse as if my message might get through. I tell you once again how grateful I am for our twenty years of intimacy, fifteen of them as man and wife. I wonder: what did you make of our last meeting? Did you learn that it was no offence to your present loyalties to love me in my proper context, our past? I regret that you never knew my better, wiser self, yet even as I form this thought I know you were attracted to my troubled spirit. I, your flock of one, your rescuee, was also your shadow, your sinner, your way of contacting your own rebelliousness, too deeply buried to touch. You lost a vital and valid part of yourself on the slippery slope to perfection. That part you found in me.

Why do people have to die before we begin to see them whole? Well, we played happily together, we worked hard together, we had adventures together, we took risks together. We laughed at the same things, had dozens of private jokes and code words, spent hours and days and years with our hands on each other. You called me your Little Friend, and for many years I was. I sensed—as you did—that yours would be a short life while mine would not. Some fragility there, not a long-lived family, whereas my great-grandfather bought his last motorcycle at age eighty.

My companion joins me at the casket. She speaks of you as a gentleman. That epithet surprises me. It's a word reserved for our elders—but now, of course, we are the elders. I take a step back, see you through her eyes. Yes, it's the right word, meaning far more than your three-piece navy suit, your red tie and matching handkerchief. A gentle man. One who practiced the truth of good manners—formalized compassion.

I take another step back to explore your habitat. A photograph offers the confirmation I have been seeking—there you are, exactly as you should be, beaming with optimism and good cheer, your arm proudly encircling your son, age six, with your young wife embracing a daughter, age four. I don't recognize many of the names on your floral tributes. That gives me no pang. It's as it should be. Another life.

You are to be buried at eleven o'clock the next morning. I wasn't going to attend; finally, to stay away is unthinkable.

Dressing for the occasion is fraught with pathos—the black bride, ritualistically preparing for her last date. The stockings I will wear, the dark print dress, the black velvet coat, black muff, checked scarf, black boots—all acquire a mystique through association. My companion picks me up in ample time for your service. At 10:48, we discover that we are at the wrong church. An anxious race across town brings us to the right church at the wrong time—simultaneously with the casket. I had intended to arrive with everyone else, sit toward the back, participate with stoicism and leave with dignity. Now, a side door allows us to slip into the very back row. Another friend, male, slides into the pew beside me. Your official mourners are on the aisle front left. I am on the aisle back right, supported in compassion by both the male and female principle. Appropriate, but a little too showy.

Yours is an Anglican church with Gothic ceiling and an altar arched in stained glass. Now your casket moves slowly up the long central aisle, led by a white choir carrying a golden cross. At the first sound of those voices, high and haunting, I am lost . . . I am lost . . .

The hymns are unfamiliar. Did they mean anything to you? Last I knew you saved your skepticism for heaven and your good deeds for the earth. Did you change? The eulogy, given by your legal mentor, gracefully states your creed. "Daniel loved people. He saw the best in everyone . . ."

Your casket is drawn from the church, followed by your children, eyes sweeping the crowded pews, still unaware their father lies in that shiny box, stone cold. Your young widow is dressed in white. She has a lovely face, full of an unspeakable sorrow. I, above all others, know the measure of her loss. My grief today is sharp and deep and clean, like the cutting of a knife through flesh to bone. Her grief has yet to die a thousand deaths. For me, this is closure.

As your long procession of mourners passes, I see that most of their faces, like the names on your wreaths, are unknown to me. Legal faces, correct and clear-eyed, used to containing grief. A few dear friends from our past. Probably most don't even know you're dead. I am still trying to be inconspicuous, but so obviously in pain, as I grip one male hand and one female, that I'm becoming harder to miss. One or two mourners do make that difficult crossover from the formal line to embrace me, to say: "I'm glad you came." Their unexpected kindness, though deeply appreciated, unhinges me. It's been a cruel time, as well as a sorrowful one. Nobody's fault, no callousness intended. Your death took us all by surprise. I'm one wife, one widow too many. No one knows what to do with me. I don't know what to do with myself. I'm not supposed to feel pain while your funeral procession, with measured step, marches over me.

The last mourner leaves the church. No more need for artifice. I break.

I'm going to the cemetery, against all advice. It's necessary to see your body go down into the earth. Both of my companions have other engagements. I'm left outside the gate of Mount Pleasant Cemetery, watching your long cortege, headlights lit, from the wrong side of the street. By the time I make it through the traffic, the last car is rounding the first turn. I struggle to catch up. Now that last car is rounding a second turn. Now I am running, in full awareness of my absurdity, spared nothing there, the shadow of the lady in white, stumbling after your hearse, twelve years late.

Dare I cut across the graveyard, avoid some of the loops of the road? Wouldn't that be even more absurd, to come groping through tombstones? What will the neighbors think?

The truth is, yours is the only prohibition still with the power to hurt. Yours was the voice that laughed away my social outrages, for which I'm sure this qualifies, yet yours is also the voice that told me I was no longer wanted in your life. And yet, and yet, no one can possess all of someone else. Not one wife or another. Not a mother or a father. Not a child. No one. I will be burying a different set of memories, a different person from everyone else. What I'm doing now is no one's business but my own. Not even yours.

The braking of wheels on gravel. I stop running, grab for the tag ends of dignity. A blue sports car, door open. "Come on. Get in." A colleague of yours, someone we both like. He rescues me, as I believe you would have done, drives me to the right place as your surrogate, steers me to the edge of the crowd gathered under your canopy while a few more words are said and your coffin plunges into the earth.

Afterward, we talk about you.

It's not quite over, not yet, not this long day. I've finished with one funeral in time for another—a memorial service for the compassionate friend and fine novelist to whom this book is dedicated: Margaret Laurence, 1926–1987. Ironically, here I am to sit with the family. As I walk up the aisle, no longer needing to be invisible, I encounter a rope marking off the first four rows. Paralyzed, I stare at it, unable to breach one more barrier, feeling myself begin to faint. A friendly arm reaches out, pulls me in. Now I can cry fully and freely—for Margaret, for you.

I believe the only way to overcome loss is to absorb the good qualities of that which is lost. Surely that is the meaning of the Eucharist: "This is my body, this is my blood." I await the dubious blessing of old age with your gentleness smoothing my rough edges, with your voice still sweet and clear in my ear: "It's okay, Little Friend. Now, try again."

Looking at my life from one vantage point, I see nothing but devastation. A blasted childhood, an even worse adolescence, betrayal, divorce, craziness, professional stalemate, financial uncertainty and always, always a secret eating like dry rot at my psyche. That is the dark side, the story I have told in this book. Yet, like the moon, my life has another side, one with some luminosity.

I have been loved once, unconditionally, and I have loved in return. That, like the gift of air, can never be withdrawn. The disguises I assumed—cheerleader, philosopher, princess, journalist, author—all had something to teach me about sorrow and about laughter. Since I had early been damaged by love, my ruling passion became curiosity—the desire to experience and to know. Since I could not trust what happened inside my father's house, I turned for adventure outside it. Since I dared not parent children, I created books.

Mine was a story of early loss—of innocence, of childhood, of love, of magic, of illusion. It was a hazardous life, which began in guilt and self-hate, requiring me to learn self-forgiveness. This meant discovering the difference between fixing blame and taking responsibility. The guilty child was me, though I didn't know her existence. Her actions were mine, for which I must assume responsibility.

My life was structured on the uncovering of a mystery. As a child, I survived by forgetting. Later, the amnesia became a problem as large as the one it was meant to conceal. However, I did not remember my past until the homemade bomb was defused, until the evil was contained, until I was stable enough and happy enough that sorrow or anger or regret or pain was overwhelmed by joy at my release. To reach this state, I needed the help of friends and healers. This I had in abundance.

Mine turns out to be a story without villains. Children who were in some way abused, abuse others; victims become villains. Thus, not to forgive only perpetuates the crime, creates more victims. Like Sleeping Beauty I was both cursed and blessed at birth. I was given the poison and the antidote at the same time and by the same people. The well that poisoned me also provided me with the ability to resist that poison. Specifically, I was of the first generation of my family to receive the education and the social resources and the personal support to fight back.

Mental institutions and prisons and hostels and shelters and addiction centers are full of persons who were sexually abused and who did not recover. Sex between an adult and a child always involves emotional and physical brutality. It is a crime that cripples, usually for life. That some people do survive, that emotional health often requires the abused to forgive the abuser does not make the crime more acceptable.

A volunteer at a women's shelter told me of discovering a nine-month-old girl who had been raped. The mother's live-in lover who did this was an alcoholic. The family was on welfare and the baby was undernourished. By contrast, mine is a middle-class story with built-in loopholes and rescue stations and options and timelocks and safeguards.

In retrospect, I feel about my life the way some people feel about war. If you survive, then it becomes a good war. Danger makes you active, it makes you alert, it forces you to experience and thus to learn. I now know the cost of my life, the real price that has been paid. Contact with inner pain has immunized me against most petty hurts. Hopes I still have in abundance, but very few needs. My pride of intellect has been shattered. If I didn't know about half my own life, what other knowledge can I trust? Yet even here I see a gift, for in place of my narrow, pragmatic world of cause and effect and matter moving to immutable laws, I have burst into an infinite world full of wonder. The whole mystery of the universe has my reverence. Nothing is sure but nothing can be dismissed. I pay attention.

All of us are haunted by the failed hopes and undigested deeds of our forebears. I was lucky to find my family's dinosaur intact in one deep grave. My main regret is excessive self-involvement. Too often I was sleepwalking through other people's lives, eyes turned inward while I washed the blood off my hands. My toughest lesson was to renounce my own sense of specialness, to let the princess die along with the guilt-ridden child in my closet, to see instead the specialness of the world around me.

Always I was traveling from darkness into the light. In such journeys, time is our ally, not our enemy. We can grow wise. As the arteries harden, the spirit can lighten. As the legs fail, the soul can take wing. Things do add up. Life does have shape and maybe even purpose. Or so it seems to me.

It is July 6, 1987. My mother debarks from a Greyhound bus after a weekend visit to her niece's. Typically, she has decided to walk the four blocks home instead of taking a taxi from the bus terminal. Though it's a muggy ninety degrees, she is wearing her raincoat so she won't have to carry it, and toting her overnight case. Her gait is slow, sometimes uncertain, as she greets acquaintances en route, complimenting them on their flowerbeds, making this small journey an occasion for the exchange of pleasantries, embuing each moment and everyone encountered in it with a sense of importance as she always has.

My mother is enjoying the final years of a productive life, still supported by a network of aging friends stitched together—like everything in her house—by eternal optimism. Despite failing eyesight, she reads the newspaper each evening through a giant magnifying glass, then bundles it up with the rest for recycling, accompanied by the tin cans she has flattened in the basement. She climbs the stairs of her three-storey house a dozen times a day. Only reluctantly, in the past few years, has she given up shoveling snow and cutting grass. She still refuses a cane. When anyone suggests she slow down, she insists: "I'm fine! Don't worry about me." To my mother, approaching her eighty-eighth birthday, ninety seems old.

Now, as she turns the corner onto her own street, she looks with relief toward her home of more than fifty years, just a few doors away. The gradient, though not steep, has been steady, all the way from Main Street to the Mountain. Soon she is mounting her own front steps, three of them, to her veranda. She sets down her little embroidered case, frankly exhausted, slips her key into the lock, opens the door leading into the cool sanctuary of her own home. She sits down on her favorite chair, still wearing her coat, and unclasps her earrings.

In the next few hours, the phone rings several times, unanswered. Friends, well-rehearsed for catastrophe, are becoming alarmed. Simultaneously, a neighbor grows suspicious of that still-ajar door and investigates. My mother, her final journey completed, has run out of breath.

OTHER VIRAGO BOOKS OF INTEREST

CRY HARD AND SWIM

The Story of an Incest Survivor

Jacqueline Spring

'This is the true story of the childhood and therapy of an incest survivor – myself.' Jacqueline Spring (a pseudonym) was the youngest of seven children, born into a Glaswegian family that appeared conventionally at ease both emotionally and materially. But the picture that emerges here in letters to her mother, in poems and narration is one of pain and immense bewilderment caused by her father's sexual advances. The frightened compliant child was pressured by family silence never to refer to what was going on inside or outside the family. It was only years later, in therapy – an experience that was to be profoundly transforming – that she began to confront her own psychological mutilation. Her therapist, Eve, through her warmth and acceptance, helped Jacqueline to rid herself of her guilt and self-hatred. And she began to learn how common her feelings and conflicts were in talking to other women in incest survivors' groups. It is for them and for the many workers who deal with survivors that she has described what was for her this 'beautiful and ultimately healing journey'.

FOR YOUR OWN GOOD

The Roots of Violence in Child-rearing

Alice Miller

'Child abuse is still sanctioned – indeed, held in high regard – in our society as long as it is defined as child-rearing. It is a tragic fact that parents beat their children in order to escape the emotions stemming from how they were treated by their own parents.'

Expanding on issues raised in her first book. *The Drama of Being a Child*, Dr Alice Miller here explores the sources of violence within ourselves and the way these are encouraged by orthodox child-rearing practices. Challenging the way in which we rationalise punishment and coercion as being for the child's 'own good', she illuminates the cost in compassion and humanity in later life, both in the private and public domain. Her message is clear: 'People whose integrity has not been damaged in childhood . . . will feel no need to harm another person or themselves.'

'She makes chillingly clear to the many what has been recognised only by the few: the extraordinary pain and psychological suffering inflicted on children under the guise of conventional child-rearing and pedagogy . . . This book can change lives' – *Maurice Sendak*

THE DRAMA OF BEING A CHILD

Alice Miller

The startling insights into child development gained by psychoanalyst Dr Alice Miller in twenty years of practice are shared with us in *The Drama of Being a Child*. Here she explains her conviction that violence and cruelty in society have their roots in conventional child rearing and in education – a discovery that has profound implications for us all. She shows how many children, adapted from birth to the needs and ambitions of their parents, lose the ability to experience and express their true feelings, eventually to become estranged from their real selves. She uncovers, too, the means by which many children now, and throughout history, have sublimated their full potential in order to fulfil the desires of their parents, impeding the creativity, vitality and integrity that is authentically their own. Alice Miller asks searching questions about the bringing up of children and gives us a unique understanding of the parent-child relationship.

'Full of wisdom and perception' – Anthony Storr, *The New Republic*

UNOFFICIAL SECRETS

Child Sexual Abuse – the Cleveland Case

Beatrix Campbell

When in July 1987 the diagnosis of child sexual abuse in some forty families in Cleveland hit the national headlines, society was confronted not only with the spectre of a much wider crisis, but also with a challenge to our stereotypes of both victims and perpetrators. For the children at the centre of the controversy were not the teenagers of popular mythology: they were as young as four years, even four months, from every class, boys as well as girls. When Cleveland Council made child sexual abuse a priority, it led to the appointment of specialist consultants and paediatricians trained in radical new approaches to diagnosis. It was they who uncovered what few others in Britain had seen, or wanted to see, throwing professional services and private lives into turmoil. In this important and timely study of the circumstances and implications of the Cleveland case, Beatrix Campbell examines in detail the ways in which the different professions – police, doctors, social workers, health visitors, bureaucrats, educators – interpret the problem according to their particular stake in it. She looks too at the issues raised for every one of us by the evidence of the Cleveland findings: that our assumptions about the nature and frequency of child sex abuse must change before solutions can be found.

HEROES OF THEIR OWN LIVES

The Politics and History of Family Violence

Linda Gordan

'Gordan's pioneering research into a crucial topic leads her to the very heart of beliefs about parents and children, men and women . . . The book is essential reading for anyone concerned about children's rights and parental responsibility.' – Claudia Koonz.

Heroes of Their Own Lives is a history of family violence from the point of view of its victims. Covering child abuse, child neglect, wife-beating and incest throughout the period 1880–1960, it is based on a new source for historians – the case records of social work agencies. From these, Linda Gordan has constructed an intimate and complex narrative of family violence itself – how it occurred, how family members reacted to it and how the agencies responded. She argues that, 'Family violence is a problem inseparable from the family norms of a whole society or from the overall political conflicts in that society. It is a changing historical and cultural issue, not a biological or sociobiological universal.' Her conclusions shatter many long-held assumptions about American social history, class and family structure and have profound implications for us all.

Linda Gordan puts contemporary family violence into a new perspective, drawing out the ways in which wife-beating and child abuse must be seen as issues of power and domination, and holding up a mirror to present social policy. Moving, provocative and meticulously researched, it is a unique social document and an invaluable contribution to current debate.

PUNISHMENT

Anna Mitgutsch

'*Was your mother like you?*' Her daughter's simple question
provokes in Vera memories of a childhood blighted by fear,
humiliation and physical violence at the hands of her
mother, Marie. Cold, unapproachable, frustrated in her
marriage to the war-scarred Friedl, Marie's energies found
their only outlet in ambition for her daughter, whose every
failure was punished with a beating. It was a means of
reproach chilling in its familiarity, and futility. For Marie, in
turn, had endured a loveless childhood. Brought up in an
austere Austrian farming community during the Depression,
she too had borne the brunt of her mother's
disappointments, as well as of her father's rages, unable to
repay the debt of gratitude they felt she owed them:
'Gratitude for what?' Marie had asked defiantly. 'For being
alive' was the reply.

Weaving together the lives of three generations of women,
Punishment moves from the physical hardships of rural life
to the banalities of small-town existence, from the Nazi era
and the deprivations of war to the ease of post-war
prosperity. A brilliant portrayal of the pathology of child
abuse − the ambiguous relationship between tormentor and
tormented, the confusion of love and power which lies
behind their mutual dependence and hostility − it is a first
novel of extraordinary power.